The Cuban Missile Crisis:

When Intelligence Made a Difference

Regis D. Heitchue

Dorrance Publishing Co
585 Alpha Drive
Suite 103
Pittsburgh, PA 15238
Visit our website at *www.dorrancebookstore.com*

ISBN: 979-8-8868-3139-9
eISBN: 979-8-8868-3997-5

Acknowledgements

Association of Former Intelligence Officers (AFIO)

AFIO is a non-profit tax exempt §501(c)(3) educational association, formed in Maryland in 1975 and incorporated in Virginia in 1977. AFIO conducts and supports public outreach education programs focusing on the role and importance of US intelligence for national security, and providing perspectives on intelligence issues and related events.

AFIO publishes Weekly Intelligence Notes (WINs) and a semi-annual journal, *The Intelligencer*, for members and subscribers. AFIO's website (www.afio.com) contains many articles and resources for educators, students, and interested individuals.

The Cuban Missile Crisis: When Intelligence Made a Difference was a team effort by the author and the Association of Former Intelligence Officers. AFIO supported this project in many ways. Managing editor Elizabeth Bancroft oversaw the work and dedicated AFIO editorial staff to create a finished, professional product. The author extends special thanks to AFIO senior editor Peter Oleson for his assistance with this project. Peter provided the encouragement, support and editorial expertise that made it possible. As a former intelligence officer, he offered numerous ideas and suggestions that immeasurably enhanced the telling of this story.

And to my dear wife Susan, thank you ever so much for graciously enduring my two-year marriage to a computer.

Regis D. Heitchue

The opinions expressed in this monograph are those of the author and do not necessarily represent the position or endorsement of AFIO, its members, boards or officers, or any US Government organization.

This manuscript has been reviewed by the Prepublication Classification Review Board of the Central Intelligence Agency (CIA) to ensure it contains no classified information.

Contents

List of Acronyms and Terms

ABC	American Broadcasting Company
ASW	Anti-submarine warfare
CJCS	Chairman of the Joint Chiefs of Staff
CIA	Central Intelligence Agency
CNO	Chief of Naval Operations
COMINT	Communications intelligence
COMOR	Committee on Overhead Reconnaissance
CORONA	First U.S. photographic satellite
DCI	Director of Central Intelligence, responsible for both the CIA and the broader Intelligence Community
DDCI	Deputy Director of Central Intelligence
DIA	Defense Intelligence Agency, responsible for foreign military intelligence
DOD	US Department of Defense
ELINT	Electronic intelligence
Ex Comm	Executive Committee, supporting President Kennedy during the Cuban Missile Crisis
FCD	KGB First Chief Directorate, responsible for foreign spying
FKR	Soviet nuclear-capable cruise missile
FROG	Soviet short-range missile (Soviet name: Luna)
GCHQ	Government Communications Headquarters, responsible for signals intelligence in the United Kingdom
GRU	Soviet military intelligence
HUMINT	Human intelligence gathered through agents or witnesses
ICBM	Intercontinental Ballistic Missile
IG	Inspector General
IRBM	Intermediate Range Ballistic Missile
JCS	Joint Chiefs of Staff

JMWAVE	Cryptonym for CIA's Miami station
KGB	Soviet intelligence agency
MI-6	Britain's Secret Intelligence Service (SIS)
MID	Soviet Foreign Ministry
MiG	Soviet military fighter aircraft produced by design bureau founded by Artem Mikoyan and Mikhail Gurevich
MONGOOSE	A US covert action program targeted against Castro in Cuba
MRBM	Medium-Range Ballistic Missile
NATO	North Atlantic Treaty Organization
NORAD	Northern American Air Defense Command (1962 nomenclature), responsible for warning of bomber and missile threats to the US and Canada
NPIC	National Photographic Interpretation Center, a CIA-DIA element
NRO	National Reconnaissance Office, a covert organization developing, launching, and operating US spy satellites
NSA	National Security Agency, the US's COMINT and ELINT agency
ONI	Office of Naval Intelligence
ORR	Office of Research and Reports, CIA
PFIAB	President's Foreign Intelligence Advisory Board
POPPY	U.S. signals intelligence satellite
PVO	Soviet air defense forces
SAC	Strategic Air Command of the USAF
SAM	Surface-to-air missile
SIGINT	Signals intelligence, encompassing Communications Intelligence (COMINT) and Electronic Intelligence (ELINT)
SNIE	Special National Intelligence Estimate
TAC	Tactical Air Command, USAF
U-2	High altitude reconnaissance aircraft developed by CIA and also flown by the USAF
USAF	United States Air Force
USIB	United States Intelligence Board, comprised of the most senior leaders of the intelligence community
USSR	Union of Soviet Socialist Republics

LIST OF ILLUSTRATIONS

PREFACE

The Cuban Missile Crisis—the most dangerous event of the Cold War— happened over thirteen days in October of 1962. Those thirteen days, immortalized in the book *Thirteen Days* and the movie of the same name, began with the American discovery that the Soviet Union had clandestinely placed in Cuba nuclear missiles capable of attacking the United States with a devastating blow. It ended with Soviet premier Khrushchev capitulating to what were essentially U.S. demands. The Soviet decision to install strategic missiles in Cuba was a blunder of the highest order, a massive miscalculation. Khrushchev had gambled on a fait acompli—-that he could move a massive nuclear force into Cuba and construct it rapidly thereby achieving strategic nuclear parity with the U.S. before the U.S. found out. The Soviet plan failed because they completely misjudged President Kennedy, the will of the America people, and the U.S. ability to discover the missiles.

While the finding of Soviet missiles on 15 October 1962 was a shocking and for the most part an unexpected event, historians generally believe that the roots of the crisis had been planted at an earlier time; in April 1961 in an ill-fated effort known as the Bay of Pigs, CIA-led Cuban exiles invaded Cuba in opposition to Fidel Castro. The Cubans thereafter feared a full-scale U.S. invasion and sought Soviet assistance to protect their island nation. The Soviets provided massive numbers of troops, conventional weapons and tactical nuclear weapons to be used in Cuba's defense. Most importantly, the Soviets also installed medium range ballistic missiles, were preparing to install intermediate range ballistic missiles, and had taken steps toward a strategic submarine base in Cuba. The Soviet mission in Cuba amounted to vastly more than the defense of Cuba with conventional forces and a token nuclear missile contingent; Cuba was to become an extension of Soviet nuclear power from which it could, if necessary, wage nuclear war with America.

Studies of the Cuban Missile Crisis concentrate on the actions of President Kennedy and his advisors as they sought to achieve Kennedys objective: the complete removal from Cuba of the Soviet missiles. The role of U.S. intelligence in the management and resolution of the crisis has received limited coverage, and indeed, a comprehensive account of intelligence activities during the crisis is not to be found. Recognizing the absence of the intelligence chapter in the historical record of the crisis, the author undertook to document that story in *The Cuban Missile Crisis: When Intelligence Made a difference.* The author's account is a unique story of *what* American intelligence knew, *when* it knew it, and *how* it knew what the Soviets were doing in Cuba prior to and during the crisis.

In the annals of intelligence history, much is written about the relationship between intelligence professionals and the policy-making community. In the case of the Cuban Missile Crisis, the relationship was highly effective as documented in this accounting. The Director of Central Intelligence, John McCone, a Republican in a Democratic administration, was part of the inner circle of Kennedy's closest advisors. As a member of President Kennedy's Executive committee that had been established for the crisis, he provided intelligence reports daily that informed key decisions by the president.

Questions still linger about aspects of the crisis. One of those is why Khrushchev decided to undertake such a risky gamble. The author explores this and other unsolved mysteries of the Cuban Missile Crisis.

The Cuban Missile Crisis:

When Intelligence Made a Difference

INTRODUCTION

Former Director of Central Intelligence Richard Helms once said "... the Cuban Missile Crisis was really an intelligence crisis. The threat appeared only through intelligence sources. Only those sources confirmed that the threat had gone away." [1] While Helms identified the two key questions that have come to define the Cuban Missile Crisis, the intelligence challenge presented by the Soviets' bold venture in Cuba was about much more than just discovering nuclear missiles and confirming they left. While nuclear missiles presented an existential threat to the U.S., there were other dimensions of the overall threat that the Kennedy administration needed to understand as it sought a resolution to the crisis that would avert all-out war with the Soviets.

This is the story of what American intelligence knew, when it knew it, and how it knew what the Soviets were doing in Cuba prior to and during the crisis—and what we now know, 60 years later, quite accurately, of what the Soviets were actually doing in Cuba.

What is unique about this story is that it is an all-source story. While the U-2 photographs get the credit for the discovery of the nuclear deployment on the island of Cuba, it was but one of many sources that contributed to answering the questions that the administration posed to the Director of Central

---

[1] Richard Helms. "Intelligence in American Society," *Studies in Intelligence*, Vol. 11, No. 3, Summer 1967, pp. 1-16. Adapted from a talk given before the Council on Foreign Relations on April 17, 1987.

Intelligence, John McCone, and other intelligence professionals. The intelligence that made a difference to President Kennedy and administration leaders came from all sources: clandestine human agents, refuge interrogations, communications intercepts, electronic means, overhead photography, and open sources. DCI McCone had the temperament and the drive to bring all intelligence sources —those at the national level and those from the intelligence components of the military services—together to paint the intelligence picture for senior policymakers at a time of severe national crisis and extreme leadership stress.

The single most defining feature of the Soviet adventure in Cuba was the extreme secrecy—enveloped by measures to conceal, to mislead, to deceive, to cover up and to lie—that was integral to each and every aspect of the plan. The Soviets had long used such measures to conceal their actions and intentions, but in Operation Anadyr, as the Soviets named their Cuban misadventure, it went to extremes. Anadyr was executed brilliantly and but for one fatal flaw would have succeeded in achieving Khrushchev's objective of presenting President Kennedy with a fait accompli—nuclear missiles stationed in his neighborhood ready and able to deliver a devastating nuclear strike against most any part of the United States.

A DCI once said, the task of intelligence is to uncover that which an adversary is determined to keep secret. In the case of Operation Anadyr, U.S. intelligence was supremely challenged to penetrate the security bubble in which Anadyr was encapsulated. It succeeded remarkably well, even brilliantly in some respects. But the U.S. intelligence record is not an unblemished one.

Authors Alexander George and Richard Smoke note that most experts agree that the discovery of the Soviet missiles and the way this was accomplished must be considered a distinct success for U.S. intelligence. At the same time, they maintain that U.S. intelligence could and should have become suspicious of Soviet activities sooner than they did. "The discovery of the missiles on October 14 came none too soon. The initial batch of medium-range ballistic missiles (MRBM's) were nearing readiness; had these missiles become operational before or very shortly after they were discovered, Kennedy would have been faced with just the difficult problem the Soviets were hoping to impose on him [a fait accompli]. In this crisis the timing of the intelligence discovery of the opponent's challenge to deterrence played a pivotal role, of what must be classified as a near-failure of American intelligence, ... that came fairly close to generating a U.S. intelligence and foreign policy failure of the first magnitude."[2]

It must also be said that U.S. intelligence missed and misjudged key elements of the Soviet threat in Cuba. While not critical to the resolution of the crisis, those errors would have been devastating to U.S. forces had they invaded the island, an option seriously contemplated—and strongly advocated by the military—from the very beginning of the crisis.

---

[2] Alexander L. George and Richard Smoke. *Deterrence in American Foreign Policy: Theory and Practice*, New York & London: Columbia University Press, 1974, p. 473.

An Intelligence Leader for the Times

Following the Bay of Pigs disaster,[3] President Kennedy replaced DCI Allen Dulles with John McCone. Kennedy believed the DCI should be a strong leader of the intelligence community. A 16 January 1962 memorandum instructing McCone on his duties as DCI contained the following charge: "In carrying out your newly assigned duties as Director of Central Intelligence, it is my wish that…you undertake, as an integral part of your responsibility, the coordination and effective guidance of the total United States foreign intelligence effort."[4]

McCone believed that the DCI should be the chief intelligence officer in the U.S. government and he acted as such during the Cuban Missile Crisis. He believed that he could best serve the President by ensuring that the community, not just CIA, provided the most accurate and timely intelligence possible. With his focus on intelligence community matters, he sought to delegate day-to- day authority over the CIA to his deputy, General Marshall S. Carter, enabling him to devote as much time as he could to his role as titular head of the intelligence

---

[3] In a disastrous setback for the United States, CIA-backed Cuban exiles who invaded Cuba at the Bay of Pigs in April 1961 were soundly defeated by Cuban forces. The invasion led Cubans to fear an imminent full-scale U.S. invasion and asked the Russians for defensive weapons. The Cuban Missile Crisis began eighteen months later. Some argue that the Crisis can be traced to the Bay of Pigs disaster. (See James G. Blight and Janet M. Lang. *Dark Beyond Darkness; The Cuban Missile Crisis as History, Warning, and Catalyst*, Lanham, Boulder, New York, London: Roman & Littlefield, 2018. p. 32.)

[4] The full text of this unclassified instruction is in Michael Warner (editor). *Central Intelligence: Origin and Evolution*, CIA History Staff, 2001, p. 67-8.

community.[5] According to a former CIA Chief Historian, McCone was one of the best leaders and managers CIA—and the intelligence community—ever had. "One can make a persuasive argument that he *was* the best."[6]

In a study of DCIs as Intelligence Community leaders, Douglas F. Garthoff (not to be confused with Raymond Garthoff, later) wrote that John McCone enthusiastically welcomed the community leadership role, and he clearly believed that his talent and experience were suited to the task. Kennedy's memorandum instructed McCone to work closely with the "heads of all departments and agencies having responsibilities in the foreign intelligence field," signaling that the DCI outranked the intelligence chiefs in those units and would be expected to deal directly with their bosses. McCone recognized that DOD "owned" the intelligence elements in the military services, the Defense Intelligence Agency, and the National Security Agency (NSA), but he believed that much of what they did was "national" in character and therefore something with which he should be concerned. Kennedy's memorandum stated the expectation that the DCI would delegate much of the task of running the CIA to his deputy, thus allowing him to carry out better his primary task as Director of Central Intelligence. Accordingly, McCone had his deputy represent CIA in USIB[7] deliberations, allowing McCone to better represent the position of the whole intelligence community before the ExComm,[8] and

---

5 David Robarge. *John McCone as Director of Central Intelligence, 1961-1965,* Center for the Study of Intelligence, Central Intelligence Agency, 2005.

6 Ibid, p. vii.

7 The United States Intelligence Board was the community organization on which sat the most senior leaders of intelligence agencies and departments.

8 Immediately after the President learned of the Soviet missiles in Cuba, he asked presidential assistant McGeorge Bundy to assemble with great secrecy a select group of advisors to assist him in countering the Soviet aggression. The members of the Executive Committee (ExComm) of the National Security Council, as the group called itself, were

on occasions he did take positions that were at odds with CIA's position. McCone also used the Office of National Estimates (ONE), as an instrument through which he exercised leadership in producing intelligence estimates for the President and the ExComm. In his study, Garthoff concluded that McCone was "the most community-minded DCI up to the 1970s."[9]

As noted by Raymond Garthoff, a distinguished scholar of the Cuban Missile Crisis, "The *integrative process* of intelligence worked"[10] [author's emphasis]. Garthoff also wrote "The members of the intelligence community in Washington worked well together during the crisis… CIA played a lead role, but by no means a lone role." DCI McCone held USIB meetings every morning of the crisis. Those meetings served to coordinate intelligence activities and information across all agencies, and prepared McCone to update ExComm at the beginning of each meeting on the latest intelligence regardless of its source.[11]

In praise of the integrated intelligence effort Ray Cline, former CIA deputy director, said the main thing to note about the crisis is that CIA coordinated a

Kennedy; Secretary of State Dean Rusk; Defense Secretary Robert McNamara; Treasury Secretary Douglas Dillon; JCS Chairman General Maxwell Taylor; Attorney General Robert Kennedy; DCI McCone; the President's speechwriter, Theodore Sorenson; Bundy; and others at times.

9   Douglas F. Garthoff. *Directors of Central Intelligence as Leaders of the U.S. Intelligence Community*, Washington, D.C.: CIA Center for the Study of Intelligence, 2005, pp. 41-4, 66.

10   Raymond L. Garthoff. "U.S. Intelligence in the Cuban Missile Crisis," in James G. Blight and David A. Welch (editors). *Intelligence and the Cuban Missile Crisis*, London, Portland, Or: Frank Cass, 1998, pp. 53-5.

11   A very contrarian view, and a naïve one in this author's opinion, is that of Amy Zegart who published *The Cuban Missile Crisis as Intelligence Failure* in *Policy Review*, October 2, 2012. She wrote "The Central Intelligence Agency was central in name only." Her article is replete with comments such as "organizational fragmentation existed;" "invisible fault lines within and across intelligence agencies;" structural fragmentation; "intelligence reporting and analysis of the Cuban situation was handled by half a dozen different agencies; "structural secrecy."

comprehensive interagency collection and analysis program aimed at discovering what kinds of military weapons the USSR was sending to Cuba.[12] The Chief of NSA's operations during the crisis, Juanita Moody, observed: "The community was a cumbersomely put together thing, although I think and I agree with Mr. McCone that the community did well with what they had."[13]

---

[12] Ray S. Cline. *Secrets, Spies and Scholars*, Washington, D.C.; Acropolis Books, 1976, p. 196.

[13] Moody interview by David Hatch, et al., 16 June 1994. NSA Center for Cryptologic History Oral History Program.

THE INTELLIGENCE CHALLENGE

Moscow has always had a flair for concealing secret information and for deceiving its adversaries in what is known in Russian as *maskirovka*. Its intent is to protect Russian secrets from foreign intelligence sources, especially concerning Russian intentions about the nature, scope and timing of an operation. Soviet preparations for and execution of critical aspects of their deployment of nuclear missiles to Cuba—Operation Anadyr—is a case study in Russian *maskirovka*.

Soviet planning of the operation that began in the spring of 1962 was done under extreme secrecy and a strict need-to-know. The most senior officers brought into the plan were told that Cuba was involved in the operation, but only a few were informed of the exact nature of the mission. For reasons of security, no communications about the proposed, planned and actual Soviet deployments were sent, even by coded message; everything was hand-carried by members of the small group of senior officials who were directly involved. The Soviets even misled their own officials about the objective of the operation by naming it Anadyr, promoting a false allusion of an exercise in the far north of Russia. To aid in concealing the true destination—Cuba—some units were outfitted with winter clothing and equipment.

The secrecy and deception associated with Operation Anadyr was highly effective from its start until the nuclear missiles were discovered on 14 October.[14]

---

[14] James H. Hansen. "Soviet Deception in the Cuban Missile Crisis; Learning from the Past," *Studies in Intelligence*, 46, no. 1, 2002.

Conveniently for the U.S., the Soviets had made no attempt to conceal the sites from overhead reconnaissance, even though they were well aware of the American U-2 spy plane and its photographic capabilities following the shooting down of Francis Gary Powers on 1 May 1960. The failure of the Soviets to hide and camouflage the sites and the missiles is attributable to the Soviets following standard procedure; Soviet missiles deployed in the USSR were not camouflaged and there was little thought given to camouflaging them in Cuba. Another explanation is that Soviets did not regard the possibility of detection once the missiles had been deployed as critical to the success of the venture. The Soviets may also have thought that even if discovered, the U.S would acquiesce, or at least would not react militarily to the nuclear threat in its backyard. In the view of one student of the crisis Khrushchev believed that the U.S. government would do nothing about the deployment *if* it did not recognize what was happening until the missiles were in Cuba and on combat-ready status.[15]

Khrushchev was so committed to covertly deploying the nuclear missiles that he rejected pressure by Cuban officials in late September of 1962 to go public with the missile deployment. After all, the Soviet Union had every right to supply, and Cuba had every right to accept such weapons. Had the missile deployment been an overt one, the U.S. would have faced a much more difficult problem. The secrecy and deception practiced by the Soviets made a strong case for the U.S. to argue the missiles had to be removed, President Kennedy's singular goal throughout the crisis.

The shipment, unloading, land transport, installation, and command of

---

15 Robert M. Clark. "Soviet Deception and The Cuban Missile Crisis, When Intelligence Made a Difference" *The Intelligencer*, Vol. 26, No. 2., Winter/Spring 2021, pp. 67-9.

the missiles sent to Cuba remained entirely under tight Soviet control. At the proposed missile sites, Cuban farmers were arbitrarily evicted from their lands. Soviet troops guarded the missile construction areas around the clock—from the Cubans. Cubans were also excluded from the dock areas as missiles were offloaded from ships that had brought them to Cuba. All this effort was to ensure the security of the operation, to ensure that the Americans were unaware of what was going on, that is at least until the MRBM's were in place and ready to provide a here-and-now threat to the United States.[16]

Why did Khrushchev believe his covert plan would succeed, knowing that the deployment involved constructing facilities, clearing roads, erecting launch equipment and all manner of other activities, which created signatures easily seen by U.S. overhead reconnaissance? Scholars Blight and Welch believe the answer is that he was over-confident, and along with other Soviet leaders did not appreciate the logistical technicalities involved. An unanswered question raised by Blight and Welch is why Soviet military intelligence was not tasked to assess the likelihood of a successful covert deployment.[17]

Some have theorized that the Soviets and Cubans mounted a major campaign using HUMINT channels to bolster the deception effort. In a bold and risky move, the planners supposedly leaked accurate information about the deployment so as to mask it, to make the Americans disbelieve the truth of what they were hearing. The information was supposedly funneled through counterrevolutionary organizations in the United States, especially Miami. The

---

[16] Donald C. Wigglesworth. *The Cuban Missile Crisis: A SIGINT Perspective*, NSA *Cryptologic Quarterly, Vol. 13, No. 1, Spring 1994*, p. 82.

[17] James G. Blight and David A. Welch. *Intelligence and the Cuban Missile Crisis*, London: Routledge, 1998, p. 185.

CIA discounted the information, because it did not consider the groups and people peddling it to be credible. This strategy was highly effective, according to a former Cuban intelligence officer.[18] Blight and Welch posed the question: Did the KGB orchestrate a campaign to mask the nuclear deployment by funneling accurate information about it to the CIA through Cuban sources? They conclude it is entirely plausible to imagine, though not certain, that the KGB and Cuban intelligence did cooperate on such a campaign.

In a discussion of the Soviets' extraordinary security measures, a report of the National Indications Center of 15 July 1963 stated, "It is noteworthy, even for the USSR, that there was not a single known leak through the Soviet or satellite channels of the true nature of Soviet shipments to Cuba, that security restrictions on the movement of equipment and troops into and through Soviet ports were so rigid that no information has ever been obtained on them, and that, although thousands of Soviet troops were deployed in Cuba, there was no discernible reflection of this in communications and no leaks through operator chatter, except for a few references in mid-September to a call for military volunteers for Cuba."[19] In other words, Soviet communications security was almost perfect.

Khrushchev failed to accomplish his plan for a fait accompli. That plan called for Anadyr to remain secret until the missiles were ready to serve their intended purpose—a cheap, but temporary righting of the strategic imbalance, the deterrence of an American invasion of the island, and the reemergence of the Soviet Union as a major player on the world stage. His wishful thinking

---

[18] James H. Hansen cites *Domingo Amuchastegui, "Cuban Intelligence and the October Crisis,"* in Blight and Welch, p. 101.

[19] Donald Wigglesworth, p. 86.

blinded him to the two fatal flaws in his plan—Americans not knowing and American's acceptance. Had Khrushchev consulted those around him who knew better, they would have told him of the folly of his plan, but he felt no need to do so. Nevertheless, credit must be given to the Soviets for having been almost successful in this difficult task despite the zealous efforts of the American intelligence establishment.

THE EARLY PERIOD; 16 – 22 OCTOBER

Tuesday morning, 16 October 1962, President Kennedy was told of the nuclear missiles that the Soviet Union had installed on the island of Cuba. On 22 October, Kennedy would go on nation-wide television to announce it to the American public and the world. The crisis ended Sunday morning 28 October with the Soviet agreement to remove the missiles. Those thirteen days between the beginning and the end of the crisis, immortalized in Robert Kennedy's book *Thirteen Days*, were a supreme test of U.S. intelligence as it sought to understand what Khrushchev was doing in Cuba using every means possible to find out.[20] What follows are the questions that President Kennedy and his advisors asked, or should have asked of intelligence, and *how*, and *how well*, the intelligence community answered them. In answering the "how well" we are able to compare the intelligence of the period with what we now know the Soviets were actually doing in Cuba at the time based on Russian revelations.

Khrushchev's Intentions?

Post mortems of intelligence performance in the crisis tend to highlight the estimative failure—the failure to estimate that Soviet leadership would deploy nuclear missiles to Cuba. A crucial estimate said, in effect, that a missile de-

---

[20] Robert F. Kennedy. *Thirteen Days: A Memoir of the Cuban Missile Crisis*, New York: W.W. Norton, 1971.

ployment to Cuba was unlikely, though not impossible, although the "not impossible" was not included in the estimate's conclusions.

The intelligence estimate that would come in for extensive criticism for how it misjudged Soviet intentions was occasioned by a steep acceleration in Soviet deliveries of weapons to Cuba in the summer of 1962. Special National Intelligence Estimate (SNIE) 85-3-62 judged it unlikely the Soviets would introduce strategic offensive weapons into Cuba although it did not entirely dismiss the possibility, just that it was unlikely.[21]

In preparing the SNIE, the estimators searched for information indicative of the nature of Soviet weapons, but lacking such hard evidence they concluded that the military equipment piling into Cuba indicated a Soviet attempt to give Castro a formidable defensive capability to serve as a deterrent to U.S. military moves to overthrow him. The estimators also gave thought to how the Soviets might perceive American attitudes to basing strategic missiles in Cuba and concluded that the Soviets would have estimated that the American people and government would be outraged by such action, leading the estimators to the judgment that the Soviets would not undertake the great risks involved in such a deployment.

As the SNIE was being prepared, it was clear to U.S. intelligence that shipping of armaments to Cuba had dramatically increased after mid-July. But in a report of intelligence performance, the CIA Inspector General concluded that the intelligence analysts and the estimators never carried their analyses and estimates to the point of asking themselves: "Is it reasonable to believe

---

[21] Special National Intelligence Estimate SNIE 85-3-62, *"The Military Buildup in Cuba,"* was prepared by CIA's Board of National Estimates (BNE). It was issued by USIB on 19 September 1962 without dissenting opinions with the full support of intelligence community leaders.

that so costly a defensive apparatus would be constructed against a nebulous invasion threat, particularly since the defensive structure would not halt a determined invader?"[22]

Once the nuclear missiles were discovered, Sherman Kent, who as Director of the Office of National Estimates was responsible for the erroneous estimate, realized that the estimate of the Soviets understanding of the mood of the United States and its probable reaction was wrong. The Soviets had misjudged the United States. Kent noted that "we verified that our own feeling for the mood of the United States and its probable reaction had been correct. In a way our misestimate of Soviet intentions got an ex post facto validation." In defense of the estimate, Kent wrote that no estimate can be expected to divine when the enemy is about to make a dramatically wrong decision. "We missed the Soviet decision to put missiles in Cuba because we could not believe that Khrushchev could make such a mistake."[23]

Khrushchev's miscalculation was based in part on wishful thinking. He seems not to have imagined that if the Soviet gains from a successful venture were to be so great, it was probable that the U.S. would recognize what was at stake and therefore probable that the U.S. would react to deny such gains to its principal antagonist. Khrushchev was his own analyst. He didn't ask the KGB for an assessment of a probable U.S. reaction, nor Soviet military intelligence, the GRU, for an assessment of how likely it would be that the missiles would not be discovered until the deployment was complete.[24]

---

[22] *Inspector General's Survey of Handling of Intelligence During the Cuban Arms Build-up August to mid-October 1962*, 12 November 1962, from the National Security Archive "The Cuban Missile Crisis at 55," p. 35.

[23] Sherman Kent. "A Crucial Estimate Relived," *Studies in Intelligence*, Vol. 8, No. 2, Spring 1964.

[24] Aleksandr Fursenko and Timothy Naftali. "Soviet Intelligence and the Cuban Missile Cri-

In preparing SNIE 85-3-62 the estimators had limited hard intelligence. The U.S. did not have a secret source high in the Soviet leadership with access to Soviet thinking and deliberations. Hard intelligence on the dramatic increase in Soviet deliveries to Cuba after July 1962 was limited as the nature of the ships' cargo was unknown. Despite numerous reports from secret agents in Cuba and refugees at the Opa Locka Interrogation Center, most of what was reported was considered soft, not hard intelligence. Lacking hard intelligence, the estimators turned to assessing Soviet *intentions* as the basis for the estimate. Unable to read the minds of Soviet officials, the estimators reviewed past Soviet actions as a way to predict future actions. However, the Soviet Union had never before deployed nuclear missiles beyond its borders.

Blight and Welch cite the problems of this approach: Using past behavior, how could the estimators assess the likelihood of something that had never happened before? One cannot infer future intentions from present behavior, nor infer present intentions from past behavior. Further, past Soviet behavior was a composite of the behavior of several Soviet leaders, only one of whom was Khrushchev, and he had not yet had much of an opportunity to leave his imprint.[25]

The President's Foreign Intelligence Advisory Board (PFIAB) in its after crisis report to Kennedy took aim at SNIE 85-3-62 saying that senior U.S. officials were ill-served by the "mistaken judgment." The report attributed the mistaken judgment to a lack of adequate coverage of Cuba, the rigor with

---

sis" in James G. Blight and David A. Welch (editors), *Intelligence and the Cuban Missile Crisis*, London: Frank Cass, 1998. Blight's and Welch's volume is a unique collection of articles on the activities of U.S., Soviet, and Cuban intelligence services during the crisis.

[25] James G. Blight and David A. Welch, "The Cuban Missile Crisis and Intelligence Performance" in *Intelligence and the Cuban Missile Crisis*, p. 195.

which the view was held that the Soviet Union would not assume the risks of such a deployment, and the absence of an imaginative appraisal of the intelligence indicators which, while limited in number, were contained in reports disseminated by intelligence agencies.[26]

In his response to the PFIAB report DCI McCone wrote that intelligence community analysts including the State Department "were so convinced that the Soviets would not accept the inevitable confrontation resulting from placing missiles in Cuba that they were inclined to dismiss such evidence as there was to the contrary. This, I find, is one of the difficulties of dealing with the imponderables of what the other fellow will or will not do."[27]

In forming their conclusion that the Soviets would not put missiles in Cuba, U.S. analysts noted the risks the Soviets would be taking in the form of a strong American response. What they failed to see were the benefits that would accrue from such a risky endeavor. Roger Hilsman, who served as director of the Bureau of Intelligence and Research in the State Department, has argued the one big intelligence failure was the inability to see the "missile gap in reverse." A speech by Deputy Secretary of Defense Gilpatric had made abundantly clear to Soviet leaders that they were in a horrible strategic position vis-à-vis the U.S. The Soviets knew they were in a weak strategic position, and they knew the U.S. knew they were weak. Surely the Soviets would take action to deal with the imbalance. What U.S. intelligence didn't imagine was the manner by which the Soviets chose to address the problem. "The single most

---

[26] The White House President's Foreign Intelligence Advisory Board Memorandum for the President, dated February 4, 1963. Mary S. McAuliffe, editor. *CIA Documents on the Cuban Missile Crisis 1962,* CIA History Staff, October 1992, pp. 361-71.

[27] McCone Memorandum for the President, 28 February 1963. McAuliffe, pp. 373-4.

important failure of the entire American effort in dealing with the Cuban Missile Crisis was the failure to recognize that putting missiles in Cuba was a cheap, if only temporary, solution to what everyone recognized the Soviets would regard as a very serious problem." According to Hilsman, if the intelligence community had recognized this possibility and brought it forcefully to the attention of senior officials, it is very probable that the president would have warned the Soviets of the dire consequences of such action. Had the president issued such a warning ahead of the Soviets fateful decision in the spring of 1962, they might have been dissuaded from sending missiles to Cuba, and there would therefore have been no missile crisis at all.[28, 29]

In hindsight, the much-maligned SNIE could have said the Soviets probably would not put missiles in Cuba, while giving more acknowledgment to the possibility they might. Either way, it seems it would have made little difference as to how U.S. leaders responded to the crisis, or to intelligence operations. As Blight and Welch wrote: "It is ironic that the U.S. intelligence community made such an intense effort to look for something that they did not expect to see."[30]

Another report concerning intelligence performance said "For the record, there is no evidence that the existence of SNIE 85-3 [*sic*] had any inhibiting influence on later decisions. It was not, for instance, cited to support an argument against continuing overflights. Nor did it affect current intelligence reporting."[31] A somewhat contrary view is that of the IG report: "Although proof

---

[28] Roger Hilsman. *The Cuban Missile Crisis; the Struggle over Policy*, Westport, CT: Praeger, 1996, p. 63.

[29] President Kennedy had made a public statement on 13 September warning the Soviets, but at that time Operation Anadyr was well underway. Kennedy Library archives, Papers of John F. Kennedy. Presidential Papers. President's Office Files.

[30] Blight and Welch, Intelligence and the Cuban Missile Crisis, p. 198.

[31] CIA memorandum, Richard Lehman to Director of Central Intelligence, "CIA Handling of

is lacking and evidence is scanty, we believe SNIE 85-3 [*sic*] and the political and operational climate from which it grew did have a significant effect on the use made of raw information during late September and early October. Not only do we believe that the estimators influenced the analysts, but that the analysts influenced the reporters." The report cited one example: Concerning the report of surface-to-surface missiles [meaning nuclear missiles] in Cuba on 19 September, headquarters commented that it is more likely that the missiles were SA-2's. The report as written was probably accurate."[32]

The U.S. "failure" to predict Soviet missiles going to Cuba sits alongside the Soviets real failures: the inability to accurately assess the American response to the missiles and the belief that they would remain undiscovered until they were operational. The Soviet misestimation cannot be attributed to the KGB, but rather to Khrushchev himself who operated as his own intelligence analyst. KGB Chairman Vladimir Semichastny enjoyed far less influence as Russia's spymaster than his nominal equivalent in the Unites States, the Director of Central Intelligence. Consequently, in the Cuban Missile Crisis the Chairman of the KGB would neither be invited to a Presidium meeting nor have a single face-to-face meeting with Khrushchev. Unlike the U.S. misestimate, the Soviet misestimate had dire consequences: A huge embarrassment to the Soviet Union and to Khrushchev personally, and the exposure for all to see of the weak Soviet strategic position.[33]

---

the Soviet Build-up in Cuba, 1 July- 16 October 1962," 14 November 1962 with cover memorandum attached 15 November 1962, from the National Security Archive "The Cuban Missile Crisis at 55," p. 16.

[32] *Inspector General's Survey*, p. 31.

[33] Fursenko and Naftali. "Soviet Intelligence and the Cuban Missile Crisis," in Blight and Welch, p. 65.

What the intelligence estimators failed to see; DCI McCone saw clearly. He believed that offensive missiles had been deployed to Cuba. Throughout the period of the Cuban arms buildup, he urged an interpretation of its significance that received little or no acceptance elsewhere in the community. In mid-August, McCone on several occasions speculated on the probability of medium-range ballistic missiles. On 23 August, in a meeting with the President and other senior officials, the Director questioned the need for the extensive surface to air SA-2 missiles unless they were there to make possible the concealment of offensive missiles. In his view they were installed to prevent observation by U.S. overhead reconnaissance of the offensive missiles. During September, McCone repeated his belief that offensive weapons would be installed in Cuba, urged frequent reconnaissance missions and suggested that the Board of National Estimates study the motives behind the defensive missile measures. Were they there to blind U.S. reconnaissance? Ironically, the fear that SA-2 missiles might shoot down a U-2 reconnaissance aircraft led senior officials to scale back plans for U-2 coverage of the island, a self-induced blindness.

Of note in this regard is an after-action report by the commander of the offensive missile forces in Cuba, Major General Igor Statsenko who wrote that the air defense system of the group of forces in Cuba was brought to combat readiness on 10.01.62 [*sic*] and was on combat duty, but for some reason it was allowed to turn on its radar tracking system only on 10.26.62 [*sic*]. Thus, the debarkation of the troops in Cuba and their actions were constantly monitored from the air. "*We believe that the air defense units of the Soviet Group of Forces in Cuba did not fulfill their mission in Cuba, which was to cover and secure the main strike force—the missile forces* [Statsenko's emphasis]. Naturally, this allowed the U.S. to partially uncover the formation and location of our troops during the most demanding and stressful period."[34] Major General Statsenko's complaint about the poor performance of the Soviet air defense is interesting in light of McCone's thesis that the SA-2 sites were there to protect the nuclear missiles from being detected by the U-2. McCone was, of course, right all along about the Soviets deploying nuclear missiles to Cuba.

McCone's beliefs had no evidentiary basis. They were apparently a reflection of his instincts and fears and did not influence the estimators who were unprepared to believe that the Soviets might install offensive weapons in Cuba or that the Soviets would grossly underestimate the United States ability to detect an offensive buildup and to react to it with forthright resolution.[35]

A CIA Clandestine Services officer posited a surprising reservation concerning the estimators' view of the Soviet attitude towards the Cuban venture as reflected in SNIE 85-3-62. J.J. Rumpelmayer wrote that "neither the U.S. estimate of the Soviet view of a U.S. reaction nor that Soviet view need have been wrong." "On the contrary, there is evidence that the Soviets did show, as the estimate put it, 'a far greater willingness to increase the level of risk in U.S.-Soviet relations than the USSR had displayed thus far'—because the stakes were higher than ever before—but were prepared to back down if caught." He cites as an indicator that the Soviets were prepared to pull out of Cuba if detected in the promptness with which they executed the disengage-

---

[34] Report of Major-General Igor Demyanovich Statsenko, Commander of the 51st Missile Divisions about the Actions of the Division from 07.12.62 through 12.01.1962, National Security Archive Electronic Briefing Book, No. 449, p. 19.
[35] *Inspector General's Survey*, pp. 33-6.

ment operation as soon as they were convinced that the U.S. was ready to act. "They recalled to Soviet ports all vessels suitable for missile loadings…without even waiting for the blockade to be put into effect, evidently acting on a contingency plan they would presumably not have had ready if they had really underestimated the U.S. reaction." Rumpelmayer says the Soviets judged the United States correctly but were not taking irrevocable action and considered the possibility of a radical improvement in their strategic position worth the risk involved.[36]

Rumpelmayer's theory was thoroughly debunked by CIA analysts who issued (but are not named as authors) the classic retrospective works of the crisis.[37] They say that Rumpelmayer's contention that the Soviets were willing to increase greatly the level of risk because the gains to be made were so great—but they were prepared to withdraw if caught—is manifestly false unless one assumes the missiles were to be used solely for a surprise attack on the United States. Their usefulness for anything else depended on their being caught or their presence being known when the program was completed.

The authors of the above cited retrospective studies both said that Khrushchev recognized from the start that there was some degree of risk of an American attack at one or another point in the venture but believed this risk to be small. Furthermore, that Khrushchev recognized from the start a possibility of failure but believed at least until September—perhaps until mid-October—that the United States would probably acquiesce, and until late

---

[36] J.J. Rumpelmayer. "The Missiles In Cuba," *Studies in Intelligence*, Vol. 8, Fall 1964, pp. 87-92.

[37] *Cuba 1962: Khrushchev's Miscalculated Risk*, CIA/ORR DD/I Staff Study, 13 February 1964 *and* "The Soviet Missile Base Venture in Cuba," CIA/RSS, DDI Staff Study/RS, Spring 1964.

October that the venture could be managed to his profit even if the United States did not acquiesce. They agree that Khrushchev had something of a contingency plan for withdrawal, but his improvised and erratic behavior in the week of the crisis seemed to indicate that he did not expect to fail. The authors agree with Sherman Kent that Khrushchev made a serious mistake in judgment. He seems not to have recognized that the United States would act to prevent its principal antagonist from a fait accompli, just as Kennedy had repeatedly told him.[38]

What Are Those Ships Carrying?

Soviet shipping to Cuba began to increase dramatically in mid-July 1962, leading intelligence analysts to conclude that something unusual was happening. Arms shipment to Cuba had averaged about two shiploads a month during the first half of 1962, but jumped to 125 voyages involving *military* cargoes in the three months between the last days of July and the establishment of the U.S. quarantine on 22 October. The Soviet pattern of arms deliveries to Cuba had changed so dramatically and abruptly that U.S. leadership could have concluded that the armaments being delivered represented more than could be justified for the defense of the island nation.

The U.S. was unable to definitively ascertain the types of weapons the Soviets were shipping despite intelligence that was collected through communications intercepts, maritime surveillance, and human sources when the ships

---

[38] Harlow T. Munson and W. P. Southard. "Two Witnesses for the Defense," *Studies in Intelligence* Vol. 8, 1964, pp. 93-8.

were approaching Cuba or in port being off loaded. Photographs of ships bound for Cuba were acquired from a variety of sources, especially U.S. Navy ships and aircraft, and were sent to the National Photographic Interpretation Center (NPIC) in Washington for interpretation.[39] As the ships approached Cuba, they were picked up by the Marine photo squadron based at Guantanamo and by Coast Guard planes operating out of Miami.[40]

Despite the lack of definitive evidence that nuclear missiles were being carried by the Soviet ships, there were indications to that effect. Photographs of ships at sea were taken from all aspects and would have clearly shown that some of the ships were riding high in the water, indicative of a cargo that took up a lot of space but was not very heavy—like a big missile empty of fuel. The ships that sailed to Cuba after mid-July included a group of large-hatch ships, the only Soviet-flag vessels capable of transporting nuclear missiles below decks. U.S. intelligence knew (perhaps retrospectively) about the large-hatch ships and some of the details of their construction. As far as could be determined none of those ships were built for the purpose of clandestinely transporting the missiles. However, that probably could not have been accomplished before these large-hatch vessels became available.[41]

Soviet military equipment being shipped to Cuba was frequently carried on deck in packing crates. Those crates were photographed and the images measured, analyzed and compared with crates and their contents that U.S. intelligence

---

[39] NPIC was an intelligence community organization, administered by CIA, and staffed with photographic interpretation experts from CIA, DIA and the military services, located in Washington, D.C.

[40] Dino A. Brugioni. *Eyeball to Eyeball; The Inside Story of the Cuban Missile Crisis*, New York: Random House, 1995, p. 73.

[41] "Cuba 1962: Khrushchev's Miscalculated Risk," pp. 22-3. Declassified June 2017.

had earlier photographed elsewhere (a technique known as *cratology*). On 28 September 1962 photographs of the Soviet ship *Kasimov* showed crates loaded on deck that U.S intelligence recognized and were associated with Russian IL-28 bombers. The U.S. considered the arrival of IL-28 bombers in Cuba as significant (they would play a major role in the concluding stages of the crisis). Though the Russian IL-28 bombers were obsolescent, they were capable of carrying nuclear bombs and were therefore considered to be offensive, the category of weapons that Washington was determined to eliminate from Cuba. While the crates had been photographed on 28 September, the photographic intelligence did not reach Washington until October 9. When Deputy CIA Director Ray Cline informed McCone of this important piece of information, McCone remarked, "How the hell did the Navy get them to Washington, by rowboat." Then McCone asked Cline when the *Kasimov* had reached Cuba and when told it had arrived on 4 October, McCone said the information wasn't intelligence, it was history.[42]

Moscow, apparently concerned about the U.S. photographing deck cargo on their Cuba bound ships, attempted to solve the problem diplomatically. At the time when shipping to Cuba was accelerating, in July 1962 the Soviets complained that U.S. reconnaissance missions conducted in international waters amounted to harassment and requested that the flights be stopped for the sake of better bilateral relations. This appears to have been an effort by Khrushchev to delay the discovery of weapons related to Operation Anadyr.[43] Fursenko and Naftali wrote that Kennedy missed the significance of Khrushchev's interest in reducing U.S. intelligence collection on Soviet shipping.[44]

[42] Brugioni. *Eyeball to Eyeball,* pp. 172-3.
[43] Hansen. "Soviet Deception."
[44] Aleksandr Fursenko and Timothy Naftali. *One Hell of a Gamble: Khrushchev, Castro &*

Something that was overlooked at the time was that two of the Soviet ships, the *Omsk* and the *Poltava*, were diverted from their normal tasks to carry arms to Cuba and had exceptionally large hatches. Also significant in hindsight was the fact that the intelligence reports routinely noted they were riding high in the water. Neither of these facts was brought to the attention of either policymakers or the top levels of the intelligence agencies until after the missiles had been discovered. Roger Hilsman has written that the shipping experts did not see those facts as unusual or disturbing enough even to call attention to them, much less explain them away. He sees this as clearly an intelligence failure—a failure of imagination, a failure to probe, speculate, and ask perceptive questions of the data. But he also says that no action would have been taken on the basis of this "suggestive," soft information, and that it would have made little difference because top officials were already so sensitive to the possibility of missiles that they were "quivering."[45]

Communications intelligence was a key source of intelligence on Soviet shipping. NSA routinely monitored Soviet naval and commercial ship radio traffic in the North Atlantic in conjunction with GCHQ and the Canadian SIGINT agency.[46] SIGINT provided intelligence on daily ship positions, tonnages, destinations, and cargoes, as well as Soviet attempts to deny or falsify this information. This led NSA analysts to conclude that there was something secret and unusual going on. The record shows that NSA did an excellent job tracking Soviet merchant ships, although the author of *The Secret Sentry* fails

---

Kennedy 1958-1964, New York: W.W.Norton, 1997, p. 194.

[45] Hilsman, p. 53.

[46] GCHQ (Government Communications Headquarters) is the British SIGINT agency. The Canadian SIGINT agency in 1962 was the Communications Security Establishment Canada (CSEC).

to recognize the other sources that contributed significant intelligence when he states "…virtually everything that the U.S. intelligence community knew about Soviet shipments came from SIGINT."[47]

CIA had kept abreast of the intelligence on Soviet shipping that was coming in from NSA and NPIC, and it had established a shipping task force in the Office of Current Intelligence. CIA efforts to report that Soviet ships were carrying military equipment was met with stiff resistance from DIA and the Pentagon. JCS Chairman General Maxwell Taylor[48] challenged CIA's statement that "Many Soviet ships are involved in hauling military gear [to Cuba]." In his challenge he cited from the DIA *Intelligence Summary*: "The high volume of shipping probably reflects planned increases in trade between the USSR and Cuba." General Taylor was quoted as saying he had seen no hard evidence of armaments going to Cuba…that in his opinion the Soviet aid to Cuba was purely economic. Furthermore, Taylor asked the State Department to withdraw a memo which noted an upsurge in Bloc vessels traveling to Cuba under conditions suggesting increasing deliveries of arms. These incidents illustrate the disagreement which prevailed throughout August between CIA and the defense establishment over interpretation of intelligence on the movement of shipping to Cuba. DIA publications of August and September insisted that increased shipping reflected an increased flow of economic aid. Disagreement between CIA and DIA over the interpretation of evidence persisted until 10 October. While speculative, DIA's actions could certainly have had a chilling

---

[47] Matthew M. Aid. *The Secret Sentry; The Untold History of the National Security Agency*, New York: Bloomsbury Press, 2009, p. 64.

[48] President Kennedy brought General Taylor back to active duty in a newly created post of military representative to the President. On 1 October 1962, Taylor became Chairman of the Joint Chiefs of Staff.

effect on efforts to better understand the nature of what Soviet ships were transporting.[49]

The Soviets largely succeeded in concealing the immense task of transporting thousands of personnel—41,900 as later revealed by the Russians—and huge amounts of military equipment to a far off place thousands of miles from home[50]. U.S. inability to better understand what the Soviets were shipping to Cuba can be seen as an intelligence failure because analysts knew there was something more secret being shipped than conventional military weapons as evidenced by unusual secret off loadings at night. U.S. intelligence clearly saw that Soviet ships were lightly loaded but with large hatches, and the pace of weapons delivery was much more than needed for a conventional defense of Cuba. It knew the immense magnitude of the shipping from SIGINT which also indicated that shipping information was being falsified. The unusual aspects of the ships and other key indicators were revealed by photographic reconnaissance, and clandestine human sources reported something highly secret was going on at the Cuban ports when Soviet ships unloaded.

The actual details of the Soviet deployment are now known based on an after-action report by Soviet Major General Igor Statsenko who commanded the MRBM and IRBM missile regiments on Cuba.[51] His report describes the cover stories—"agricultural specialists"—used by Soviet reconnaissance teams as they mapped out the MRBM sites, and how the purpose of the operation was

---

[49] *Inspector General's Survey,* p. 8.

[50] The Attachment is a translation of a top secret 24 May 1962 memorandum prepared by the Soviet Ministry of Defense for Khrushchev. It lists the troops, weapons and equipment to be sent to Cuba.

[51] *Report of Major-General Statsenko,* National Security Archive Electronic Briefing Book, No. 449.

held in the strictest confidence with only a strictly limited number of members of the Cuban Army having been informed. The missiles were unloaded from the ships only at night, under total blackout on the ships and in the ports. While the missiles were being unloaded, all external approaches to the ports were guarded by a squadron of 300 men. The missiles and parts were transported to the deployment areas only at night in small columns, the secrecy of which was aided by use of a decoy convoy and the staging of fake car accidents.

Statsenko's report identifies the *Omsk, Kimovsk, Poltava, Krasnograd*, and the *Orenburg* as having delivered 42 missiles, six of which were for training, to the Ports of Casilda and Mariel between September 9 and October 16. (A retrospective analysis of intelligence available at the time identified the same ships as those in Statsenko's report.[52])

Are There Offensive Missiles in Cuba?

CIA agents in Cuba and Cubans who fled to the U.S. were in positions to see the movement of military equipment from the ports and reported this information as soon as they were able. Agent reports were delayed because the information had to be concealed in secret writing and mailed to accommodation addresses used by the CIA for secret communications. Refugee reports were delayed because they needed to make their way to the U.S. and arrive at the interrogation center in Florida.

Soon after Castro's triumphant arrival in Havana, the intelligence community had been flooded with reports of Soviet weapons and missile installa-

---

[52] *Inspector General's Survey, Annex K.*

tions. To process the flow of information, CIA established a Joint Interrogation Center at a former Marine Corps air base at Opa Locka near Miami. The Center was known as the Caribbean Admission Center and manned by trained interrogators from the military and CIA. It was administered by CIA, and in internal CIA organization structure was known as a field office of the Domestic Contact Division in the Directorate of Intelligence. The Center was established under presidential authority and began operation on 15 February 1962. Opa Locka did not operate like a typical CIA station. It brandished its overt status and drummed up business by listing the phone number in the local telephone book.[53]

By September 1962, the volume of agent and refugee reporting had become very large. A substantial proportion of these reports concerned defensive missiles and related activities. However, CIA analysts recognized and correlated the first authentic reports of MRBM equipment and took action on them. Two reports targeted the San Cristóbal area as a suspect SS-4 (MRBM) site. The two reports were: 1) An observation on 12 September in Havana of a convoy carrying long canvas-covered objects, which the source identified as resembling SS-4's based on photographs of the missile he was shown (the CIA photographs of the SS-4 missile were obtained during a Moscow parade). This report, which was disseminated by CIA on 27 September, contained sufficiently accurate detail to alert intelligence analysts; 2) An observation on 17 September of a convoy moving toward the San Cristóbal area. This information, received on 1 October, dovetailed in many respects with the earlier report.

---

[53] Justin F. Gleichauf. "A Listening Post in Miami," *Studies in Intelligence,* Winter-Spring 2001.

The arrival of the second report led CIA analysts to a tentative conclusion that the two observers had in fact seen the same convoy, and that there was a possibility of the SS-4 identification being genuine, leading analysts to request U-2 reconnaissance of the area. The justification for the U-2 coverage read: "Collateral reports indicate the existence of a restricted area in Pinar del Rio Province which is suspected of including an SSM [Surface-to-Surface Missile] site under construction, particularly SS-4. The area is bounded by a line connecting the following four towns: Consolacion del Norte; San Diego del Los Banos; San Cristóbal; and Las Pozos."[54]

A report by a secret CIA agent in Cuba that was disseminated on 18 September grabbed the attention of Ted Shackley, chief of CIA's Miami station (cryptonym JMWAVE). It was the largest CIA station outside its Langley headquarters, located on land owned by the University of Miami and operated under the flimsy cover of "Zenith Technical Enterprises." The secret agent had been recruited under the MONGOOSE (see later) covert operation element at CIA, and in secret writing he conveyed information about what he observed on 7 September of a mountainous area near San Cristóbal, 60 miles west of Havana, where "very secret and important work" believed to involve missiles was in progress. What made this agent report intriguing was that it coincided with the two refugee reports that described large missiles last seen heading west from Havana. The secret CIA agent was probably Esteban Marquez Novo whose case officer was Tom Hewitt of the Miami station. Hewitt's work with Marquez Novo was recognized by Jack Downing, former CIA dep-

---

[54] Mary S. McAuliffe (editor). *CIA documents on the Cuban Missile Crisis, 1962*, CIA History Staff, October 1992.

uty director of operations. (See Vignettes, Operation Cobra, for a description of agent AMBANTY's efforts.)

DIA analysts were also closely monitoring reporting of military equipment in Cuba and were particularly struck by the deployment pattern of SA-2 defensive missiles. DIA analyst Col. John R. Wright, Jr. and his staff became increasingly interested in the SA-2 sites near San Cristóbal. Most significant to them, the U-2 photography indicated that these sites formed the outline of a trapezoid. This suggested that the sites were forming a "point defense" to protect some extremely important weapons emplacements. This deployment pattern was similar to those identified near ballistic missile launch sites in the Soviet Union. The stationing of these SA-2's, together with human-source reporting of missiles in western Cuba, strongly suggested that there were offensive Soviet missiles to be found within the San Cristóbal trapezoid. This led DIA to establish requirements for reconnaissance of the San Cristóbal area.[55] (It later became apparent that the Soviets deployed their SA-2 sites around the entire periphery of the island and not particularly close to the MRBM and IRBM sites; the SAMs were clearly meant for an island-wide, not a point defense.)

CIA pressed for U-2 reconnaissance of the areas identified by the agent and interrogation reports. But the agency was concerned that overflights might not be approved by the White House. (CIA had presented a plan for extensive U-2 coverage of the island at a White House meeting on 10 September. Sec-

---

[55] John T. Hughes with A. Denis Clift. *"The San Cristóbal Trapezoid," Studies in Intelligence,* 1992; Michael B. Petersen, *"Legacy of Ashes, Trial by Fire: The Origins of the Defense Intelligence Agency and the Cuban Missile Crisis Crucible."* DIA Historical Research Support Branch, published 2011. https://www.dia.mil > Documents > About > History.

retary of State Rusk objected to CIA's plan such that the plan that was approved provided much less coverage than what CIA had requested. There were also indications that CIA's future requests would be met with resistance.) This led the Agency to avoid having only CIA fingerprints on the intelligence concerning suspect missile sites since it worried about it being discounted as the product of an overly aggressive Agency. Consequently, in late September, Col. Wright, DIA's analyst and head of the MONGOOSE component at DIA, was invited to a briefing at CIA. Based on the coordinates provided by the MONGOOSE agent, CIA officers had marked off a Trapezoid-shaped area and they asked Wright to push a request for U-2 surveillance up his chain of command. Samuel Halpern, Executive Officer of Task Force W (the organization responsible for Agency MONGOOSE operations) recalled that the maneuver got CIA out of the line of fire and let DIA take the lead. The downside was if the U-2 found anything, DIA would get the credit for having astutely assembled the crucial intelligence.[56]

According to Roger Hilsman, Col. Wright and Navy Captain Charles R. Clark were later credited with suggesting that the San Cristóbal-Guanajay area was a likely missile site.[57] Max Holland noted that DIA Director Lt. General Joseph Carroll, USAF, was taking the lion's share of the credit for piecing together the intelligence that prompted the 14 October flight. Carroll presented the discovery of the Soviet missiles as a seamless example of intelligence collection and analysis.[58]

---

[56] David M. Barrett and Max Holland. *Blind Over Cuba; The Photo Gap and the Missile Crisis,* College Station, Texas: Texas A&M University Press, 2012.
[57] Hilsman, p. 45.
[58] Barrett and Holland. *Blind Over Cuba,* p. 94.

(The attentive reader will no doubt notice the two versions of how the suspect site was targeted for coverage by the U-2: one by DIA's Col. Wright, who, based on the configuration of SA-2 sites, sent the recommendation up his chain of command; the other that CIA had figured out the location to be targeted and used Wright to push it forward thinking that it would more likely be favorably considered than if CIA pushed it.)

Well before the Cuban Missile Crisis CIA had been flying the U-2 over Cuba gathering intelligence. Those flights had begun in 1960 as CIA was preparing for the counterrevolutionary (Bay of Pigs) invasion of Cuba. To support the effort, the Agency asked the National Security Council Special Group to approve U-2 overflights of Cuba. Known as Operation Kick Off, these flights were designed to obtain intelligence on Cuban air and ground order of battle and for choosing an invasion site. The authorization was given and the Agency conducted several overflights in the latter months of 1960.

Overflights of Cuba continued under the new Kennedy administration with two missions in March of 1961 to aid final preparations for the Bay of Pigs operation. Beginning in early April, numerous missions were flown to provide coverage of the ill-fated invasion and its aftermath. Cuba remained a high priority target even after the Bay of Pigs, with CIA flying monthly missions. By the spring of 1962, having received reports of increased Soviet activity in Cuba, CIA requested and was granted permission by the White House Special Group to increase Cuban overflights to at least two per month beginning in May 1962.

By early August, CIA analysts had noted a substantial increase in Soviet military deliveries to Cuba during the preceding weeks. Missions were flown on 5 and 29 August, the latter having been postponed from 8 August due to bad weather. The flight of 29 August provided the first hard evidence of the nature of the Soviet buildup—the discovery of SA-2 surface to air missile sites in the western part of the island. The next overflight on 5 September showed more SA-2 sites.

The discovery of the SA-2 sites made the administration far more cautious when considering Cuban overflights. The shooting down of Francis Gary Powers' U-2 by an SA-2 on 1 May 1960 was fresh on the minds of administration leaders. Concern that a loss of a U-2 over Cuba would cause a major diplomatic crisis was increased by two incidents in other parts of the world: On 8 September 1962 a U-2 flown by a Nationalist Chinese pilot was shot down over the Peoples Republic of China. And on 30 August 1962 a Strategic Air Command (SAC) U-2 on an air sampling peripheral mission mistakenly overflew Sakhalin Island.[59] Khrushchev would later refer to this intrusion in his message to President Kennedy of 28 October 1962: "…During your term of office as President, a second case [the Powers 1 May 1960 U-2 flight being the first case] of violation of our frontier by an American U-2 aircraft has taken place in the Sakhalin area. We informed you of this violation on 30 August. You then replied that this violation had occurred as a result of bad weather and you gave assurances that it would not be repeated."

(Another errant U-2 flight has received little historical interest despite its having occurred at a critical time in the crisis. In the early afternoon of Sat-

---

[59] Garthoff in *Reflections,* pg. 28, and Brugioni, pg. 108, correctly refer to the Sakhalin intrusion of 30 August, while Hilsman, p. 35, and a CIA MFR cite 7 September as the date of the incursion. See Memorandum for the Record, Subject: Notes on Factors Bearing on Reconnaissance of Cuba dated 28 October, 1962, unknown author, CIA files.

urday, 27 October, news arrived in Washington that a U-2 on a mission to collect air samples from Soviet nuclear tests near the North Pole had gotten lost near Alaska. Expressing sharp alarm about the danger of war, McNamara left the Pentagon briefly to talk to Rusk. They learned that, as a result of navigation difficulties, the U-2 had gone off course into Soviet air space. Soviet MiG fighters had tried to intercept the aircraft. Then U.S. fighters based in Alaska had been sent aloft to protect the U-2 as it reentered U.S. airspace. In his message to Kennedy on 28 October Khrushchev refers to this incident; "An even more dangerous case [the earlier case being the 30 August one] occurred on 28 October, [27 October in the U.S.] when your reconnaissance aircraft invaded the northern area of the Soviet Union, in the area of the Chukotski Peninsula, and flew over our territory."[60] In Kennedy's message to Khrushchev of 28 October he says "You referred in your letter to a violation of your frontier by an American aircraft in the area of the Chukotsk [*sic*] Peninsula. I have learned that this plane, without arms or photographic equipment, was engaged in an air sampling mission in connection with your nuclear tests. Its course was direct from Eielson Air Force Base in Alaska to the North Pole and return. In turning south, the pilot made a serious error which carried him over Soviet territory. He immediately made an emergency call on open radio for navigational assistance and was guided back to his home base by the most direct route. I regret this incident and will see to it that every precaution is taken to prevent recurrence.)" [61,62]

---

[60] Ronald R. Pope (editor and commentator). "Soviet Views on the Cuban Missile Crisis; Myth and Reality," *Foreign Policy Analysis,* Lanham, Md and London; University Press of America, 1982, p. 62.

[61] Ibid, p. 66; see also Kennedy, *Thirteen Days,* p. 170.

[62] Author Michael Dobbs shows the U-2 flight path of 27 October on page 261. (Michael

These concerns (the U-2 loss over China and the Sakhalin Island violation) led to an impromptu 10 September meeting of Secretary of State Rusk, National Security Advisor Bundy, and DDCI Carter (McCone was in France on his honeymoon). CIA's plan for extended overflights of areas of Cuba not covered by the last two missions were objected to by Rusk and Bundy, and with the acquiescence of Carter, the Agency's plan was revised to greatly reduce the vulnerability of the U-2, but in so doing the collection of photographic intelligence was also greatly reduced.

Roger Hilsman defended the 10 September meeting decision after McCone instituted a study to determine if the missiles would have been discovered sooner if the Secretary of State had not suggested substituting peripheral flights for the CIA's planned flights. Hilsman said it was not difficult to show, first, that any delay caused by making four flights instead of one was negligible; second that the risk of a U-2 being lost and an international crisis that would make it difficult to continue having any U-2 flights at all was real; and third, that there had never been a turndown of any flight that the intelligence community had proposed, but that on the contrary both the White House and the State Department had actually pushed for more intelligence all along.[63]

Caribbean weather proved to be a major problem during the month of September. Together with the cautiously-designed mission plans, the September flights turned up many more SAM sites but no concrete evidence of surface-to-surface missiles. DCI McCone upon his return from his European

Dobbs. *One Minute to Midnight: Kennedy, Khrushchev, and Castro on the Brink of Nuclear War*, New York: Random House, 2008.)

[63] Hilsman, pp. 56-7.

trip learned of the paucity of Cuban coverage. Frustrated with the restrictions that had been placed on U-2 Cuban overflights, he questioned the Special Group on 4 October whether their policy of using the U-2 only in Cuba's southeastern quadrant was a reasonable restriction, particularly since the SAM's were almost certainly not operational. The Special Group then requested that the National Reconnaissance Office (NRO) prepare an overall plan for Cuban reconnaissance for its next meeting on 9 October.[64]

The conclusion from the Special National Intelligence Estimate of 19 September that offensive missiles were unlikely to be found in Cuba may have contributed to a lack of urgency by U.S. officials. But it is also reasonable to conclude, as Hilsman does, that there might have been a greater sense of urgency to continue full coverage of Cuba if the overall judgment had been that the Soviets probably would put missiles in Cuba rather than not. Even so, he says, as a practical matter, the difference at most would probably have been no more than a few days.[65]

In response to the Special Group action levied at the 4 October meeting, the Committee on Overhead Reconnaissance (COMOR)[66] on 6 October provided a memorandum to the NRO citing the need for renewed coverage of western Cuba. It included the statement that "Ground observers have, in recent instances, reported sightings of what they believe to be Soviet MRBM's

---

[64] Hilsman is incorrect when he writes on p. 60 that there was a decision at the 4 October meeting to fly again over western Cuba. In fact, the decision coming out of the 4 October meeting was to develop a reconnaissance plan to be considered at the next meeting on 9 October. The National Reconnaissance Office was the joint CIA-DOD covert organization for operating reconnaissance satellites and reconnaissance aircraft established in August 1960. Its existence was declassified in 1992.

[65] Hilsman, p. 61.

[66] COMOR served to integrate requirements from intelligence community elements for transmittal to the USIB.

in Cuba. These reports must be confirmed or denied by photo coverage.". Attached to the memorandum was a list of targets, with the area around San Cristóbal at the top.[67]

On 9 October the Special Group discussed COMOR's recommendations, the most important of which was to cover the suspect MRBM site. The mission was also designed to pass over one of the SA-2 sites that was thought to be most nearly operational in order to determine the status of SA-2 defenses of Cuba. The danger posed by overflying the SA-2 site was an obvious concern of the Special Group which McCone addressed; a CIA expert on the U-2's vulnerability gave his estimate of the loss of a U-2 over Cuba at 1 in 6. The Special Group approved the recommended mission.

The Agency's cover story for its missions over Cuba had been that its pilots were Lockheed employees on ferry flights to Puerto Rico. DOD and the Air Force though it would be better to use Air Force pilots, and that in the event of a mishap, that the overflight was a routine Air Force peripheral mission that had gone off course. The CIA expert agreed but noted that SAC's U-2s were much more vulnerable than the CIA's because the Agency's had more powerful engines and thus a higher altitude capability. McCone and Gilpatric met with President Kennedy after the 9 October meeting at which time Kennedy approved the use of Air Force pilots.

While the President had approved using Air Force pilots, there were still issues associated with the transfer of responsibility, specifically who, the CIA or the Air Force (really the Strategic Air Command—SAC) should fly the upcoming mission. The DOD strongly favored the Air Force and gained

---

[67] Lehman pp. 30-1.

McCone's consent. Air Force control became official on 12 October when Kennedy transferred "responsibility, to include command and control and operational decisions, with regard to U-2 reconnaissance of Cuba" from CIA to the Department of Defense.

Acting DCI Carter (McCone was in California for the funeral of his wife's son) reacted strongly to the Air Force takeover, and argued against changing command and control at such a crucial time. He told Gilpatric "To put in a brand-new green pilot just because he happens to have on a blue suit and to completely disrupt the command and control and communication and ground support system on 72 hours' notice to me doesn't make a God damn bit of sense, Mr. Secretary." Carter's efforts were in vain. The Air Force insisted on immediate control of the operation and administration officials were unwilling to become involved.

Carter was clearly disappointed and concerned over the abruptness of the change and he told McCone that the immediate turnover was "a hell of a way to run a railroad." McCone then told Carter: "If that's the way they're going to run the railroad, let them run the goddamn thing."[68]

Once the decision was made, the Agency's U-2 detachment at Edwards Air Force Base supervised the training of Air Force pilots in the CIA version of the U-2, the U-2C. And on 13 October the CIA's Edwards detachment deployed to McCoy Air Force Base, Florida, near Orlando, to support SAC as instructed by an Agency official: "Continue to regard yourself as being under SAC control." And later: "You are urged to support SAC fully in the manner

---

[68] Robarge history of McCone, p. 110.

you have done so well these past few days."[69]

By 14 October the weather over Cuba had cleared (it was unfavorable on 10, 11, and 12 October while SAC pilots were being trained) and the first SAC overflight of the island took place in a U-2C that SAC had "borrowed" from the Agency.[70] Major Richard Heyser departed Edwards Air Force Base and flew the mission that had been planned by CIA. After landing at McCoy, the film from the historic mission was rushed to NPIC for interpretation. By the evening of 15 October, experts had found evidence of MRBM's in the San Cristóbal area.[71] Senior officials were immediately notified and on 16 October, DDCI Carter briefed the President.[72]

Much has been written about the gap in U-2 photographic missions between 5 September and the eventful one of 14 October when Soviet MRBM's were discovered.[73] Often cited as one of the reasons for the gap was a supposed dispute between CIA and the Air Force over control of U-2 Cuban missions. McGeorge Bundy's 1988 memoir attributed the gap to an unworthy squabble between CIA and the Air Force.[74] A *Newsweek* article of 4 March 1963 read in

---

[69] Scoville cable to KWCACTU.S, 13 October, and Cunningham cable to KWCACTU.S, 16 October. CIA archives.

[70] Helen Kleyla. "History of the Office of Special Activities; Operation NIMBUS: Cuba During the Missile Buildup," CIA Directorate of Science and Technology History (later referred to as the OSA history), p. 24.

[71] The San Cristóbal MRBM site was actually three sites designated the San Cristóbal MRBM sites 1, 2 and 3. The name San Cristóbal was used because it was a larger town than others in the area.

[72] The primary source for the above is Gregory W. Pedlow and Donald E. Welzenbach, *The Central Intelligence Agency and Overhead Reconnaissance; the U-2 and Oxcart Programs, 1954-1974,* History Staff, Center for the Study of Intelligence, 1998, pp. 197-201, 205-21. https://www.cia.gov/static/37e56c57ddf41f9c85f357a04900e1e8/CIA-and-U2-Program.pdf .

[73] In reality the photos from the 14 October mission did not show MRBM missiles. Rather the photos showed transporters and other equipment that were known to be associated with Soviet MRBM's leading the photo interpreters to conclude there were Soviet MRBM's in Cuba.

part: "Though he [Bundy]…will not discuss the matter, there is firm basis to credit him with breaking a deadlock in a dispute between CIA and the Strategic Air Command as to which agency would conduct U-2 flights over Cuba. According to this account, it was that dispute—not bad weather—that left a gap of some two weeks in the U.S. overflights…"[75] In fact, there was no delay caused by a "dispute." CIA not only accepted but facilitated the transfer of responsibility and that included expedited training of Air Force pilots.

Much of the photo gap can be attributed to weather where cloud cover over Cuba in September and October precluded useful photography by the CIA BRASS KNOB U-2 flights much of the time. Still, the timidity of senior U.S officials Bundy and Rusk who feared the consequences if a U-2 were to be shot down has received the criticism. In *Eyeball to Eyeball*, Brugioni noted "it wasn't the weather, but rather the dereliction, bumbling, and intransigence of Rusk and Bundy."[76]

According to Max Holland the Kennedy White House had not wanted the issue of a photo gap to be known for it would damage the image of its masterful crisis management. It promulgated the idea that no request for photographic coverage was ever denied by the White House. While technically true, it was disingenuous; COMOR representatives had resisted submitting requests for U-2 coverage after being told, in effect, they would not be approved. Indeed, the president could technically claim (and on his behalf, Bundy did) that he approved every overflight request.[77]

---

[74] Holland, p. 131.
[75] From OSA History.
[76] Brugioni, p. 132.
[77] Holland, p. 105.

Have You Found the Nuclear Warheads?

President Kennedy often asked McCone and NPIC chief Arthur Lundahl that question. The answer was always *no*, but today, thanks to retrospective research, after-action reports and statements by former Soviet officials, we know there were nuclear weapons in Cuba, where they were located, when they arrived in Cuba and when they were withdrawn. While *direct* evidence concerning the presence of warheads has never been found, and given the limitations of overhead photography and Soviet security measures, probably could not have been, there is now little question that the USSR did have a nuclear capability in Cuba.

Virtually all evidence concerning possible nuclear weapons in Cuba came from overhead photography, first from the U-2, and beginning on 23 October, from low-level, unarmed Navy supersonic jets under a secret operation code-named *Blue Moon*, and a little later by U.S. Air Force low-level reconnaissance aircraft.[78]

After the Cuban Missile Crisis, CIA's Office of Research and Reports (ORR) conducted a study to review the evidence concerning the nature, scope, and timing of the Soviet buildup in Cuba in 1962. The study was published in February 1964, but not declassified and released until 2017. This retrospective study provides an accounting of what U.S. intelligence knew at the time.[79] What follows is information from that study concerning possible nuclear weapons in Cuba.

---

[78] Capt. William B. Ecker, USN (ret.) & Kenneth V. Jack. *Blue Moon Over Cuba; Aerial Reconnaissance during the Cuban Missile Crisis*, Oxford: Osprey Publishing, 2012.

[79] *Cuba 1962: Khrushchev's Miscalculated Risk*, CIA/ORR DD/I Staff Study; pp. 3, 68-74.

The precise degree of combat readiness of the 24 MRBM launch positions in Cuba at the time of the crisis cannot be determined from available evidence, even in retrospect. The principal uncertainty concerns the presence or absence of nuclear warheads; the evidence on this aspect of the buildup is so ambiguous and inconclusive that it is not possible to reach a judgement based on factual information. It cannot be demonstrated from available evidence that the USSR had delivered nuclear warheads to Cuba by the time of the U.S. quarantine. If they had not been delivered, then the USSR probably had no capability whatever during the crisis to attack the U.S. by missiles fired from Cuba, for it is highly unlikely that the USSR would have provided conventional, high-explosive warheads for the MRBM's. On the other hand, the evidence indicates that much of the equipment believed to be necessary for the handling and on-site transportation of MRBM warheads and nosecones was present and that permanent facilities almost certainly intended for the storage of nuclear warheads were being constructed at both the MRBM and the IRBM sites. Although a thorough effort failed to uncover direct evidence concerning the presence of warheads, there is no assurance that they could have been detected by photography or other means; hence there is also no basis in evidence for concluding that the USSR did not have a nuclear capability in Cuba.

There are three bodies of evidence, all ambiguous and inconclusive, that may relate to the presence of nuclear warheads. The first of these concerns the equipment and facilities required for their handling and storage. At five of the six MRBM sites, as well as at the Mariel Naval Air Station, special purpose units were observed in photography which, because of their unique equipment and physical positioning, have been identified as probable missile nosecone handling units. In general, the equipment included: eight large vans that seemed appropriate for nosecone handling; a truck-mounted crane; and an undetermined number of dollies that appear suitable for nosecone handling and generally corresponded to descriptions of such equipment found in Soviet documents.

At the missile sites the special purpose units referred to above generally were located in an area by themselves, just as the propellant vehicles were in separate areas, indicating a special function. In some cases, they were positioned in close proximity to the arch-roofed, probable nuclear weapons facilities.

It is known from Soviet documents that nosecones and warheads normally are stored separately from the missiles for which they are intended. When an increased state of readiness is ordered, the nosecones with warheads are transported to the missile-ready facility for mating to the missile. In Cuba the MRBM nosecones probably were stored in the vans of the nosecone handling unit and would have been transported to the missile-ready tents in these vans. The presence of the vans, however, provides no assurance of the presence of warheads. No vans were observed in the immediate vicinity of missile-ready tents at any of the Cuban MRBM sites, and, for that matter, none of the missiles observed on their transporters was of sufficient length to have had nosecones (with or without warheads) attached. The only activity of the nosecone handling units at the MRBM sites that may have been indicative of some nosecone/warhead checkout consisted of a single instance of a van at one of the San Cristóbal sites being loaded or unloaded, but the cargo cannot be identified. Otherwise, little or no activity was observed.

It is likely that nuclear warheads would have been delivered to Cuba in specially hermetically sealed containers. About two dozen such containers were observed in photography of a special unit located at Mariel Naval Air Station throughout the period 15 October–10 November. These containers were located in a separately secured area at the end of the runway, together with a number of nosecone dollies and 12 or more probable nosecone vans. Although the unit at the Mariel Naval Air Station appears to have performed some unique function, there is no way of determining from the available evidence whether its activity concerned MRBM nosecones or warheads. If warheads were in Cuba, this unit may have served as a receiving and initial checkout point through which they were transshipped to the sites. It must be noted, however, that the facilities at Mariel were of a field type and rudimentary. Although they might have sufficed for a temporary receiving facility, their appearance seems somewhat out of keeping with the stringent procedures and precautions that normally surround Soviet handling of nuclear weapons, especially in view of the general availability of more appropriate facilities in Cuba.

In addition to the nosecone handling units and their special equipment, each MRBM site was evidently to have its own arch-roofed nuclear warhead bunker. The size of these bunkers suggests that they were intended for more than just storage of the warheads; probably warhead checkout and maintenance also would have been performed in these facilities. By 28 October it is unlikely that any of the bunkers had equipment installed or were actually in use. If warheads were present and operational at the MRBM sites, therefore, they must have been maintained and stored elsewhere, presumably in vans.

Bunkers were also present near the IRBM sites at Guanajay and Remedios. It is curious that both of the IRBM bunkers were virtually complete by 28 October, in contrast to those at the MRBM sites, even though the IRBM missiles had not yet arrived, whereas MRBM's had been arriving on site for well over a month. Because warheads for both systems are controlled by the same Soviet authority, it is possible that both MRBM and IRBM warheads were to be delivered to Cuba in a single shipment after completion of all of the storage and checkout facilities, which was not planned to occur until some time in November.

A second body of evidence that may be pertinent to the presence of nuclear warheads in Cuba concerns the voyage of the Soviet ship Aleksandrovsk. *Although any shipment of military cargo to Cuba during the buildup period could have included nuclear warheads, the* Aleksandrovsk *is suspected of having had some special cargo aboard, possibly nuclear warheads, because it was the only ship that departed from and returned to a Soviet Arctic naval port during the entire Cuban buildup. On 3 October the* Aleksandrovsk *was photographed at the arctic port of Guba Okol'naya,[80] a part of the naval complex in the Severomorsk area that serves submarines and surface craft of the Northern Fleet. The* Aleksandrovsk *is the first merchant vessel known to have called at this port. After the quarantine was imposed the* Aleksandrovsk *probably remained at La Isabella for about a week, following which the vessel sailed to Mariel. The reason for the unique voyages of the* Aleksandrovsk *is not readily apparent. It can be hypothesized that the use of Guba Okol'naya enabled the vessel to reach Cuba and return with an unusually sensitive cargo, such as nuclear warheads, without risking surveillance in narrow waters under Western control, such as the passages from the Baltic or Black Seas. If this is a correct explanation for the voyage of the* Aleksandrovsk, *it must have been the first delivery of warheads to Cuba, for most all other known voyages transited the Baltic or Black Seas.*

The Aleksandrovsk *was one of the first Soviet ships to depart Cuba, leaving Mariel with a deck cargo of nosecone vans on 5 November and arriving at Guba Okol'naya in late November.*

---

[80] The 3 October photographs of the *Aleksandrovsk* did not reach Washington until January 3, 1963. The photographs of this highly significant ship were taken by the U.S. Navy but were apparently misplaced only to be discovered later. See Dwayne Anderson, "On the Trail of the Alexandrovsk [*sic*]," *Studies in Intelligence*, Winter 1966.

The CIA analysts that reviewed what we knew was going on in Cuba regarding nuclear matters during the crisis found the activities of the Aleksandrovsk quite mysterious and their analysis of its role was inconclusive. They determined that Guba Okol'naya and the Aleksandrovsk may have no nuclear significance whatever.

The only other evidence bearing on nuclear warheads consists of the statements of Soviet officials on the subject. On 8 November, Deputy Foreign Minister Kuznetsov stated to Ambassador Stevenson that nuclear warheads had been taken out of Cuba "immediately" after the decision was made to remove the missiles. Two days earlier, however, Kuznetsov had indicated that the warheads would be removed if warheads are indeed in Cuba. On 12 November, Khrushchev twice stated to British Ambassador Roberts that nuclear warheads had been removed from Cuba. Although the November assertions regarding nuclear warheads may well have been true, they cannot be taken at face value. The Soviet authorities probably judged that they would not be compelled to demonstrate the removal of nuclear warheads as they would be compelled to demonstrate the removal of the missiles. Hence statements that warheads were not present in Cuba, even if true, probably would not have served the Soviet purpose at the time, which was to reassure the U.S. that the offensive weapons were being withdrawn. Once the crisis was past, the Soviet authorities could hardly be expected to admit that warheads had not reached Cuba, had that been the case.

Since publication of the CIA ORR study much additional information has surfaced. At a January 1989 conference in Moscow,[81] Soviet General Dmitry Volkogonov, head of the Soviet Ministry of Defense Institute of Military History, said twenty nuclear warheads had arrived in Cuba in late September or early October, and twenty others were in transit aboard the *Poltava*[82] when the quarantine went into effect. According to Volkogonov, the warheads that had

---

[81] There have been a number of ex post facto conferences about the crisis. See the listing in the vignettes.

[82] This is the only known reference connecting the *Poltava* to nuclear warheads; it is never mentioned by other Soviet officials.

arrived in Cuba were kept "well away" from the missiles themselves, and at no time were measures taken to mate them, even when alerts were raised following President Kennedy's speech of 22 October. At the same conference Sergei Khrushchev, son of Nikita Khrushchev, claimed "My father would not have allowed [the warheads] to be mounted. He felt that would have made it easier for a madman to start a war."[83]

According to Admiral Gribkov writing in *Operation Anadyr*, the atomic warheads for the MRBM's had arrived in Mariel on 4 October onboard the freighter *Indigirka* from the Barents Sea military port of Severomorsk. The KGB troops on that ship, itself specially armed for the perilous trip, were also guarding eighty cruise missile (FKR) warheads, six bombs for the IL-28's and a dozen atomic charges for the "Luna" rockets. Separately, another ship, the *Alexandrovsk* [the *Aleksandrovsk*] carried the twenty-four warheads for the IRBM missiles. These stayed in the vessel's hold in the port of La Isabela, waiting for missiles that never arrived.[84]

The MRBM warheads had gone into bunkers in Bejucal, about thirteen miles south of Havana and—by road—not much more than fifty miles from the three MRBM missile regiments deployed near San Cristóbal. This central nuclear depot in Bejucal was also the storage site for forty warheads for the FKR detachment about forty miles away, west of Mariel, and for the twelve warheads for the "Luna" rocket units. Other atomic weapons—the six bombs

---

[83] Bruce J. Allyn, James G. Blight, and David A. Welch. "Essence of Revision; Moscow, Havana, and the Cuban Missile Crisis," *International Security*, Vol. 14, No. 3, Winter 1989-1990, p. 154.

[84] General Anatoli I. Gribkov and General William Y. Smith (USAF). *Operation Anadyr; U.S. and Soviet General's Recount of the Cuban Missile Crisis*, Chicago: Edition q , 1994 , pp. 45-6.

for the IL-28's and the forty warheads for the second cruise missile detachment—had been placed in well-guarded depots closer to either the bombers airfield in the central portion of the island, or to the cruise missile units in the hills above the U.S. base at Guantanamo Bay.[85]

Soviet Col. Nikolai Beloborodov was responsible for the storage of all nuclear munitions on Cuba, including those at the main depot at Bejucal. He was also safeguarding forty FKR warheads assigned, but not yet deployed to rockets and launchers in eastern Cuba and the six atomic bombs for the IL-28's. Gribkov notes that none of the "cargoes" (the Soviet term for atomic weapons) under Beloborodov's control had been released by 22 October to other commanders, nor were they released at any time during the crisis.[86]

We now know that nuclear weapons were indeed in Cuba, but confidence in such a conclusion had not always been the case. Writing in *Reflections on the Cuban Missile Crisis* in 1989, Raymond L. Garthoff explains the uncertainty about nuclear weapons when he discusses U.S. and Soviet negotiations on removal of nuclear weapons at the conclusion of the crisis.[87] The U.S. had informed Soviet negotiators in early November that "warheads" for missiles and bombers were to be withdrawn along with the missiles. Vasily Kuznetsov, the Soviet negotiator, had said on 6 November 1962 that the question of removal of warheads was "a detail," that without doubt warheads would be removed "if indeed any warheads are in Cuba." On 18 November he informed the U.S. that "he was now authorized to say that no nuclear weapons whatsoever were

---

[85] Ibid, p. 45-6.

[86] Ibid, p. 62-3.

[87] Raymond L. Garthoff. *Reflections on the Cuban Missile Crisis*, Washington, D.C.: The Brookings Institution, 1989, pp. 115-6.

any longer on the territory of Cuba," and that the Soviet government re-affirmed that "all nuclear weapons had been removed and that they were not going to reintroduce them."

Garthoff continues: "Assuming that the recent Soviet acknowledgment that some of the nuclear missile warheads had been in Cuba is correct, the record of Soviet statements in November 1962 is entirely consistent with the known facts." "While couched in terms that implied there had been warheads in Cuba, the Soviet purpose was to reassure the United States—which had raised the issue as though warheads were there. Thus, even if no warheads had ever reached Cuba, the Soviets would not have wanted to stimulate American suspicions or a new issue by stating so. For its part the United States did not want to admit that it did not know if there were any nuclear warheads in Cuba." "It did not wish to acknowledge doubt as to the presence of nuclear warheads and possibly stimulate any Soviet temptation to conceal and keep in Cuba any warheads it might have there." "The result was agreement that any [nuclear] warheads for the missiles and bombs were being returned. Although American intelligence did not conclusively detect the return of any nuclear warheads to the Soviet Union, that very fact tended (except for the most suspicious) to confirm the estimate that none had been there. That judgment may have been in error." "Assuming nuclear warheads had been there, the available evidence tends to corroborate the Soviet account of their removal."[88]

Brugioni in *Eyeball to Eyeball* claims that statements made during and after the crisis that nuclear weapons were never seen in Cuba simply weren't true. Here he makes the distinction between "seeing" and "discovering." He claims they

---

[88] Ibid, pp. 115-6.

weren't *discovered* until reviewing aerial photography after the crisis that had been acquired during the crisis. He also claims that this same post-crisis review made it obvious that the Soviets had fueled and mated the warheads and had practiced moving the missiles to the erectors. He cites photography of October 23 of the Sagua la Grande MRBM site no.1. showing missile fueling, check-out, generator, and water vans positioned and connected to a missile inside the missile-ready tents. Brugioni then makes a leap not supported by the available evidence: "It must be presumed that the warhead was also mated to the missile."[89]

U.S. intelligence had not seen actual nuclear warheads for the missiles or a nuclear bomb for the IL-28's, but it had accumulated numerous indicators of nuclear weapons in the form of "signatures" that resembled those of nuclear facilities and equipment that NPIC had seen in the USSR. At each of the MRBM and IRBM missile sites photo interpreters found either nuclear warhead storage bunkers or construction activity indicating they were being planned. Overhead reconnaissance also revealed the presence of four to eight vans at each of the bunkers that photo interpreters labeled *unidentified* meaning their purpose was unknown. But as noted by Brugioni, no particular attention was paid to the vans that were always parked near the bunkers, apparently because there was no special security fencing near them. One of the features of nuclear installations in the Soviet Union was a series of heavily guarded security fences, and it was believed that KGB security officers would exercise even more caution and physical security when nuclear weapons were deployed to Cuba. In its search for nuclear weapons indicators, NPIC photo interpreters looked for, but curiously didn't find such indicators.

---

[89] Brugioni, pp. 547-8.

The *Aleksandrovsk* had arrived in Cuba at the port of La Isabela shortly before the quarantine took effect. It remained at La Isabela until 28 October when it hurried to the port of Mariel. Interestingly, the first objects to arrive at the port of Mariel from the dismantled launch sites were not the missiles themselves but rather the "unidentified" vans. A number of vans were loaded aboard the *Aleksandrovsk* which departed the port immediately. According to Brugioni, the rapid movement and transshipment of the vans in the port revealed their real purpose: They were nuclear warhead storage vans. Brugioni continued: Further postmortem reviews of all previous photography over Cuba revealed that, indeed, the nuclear warheads were stored in the "unidentified" vans. (Subsequent to the crisis, the same type vans were seen not only at nuclear weapons storage areas within the Soviet Union but also at Soviet nuclear weapons storage areas in East European countries.) The secret of the Russian handling of nuclear warheads for the missiles was uncovered at the Mariel Naval Air Station where the short runway had fallen into disuse and disrepair. Photo coverage of 14 October revealed that a nuclear warhead processing facility had been sited at the western end of the runway. It was postulated that the warheads arrived at the port of Mariel and were carried to the runway facility in coffin-shaped nosecone containers. Measurements of the equipment by photogrammetrists showed the size was compatible with the size of SS-4 nose cones that had been seen in Moscow parade photography. None of the coffin-shaped containers remained at the Mariel facility after the *Aleksandrovsk* left. Also seen at Mariel were uniquely configured dollies for handling nuclear warheads.[90]

---

[90] Brugioni, pp. 538-48.

What U.S. intelligence had not discovered in Cuba was the central nuclear weapon storage facility. The CIA had concluded that the nuclear warheads were probably stored near the port of Mariel. As noted earlier, Gribkov had identified Bejucal as the site of such a facility, but U.S. intelligence never identified it as such in overhead photography even though low-level American reconnaissance airplanes had flown over the area on numerous missions beginning on 23 October. Decades would pass before an analysis of archival film of Bejucal by Michael Dobbs revealed that the purpose of a facility that had been photographed many times was nuclear weapons storage. The proof was in the photographs that showed special nuclear transport vans parked at the facility.

Dobbs writes that the CIA had been scouring Cuba for nuclear warheads ever since discovering the missiles. "In fact, they were hidden in plain view all along." Analysts had been following construction activity at Bejucal and by the fall of 1962 had tagged a pair of Bejucal bunkers as a possible "nuclear weapons storage site." But analysts were not convinced because the facility lacked the extra security that had been observed at nuclear storage facilities in the USSR. Dobbs's analysis of archival film revealed the locations of the Bejucal nuclear storage bunker and a similar bunker, dug into a hill overlooking the town of Managua. Dobbs concludes that the Bejucal bunker was the hiding place of the thirty-six warheads for the MRBM missile; Managua was the storage point for the twelve Luna warheads (warheads for the IRBM's were stored on the *Aleksandrovsk* awaiting the arrival of the missiles). Photo interpreters missed the significance of the Bejucal facility because they had been told to look for multiple security fences, roadblocks, and extra levels of protection. At the Bejucal facility all that they saw was a rickety fence which was not even protected by a closed gate. Dobbs explains this mindset as the tyranny of conventional wisdom. The lack of obvious security precautions around the Bejucal site was the best security of all.[91]

Secretary of Defense McNamara gave a special Cuban briefing on 6 February 1963 where he was asked by a reporter about atomic weapons in Cuba. McNamara answered, "The movement of nuclear weapons into Cuba, I believe, occurred. I believe we observed it in certain vehicles and we observed the movement of those vehicles out of Cuba, and we traced the shipment of those vehicles on ships back into the home waters of the Soviet Union."[92]

The National Security Archive at George Washington University maintains an impressive collection of declassified documents on the Cuban Missile Crisis. According to some of those documents, Soviet nuclear warheads stayed on Cuban territory for 59 days—from the arrival of the ship *Indigirka* on 4 October to the departure of *Arkhangelsk* on December 1. *Arkhangelsk* carried 80 warheads for the FKR cruise missile, 12 warheads for the Luna launcher, and 6 nuclear bombs for the IL-28 bombers—in total, 98 tactical nuclear warheads. Four other nuclear warheads, for torpedoes on the Foxtrot submarines, had already returned to the Soviet Union, as well as 24 warheads for the R-14 (IRBM) missiles, which arrived on 25 October on the *Aleksandrovsk* but were never unloaded. The available evidence suggests that the 36 warheads for the MRBM missiles came to Cuba on the *Indigirka* and that they left on the *Aleks-*

---

[91] Dobbs, *One Minute to Midnight,* pp. 174-5.
[92] Brugioni, p. 547.

androvsk, being loaded at Mariel between 30 October and 3 November.[93]

Two documents from the National Security Archive are particularly interesting in the context of nuclear weapons in Cuba. Document 1 is an after-action report written in December 1962 by Soviet Major General Igor Statsenko, the commander of the MRBM and IRBM regiments and supporting personnel. In his report he describes the movement of "warheads" to field deployment areas. Document 2 is the report written by Soviet Lieutenant General Nikolai Beloborodov who commanded the Soviet nuclear arsenal in Cuba. It describes the delivery, deployment and withdrawal of all nuclear weapons, the "special cargo" as the Soviets referred to them, which were under his command.[94]

Do the Russians Know?

Between the discovery of MRBM missiles on 15 October (from the U-2 flight of 14 October) and President Kennedy's announcement on the 22nd, those few U.S. officials who knew wondered whether the Soviets knew of the U.S. discovery. The secret of the missile discovery had been extremely tightly held and special precautions had been taken to avoid creating the appearance that something out of the ordinary was happening in Washington. The U.S. had begun frequent U-2 flights once the missiles were first discovered, but it had no way of knowing if the Soviets were aware of the intensified U-2 coverage since the SA-2 search radars were not operating at the time (They began operating on 26 October).

---

[93] The National Security Archive: "Last Nuclear Weapons left Cuba in December 1962," *Electronic Briefing Book No.449*, posted December 11, 2013

[94] Ibid. Document numbers 1 and 2.

The President learned of the missiles on Tuesday morning, 16 October, and was intent on preventing leaks and any indication that the U.S. had discovered the Soviet missiles. Secrecy was paramount and Kennedy would not disclose to anyone who lacked a rigid "need-to-know" what the U-2 had discovered. On Wednesday morning, in order to mask the discovery from the Russians, he flew to Connecticut to keep a campaign commitment. Had the discovery been widely known within the government, it would have leaked and had it leaked, the administration's diplomatic initiative, achieved by making a countermove when unmasking Soviet duplicity, would have been lost. As it turned out, this was perhaps the best kept secret in American history, but only barely. By Saturday, 20 October, the *New York Times* had the story, but a phone call from the president delayed the story until after the White House announcement on 22 October.

On 18 October, President Kennedy met in the Oval Office with Soviet Foreign Minister Gromyko, as planned. Kennedy didn't know whether the Soviet Foreign Minister knew about the missiles or whether he knew that the Americans knew. Kennedy debated whether he should confront the Soviet Foreign Minister with what the U.S. knew and finally decided that as he had not yet determined a final course of action and the disclosure of our knowledge might give the Russians the initiative, he would simply listen to Gromyko. Gromyko told the President that Khrushchev had told him to tell Kennedy that the only assistance being furnished Cuba was for agriculture and land development, so the people could feed themselves, plus a small amount of defensive arms. He said that he wanted to emphasize that the Soviet Union would never become involved in the furnishing of offensive weapons to Cuba. Brugioni wrote that after the Gromyko meeting, he and Lundahl went into the Oval Office to retrieve the briefing materials that NPIC had prepared for the meeting but which the president had chosen not to reveal to Gromyko.[95]

Alexander Feklisov, alias Alexander Fomin, was one of the KGB's top agents in the U.S. and the KGB *Rezident* in Washington, D.C. from 1960 to 1964.[96] In his book *The Man Behind the Rosenbergs*, he writes that Gromyko had to know, even though he wasn't part of the Politburo. On the other hand, Feklisov writes that Gromyko probably didn't think that the Americans had found out. Feklisov also writes that during a ball in Gromyko's honor at the State Department, ExComm was working just one floor below on two options: a blockade or a bombing raid of the island.

Feklisov, a 20-year veteran of Soviet intelligence had little success in penetrating the power centers in D.C., but he did develop a number of useful journalistic sources, one of whom was John Scali, the moderator of ABC's Issues and Answers program. (Feklisov and Scali developed a communication backchannel between Moscow and Washington that some credit with resolving the Cuban Missile Crisis.) (See Vignette.)

Soviet intelligence provided little warning of the impending crisis. In the days immediately preceding Kennedy's blockade speech, the Soviets detected unusual activity but could not determine the exact reason for it. Similarly, the GRU (Soviet military intelligence) disseminated worrisome but inexact signals of trouble ahead. As of 21 October, the headquarters of the GRU had received

---

[95] Kennedy, *Thirteen Days*, p. 31; Brugioni, pp. 286-7.
[96] Feklisov was portrayed in the 2000 movie *Thirteen Days* by Russian born actor Boris Lee Krutonog (www.imdb.com).

four different reports suggesting that Kennedy was considering some form of military action in the Caribbean. Noting unusual activity by the U.S. Air Force, the GRU reported on a convoy of military planes that had left for Puerto Rico. It also appeared that the number of bombers on duty in the Strategic Air Command had inexplicably increased. On the high seas, the Soviets detected that the U.S. Navy had increased its presence in the Caribbean as part of an exercise. The Soviet military picked up Robert McNamara's order that senior military officers remain near the Pentagon to participate in a series of intensive meetings. Finally, there were indications that this was only the beginning of some U.S. military operation.

Despite these indicators, the Soviet Presidium appears not to have had any special advance warning of Kennedy's speech to the nation on Monday, 22 October. Berlin and Cuba were both on the agenda for the scheduled Presidium meeting that day, indicating uncertainty over which Cold War volcano might be about to blow.[97]

According to Feklisov, because of the security around ExComm deliberations, Moscow didn't know that Washington was aware of the missiles. He says that all the excitement going on prior to the President's announcement affected only the highest councils of power. "None of our American agents in the State Department or elsewhere had noticed anything out of the ordinary." "By Sunday, 21 October, I knew there was a crisis. During the afternoon Ambassador Dobrynin called an urgent meeting where the military attaché said the U.S. military had been placed on DEFCON 3. The American press gave no clue that a conflict was in the offing. The next day I was trying to find an American contact who could help find out what was going on in the Oval Office."

---

[97] Fursenko and Naftali. *"Soviet Intelligence and The Cuban Missile Crisis."* pp. 77-8.

Moscow had received the text of Kennedy's speech before it was given. Khrushchev didn't know until then that the Americans knew everything and he became very angry. It wasn't only against the quarantine, which he interpreted as an act of war: he was furious at the Soviet generals for failing to hide the missiles properly. Khrushchev's initial reaction was to order the ships on their way to Cuba not to stop and to send a very terse message to Kennedy.[98]

What Should We Do with MONGOOSE?

On the morning of 16 October, the same morning that the President was informed of the missiles, Robert Kennedy was holding a meeting which he opened by expressing "general dissatisfaction of the President" with Operation MONGOOSE. He pointed out that the operation had been underway for a year, that the results were discouraging, that there had been no acts of sabotage, and that even the one which had been attempted had failed twice. While there had been noticeable improvement during the year in the collection of intelligence, other actions had failed to influence significantly the course of events in Cuba. The Attorney General spoke favorably of the sabotage paper that General Carter had presented that morning. In it the Acting DCI advocated a series of demolition and other sabotage operations including "a hit-and-run mortar and gunfire attack on the Soviet SAM site near Santa Lucia, Pinar del Rio Province."[99, 100]

---

[98] Alexander Feklisov and Sergei Kostin. *The Man Behind the Rosenbergs*, New York: Enigma Books, 2001, pp. 370-5.

[99] Memorandum for the Record, MONGOOSE Meeting with the Attorney General, 16 Oc-

MONGOOSE was a large-scale covert action program. It was a sustained campaign of sabotage, propaganda, espionage, and work with resistance networks and exile groups to overthrow Castro. John Kennedy had been disgusted with the disaster at the Bay of Pigs and was more determined than ever to get rid of Castro. MONGOOSE was set up in the fall of 1961 to overthrow Castro and was part-Pentagon, part-CIA, run out of the White House with General Edward Lansdale as the operational director, and the CIA element, Task Force W, run by William Harvey. While Lansdale was the titular head, the moving force behind the operation was Attorney General Robert Kennedy. In January 1962, the younger Kennedy declared that Castro was the administration's top priority and that no time, money, effort or manpower was to be spared to push for Castro's overthrow. According to Sam Halpern, executive officer of Task Force W, "Bobby wanted boom and bang" all over the island. MONGOOSE did produce a little boom and bang, but the biggest target, the Matahambre copper mines, went unscathed after the sabotage operation failed.[101]

At the ExComm meeting on the morning of 26 October there was a sense that the combination of limited force and diplomatic efforts had been unsuccessful and that a direct military confrontation between the two great powers was inevitable. The largest concentration of U.S. armed forces since the Korean War was massing in the southeastern United States. Several different options for air strikes were readied. Under the contingency plan prepared and preferred by the Joint Chiefs of Staff, designated Operation Scabbards, a mas-

tober 1962 by Richard Helms, McAuliffe, pp.153-4.

[100] Memorandum for: Special Group (Augmented), Operation MONGOOSE/Sabotage Proposals, 16 October 1962 by Marshall S. Carter. CIA archive.

[101] Evan Thomas. *The Very Best Men; The Daring Early Years of the CIA*, New York: Simon & Schuster, 1995, 2006, pp. 270-1, 288-91; also, Robarge, McCone history, p. 84.

sive air strike would hit Cuba 12 hours after the President gave the order. Strikes would continue for seven days, then troops would begin going ashore. These preparations fueled speculation about an imminent invasion, speculation that was featured in the newspapers delivered to the White House on Friday morning 26 October.[102]

McCone began the ExComm meeting with an intelligence briefing where, as on previous days, he read the highlights of that mornings Watch Committee report: Construction of IRBM [Intermediate Range Ballistic Missile] and MRBM bases in Cuba is proceeding; road construction around Remedios suggests a fourth IRBM site; 16 dry cargo ships having turned back toward the USSR; further indications that some Soviet and satellite elements, particularly air and ground elements in Eastern Europe and European Russia, are on alert or readiness status; Peiping [Beijing] is irritated that the Soviet response to U.S. action is not stronger; most OAS [Organization of American States] nations offered to participate in some form in the quarantine; NATO members agreed with minor reservations to deny landing and overflight rights to Soviet planes bound for Cuba.

McCone added that "rapid construction activity" was continuing, apparently directed toward achieving a full operational capability as soon as possible. ...As yet there is *no* evidence indicating any intention to move or dismantle these sites."

ExComm then turned its attention to Operation MONGOOSE. Early in the Crisis the CIA, as noted above, had been pressured, especially by Robert Kennedy, to do more with MONGOOSE against Castro. A plan had been developed to land teams of exiles in Cuba by submarine to collect intelligence,

---

[102]   ExComm meeting Friday 26 October 10:10 AM transcript introduction.

conduct sabotage operations, and perhaps even to try to destroy the Soviet missile sites. McCone decided that the CIA would not be prodded into launching this intelligence and sabotage mission on its own. He ordered that the planned operation be suspended and told the ExComm what he had done. If there was a military requirement, he said, then that requirement should be handled by McNamara and the Joint Chiefs of Staff. A meeting to decide how to proceed was arranged to take place in the Pentagon that afternoon.[103]

The afternoon following the ExComm meeting McCone, McNamara, General Taylor, Robert Kennedy, Lansdale, Harvey, and others met to give guidance to Operation MONGOOSE. McCone stated that he thought the MONGOOSE goal was to encourage the Cuban people to take Cuba away from Castro and to set up a proper form of government. It was decided that a new Cuban political office to plan for the post-invasion government would be secretly set up by the State Department. Also decided was that the infiltration of agents was to be held up pending a determination by DOD and State Department as to what military and political information was needed.[104]

As noted above, Robert Kennedy was the driving force behind Operation MONGOOSE and the sizable activities of the U.S. government to get rid of Castro by any means possible.[105] In *Thirteen Days* he paints an entirely different picture where he denies that he and the President were out to get Castro.

---

[103] ExComm meeting Friday 26 October 10:10 AM transcript introduction; also, McCone memo subject Meeting of the NSC Executive Committee, 26 October 1962; McAuliffe CIA documents, p. 317.

[104] Memorandum of MONGOOSE Meeting in the JCS Operations Room, October 26, 1962, at 2:30 PM by McCone, CIA documents, p. 319.

[105] The transcript of the 9:00 PM meeting of 27 October shows Robert Kennedy saying: "I'd like to take Cuba back. That would be nice." Kennedy's comment was followed by an unidentified ExComm member comment:" Yeah, and let's take Cuba away from Castro."

"There is a theory that John and Robert Kennedy were 'obsessed' with Castro and out to destroy him. If that had been the case, the deployment of Soviet nuclear missiles in Cuba would have provided a heaven-sent pretext—one that would have been accepted around the world—to invade Cuba and smash Castro forever. Instead, Robert Kennedy led the fight against military intervention, and John Kennedy made the decision against it. Some obsession."[106]

---

[106] Kennedy, *Thirteen Days,* p. 11.

THE HEIGHT OF THE CRISIS: 22 – 28 OCTOBER

The days between Monday, 22 October and Sunday, 28 October were days of high drama and extreme anxiety in the White House. Both Kennedy and Khrushchev were in fear that events were spinning out of control and that a conflict was almost unavoidable, a conflict that could well erupt into all-out war between their two countries. Their fears were heightened by numerous actions that took place during this critical week: Khrushchev's ships were streaming steadily toward the quarantine line; The Soviet air defense system became operational and immediately thereafter successfully shot down Air Force Major Rudolf Anderson's U-2C; Castro had ordered Cuban anti-aircraft batteries to operational status, and they began to fire on low-level U.S. reconnaissance planes; a U-2 had inadvertently strayed into Soviet air space causing Soviet leaders to fear it was a reconnaissance mission ahead of an American attack; Foxtrot submarines had been discovered near the ships transporting Soviet weapons and supplies enroute to Cuba; construction at the MRBM sites had appreciably accelerated; and Khrushchev decided to play tough demanding the dismantlement of American-controlled missile bases in Turkey.

As Kennedy and the ExComm struggled to assess the situation and decide a course of action, U.S intelligence played a key supporting role by providing answers to critical questions.

Are the Surface to Air Missiles Operational?

With the discovery of SA-2 missiles on 29 August 1962, U.S. intelligence actively sought to collect signals from the two radars associated with those systems: the SPOON REST long-range target acquisition radar and the FRUIT SET target tracking and missile control radar. Each was identifiable by experts who were trained to recognize their telltale electronic signatures.

Fear of SA-2 missiles played a major role in planning U-2 missions as noted earlier in the meeting of 10 September where Secretary Rusk scaled back CIA overflight plans. Though SAM sites had been seen as early as late August, they did not become operational until late October. Why weren't the missiles and their associated radars made operational sooner? Certainly, the Soviets were aware that the U-2 was repeatedly flying over Cuba; knowing that, and knowing their missiles sites were vulnerable to overhead observation, why didn't they get the SA-2's ready sooner to take action against the U-2. One possible reason may be the same reason the Soviets didn't make an effort to hide the nuclear missile sites: standard operating procedures.[107] Another possible reason is that the SA-2 crews were in no hurry to make them operational since Khrushchev had instructed his Soviet forces on the island not to fire on U.S. planes. Later, when they did and succeeded in downing Major Anderson's U-2, Khrushchev was angry and extremely unsettled, fearful that he had lost control, even of his own forces.

---

[107] This can be understood as Model II Organizational Behavior where large organizations function according to standard routines and patterns of behavior. See Graham Allison and Philip Zelikow, *Essence of Decision; Explaining the Cuban Missile Crisis*, second ed., New York: Longman Publishing Group, 1999, p. 143.

Understanding the operational status of the SA-2 sites largely depended on SIGINT, specifically the interception of the emissions from the radars that were associated with the SA-2 missile by electronic intelligence (ELINT) sources. Those sources were the *Oxford*, a converted WWII Liberty ship which operated under the technical direction and control of NSA, and SAC RB-47H aircraft that had been operating around Cuba in search of SA-2 radar signals under Operation Common Cause.

The intelligence community was desperate to acquire the FRUIT SET radar signals because doing so would enable implementation of electronic measures that could counter the threat, or at least warn the pilot of an impending threat. CIA developed a plan to modify a Ryan Q2C drone with special ELINT collection equipment. The drone if tracked by the SA-2 associated FRUIT SET radar would receive the signals, convert them to another frequency, and re-broadcast the data to ground or airborne receivers stationed well offshore of Cuba. It was soon decided that the time to outfit the drone was unacceptable and another plan was to have a U-2 overfly a SAM site while an ELINT aircraft in the vicinity, but safely offshore, would acquire the FRUIT SET signals. It was clearly understood that the risk of sending the U-2 over an operational SA-2 would be high, but was considered acceptable given the importance of acquiring the signal. On the 14 October SAC mission that first discovered the MRBM missiles, the FRUIT SET radar signal was not "heard" presumably because the SA-2 sites were not yet operational.[108]

The spy ship USS *Oxford* (officially termed a Technical Research Ship)

---

[108] Memorandum for the Record, Subject: Notes on Factors Bearing on Reconnaissance of Cuba, dated 28 October, 1962, unknown author, CIA files.

first detected a SPOON REST radar in Cuba on 15 September 1962, but it was evidently just a test. On 20 October it picked up signals from a FRUIT SET radar. That suggested that SAM missiles were fully checked out and could be launched at any time. Other intelligence showed that the Soviets had taken over the entire air defense network. Only anti-aircraft guns that would be used against low-flying U.S. aircraft remained under Cuban control (SAM missiles did not threaten low-flying reconnaissance aircraft because they were too low for SAM's to be effective).[109]

Around midnight on Friday, 26 October a SPOON REST radar came on-line, was picked up by the *Oxford* and immediately reported to NSA headquarters via dedicated circuits.[110]

Major Rudolf Anderson, Jr., who along with Major Heyser had been checked out by the CIA in the U-2C model and was designated as backup pilot to Major Heyser for the 14 October mission, had flown several Cuban U-2 missions, and was flying one the morning of Saturday 27 October, a tragic day that would be remembered as "Black Saturday." Major Anderson took off from McCoy Air Force Base in one of two U-2's that SAC had "borrowed" from the CIA and repainted with Air Force insignia. CIA's U-2C was less threatened by SA-2 missiles than Air Force versions, but even at seventy-two thousand feet they were still vulnerable as senior U.S. officials well knew.

Word reached Washington the evening of 27 October that Anderson had been shot down. The *Oxford* had intercepted a teletype message saying that the Cubans had recovered his body and the wreckage from his plane. NSA

---

[109]   Dobbs, *One Minute to Midnight*, p. 185.

[110]   Col. H. Wayne Whitten. *Without a Warning: The Avoidable Shootdown of a U-2 Spyplane During the Cuban Missile Crisis,* Whitten and Associates (self-published), 2017, p. 70.

also possessed a couple of minutes of Soviet air defense tracking suggesting that the U-2 went down somewhere near Banes.[111] Major Anderson's body was returned to the U.S. from Havana aboard a Swiss airplane.[112]

The order to attack Anderson's U-2 was given by Lt. General Stepan Grechko, the commander of Soviet air defenses on the island. Grechko had brought the entire air defense radar network into full combat mode the night before and was following Anderson's U-2 in real time since before it entered Cuban air space. He became concerned when the U-2 made the turn toward Guantanamo and overflew the area where the general knew an FKR cruise missile battery had secretly moved overnight to an open firing position 15 miles from the huge American naval base and was now exposed to overhead reconnaissance.[113]

According to Alexander Orlov in *The U-2 Program: A Russian Officer Remembers*, Grechko tried—unsuccessfully—to reach his superiors but was unable to and made the decision to fire his missiles against the intruding airplane. Orlov was ever-present at the central command post for Soviet Air Defense Forces and says he vividly remembers the extremely tense time. Shortly after Anderson was shot down a message came from Moscow consisting of two sentences: "You were hasty. Ways of settlement have been outlined…"[114] Khrushchev, who had learned about the shoot down from a Pentagon report, was

[111] Dobbs, *One Minute to Midnight*, p. 301.

[112] See photograph from *"The Once-Classified Tale of Juanita Moody"* by David Wolman published in *Smithsonian Magazine*, March 2021. No page number.

[113] Whitten, p. 54. The FKR missiles had just been moved into a position from which, had conflict erupted, they would have attacked the Guantanamo base inflicting huge casualties from the nuclear warheads they carried. A map from Dobbs p. 243 shows Anderson's flight path over the FKR position.

[114] Alexander Orlov. "The U-2 Program: A Russian Officer Remembers," *Studies in Intelligence,* Winter 1998-1999.

furious as he knew that Kennedy would have no choice but to oblige his military leaders with some form of retaliation.

According to Whitten who quoted Khrushchev, the shoot down was a turning point for Khrushchev who felt the crisis was slipping out of control. Not only had he no control over U.S. actions, he saw the loss of the American spy plane as signaling his loss of control over his own forces.[115,116]

The shootdown of Major Anderson was an avoidable tragedy that could very well have had grave consequences. The U.S. had been monitoring the airwaves around Cuba to intercept signals from radars associated with the SA-2 surface to air missile. Those airwaves had largely been quiet until the night of 26 October when multiple ELINT intercepts signaled that the Soviet air defense network suddenly became active and remained so afterword. NSA would later say that on 27 October, the Cuban Air Defense System came of age; "…The operators after 27 October are much more proficient than previously noted and are obviously experienced Soviet operators."[117]

---

[115] Whitten, p. 60.

[116] A fascinating but totally untrue tale was told by Carlos Franqui, journalist and former Castro aide. In his book he claims that it was Castro that pushed the button that launched the SA-2 missile against Anderson's U-2. From the book's foreword: "During the October crisis Fidel Castro, on a visit to a super-secret, Russian-manned missile base on the western end of the island, innocently asks a technician to show him the button that fires the rockets. The Russian complies. The Russian also shows Castro a radar screen which at that very moment is tracking an American reconnaissance plane on a routine flight over Cuba. 'Is that an American spy plane' asks Castro. Da da! Suddenly the Prime Minister presses the button. Swoosh! He didn't even have to aim: that was handled by computer. The Russians, aghast, can only watch as their missile rises in the green, ghostly oscilloscope of the radar to collide with the moving spook. One second later the two shadows disappear from the screen with a flash." See Foreword by G. Cabrera Infante in Carlos Franqui, *Family Portrait with Fidel,* New York: Random House, 1985. Franqui tells the story in his own words on p. 193.

[117] Memorandum, subject: Soviet Involvement in the Air Defense Activities of Cuba, 1 November 1962 (from Whitten, p. 94).

The command center at NSA that had been established by the director for the crisis would have had the actionable intelligence hours before Anderson took off on his fateful mission. Apparently, this information had not been communicated to CIA or the Pentagon despite the fact that it was well known that Washington principals were attuned to the SAM threat given the vulnerability of the U-2. DCI McCone who in reporting on the latest intelligence at the ExComm's morning meeting on 27 October made no mention of SAM radars having been activated, clearly signaling a threat to any U-2 flights. Neither McNamara or General Taylor who were in attendance had intelligence to report in that regard.[118]

NSA is to blame for having actionable intelligence that could have been communicated to decision makers in time to have Anderson's mission canceled. But the Strategic Air Command, which was responsible for Anderson's mission, also failed. SAC, unlike when CIA was running Cuban missions, had failed to coordinate with NSA on U-2 mission timing and flight paths, when doing so would have enabled NSA listening posts to provide warning.

A SAC RB-47H had arrived on station off Cuba about an hour before Anderson's U-2 entered Cuban air space. As the RB-47H flew around the coast of Cuba the ELINT crew began picking up SPOON REST radar signals. (The *Oxford* had picked up similar signals the night before.) Then they intercepted an ominous signal, from the telltale FRUIT SET fire control radar, a clear indication of the SAM threat. The officers onboard the aircraft radioed the new threat information using the code word "Big Cigar" to the SAC Reconnaissance Center. but there was no way to inform Major Anderson that he

---

118   Whitten, p. 78.

was in imminent mortal danger.[119] As Whitten notes, both the U-2 and the

RB-47H were under the command of the SAC Reconnaissance Center. Yet

the right hand had no idea what the left hand had discovered.

The lack of coordination within the SAC Reconnaissance Center between

those knowledgeable of the RB-47H intercepts and those planning Anderson's

U-2 mission is shocking. So is the inability of the RB-47 crew to communicate

a warning directly to Anderson, and the failure of SAC to relay the warning to

him. And, unfortunately, Anderson's U-2 was *not* equipped with electronic

countermeasures equipment that could have warned him that he was under

immediate threat, enabling him to take evasive action. CIA had just completed

development of a SA-2 warning system, called System 12, but it unfortunately

was not available in time to be used on Anderson's U-2.[120]

The transfer of control of U-2 operations over Cuba from CIA to SAC

indirectly resulted in the loss of warnings from NSA's listening posts. In the

wake of the U-2 shoot down, the NSA Director claimed that SAC didn't keep

them informed about the U-2 schedules as did CIA, and consequently NSA

could not provide warnings of reactions by Soviet air defenses. SAC's failure

to protect Anderson are consistent with observations by Deputy CIA Director

---

[119]   Ibid, p. 57.

[120]   Dobbs in *One Minute to Midnight* says on p. 219 that Anderson's U-2 was equipped
with a warning device for detecting SA-2 radar signals and once detected the pilot
would attempt evasive action. See also Brugioni, p. 182. It seems that Dobbs and Brugioni are incorrect. Whitten, p. 83, writes that contrary to reports, Anderson's U-2F
[actually a U-2C] did not have a SA-2 radar warning receiver. The receiver called System
12 [System XII in CIA terminology] had completed development and was about to be
tested at Area 51, CIA's flight test facility, and was therefore unavailable for Anderson's
U-2. Installation of System 12 in USAF U-2's was delayed until January 1963 due to
SAC commanders concerns about potential compromise of the technology that was
used by the strategic bomber force. Pedlow and Welzenbach, Appendix C, *Electronic
Devices Carried by the U-2*, refer to System XII as being used by U-2's overflying China
(circa 1964) and Vietnam, but makes no mention of its use in U-2's overflying Cuba.

Major General Marshall Carter. In a memorandum to McCone, he wrote that during the period when CIA was flying U-2's over Cuba, CIA had developed a very coordinated system. That included NORAD radars, Navy and Air Force communications links, and the Air-Sea rescue services. He further noted that when the operation was turned over to SAC, the bulk of these safeguards fell by the wayside. "…when Major Anderson was shot down, he was not under radar coverage nor was SAC really on top of his problems."[121] Thomas R. Johnson also wrote in his Cryptologic history that U-2 flights over Cuba had not been receiving advisory warning support from the cryptologic community. After the Anderson shootdown, NSA directed the hurried implementation of a warning system under the White Wolf program.[122]

After the loss of Major Anderson President Kennedy and ExComm debated at length whether and how to respond despite earlier having agreed that an attack on a U-2 would be cause for an American attack on one or more SAM sites. The discussion apparently began with Rusk whose sense was that Khrushchev was not in a good position vis-à-vis the U.S. and spoke about the necessity for "enforced surveillance." "We shoot at anybody who gets in our way." "If we do have to enforce our right to overfly…the accidental fact that some Russians technicians may be around at the time we have to shoot, since they've already fired the first shot, is something that is regrettable, but it is not something that we can make a very public issue out of."

Not long after Rusk had made his point, Kennedy entered the discussion:

---

121 Memorandum for the Director by MSC [Marshall S. Carter] dated 3 November 1962. CIA archive.

122 Thomas R. Johnson and David A. Hatch. *NSA and the Cuban Missile Crisis*; NSA Center for Cryptologic History, p. 330.

"I think we ought to wait till tomorrow afternoon to see whether we get any answers if U Thant goes down there [to Cuba]. I think we ought to figure that Monday, if tomorrow [Sunday] they fire at us and we don't have any answer from the Russians, then Monday, it seems to me…we ought to, maybe consider making a statement tomorrow about the firing and that we're going to take action now any place in Cuba on those areas which can fire. And then go in and take *all* the SAM sites out. I don't think it does any good to take out, to try to fire at a 20 mm [referring to Cuban anti-aircraft guns that were firing on American low-level reconnaissance aircraft] on the ground. We just hazard our planes. On the other hand, I don't want, I don't think we do any good to begin to sort of *half* do it. I think we ought to keep tomorrow clean, do the best we can with the surveillance. If they still fire and we haven't got a satisfactory answer back from the Russians, then I think we ought to put a statement out tomorrow that we are fired upon. We are therefore considering the island of Cuba as an open territory, and then take out all these SAM sites. If we don't get some satisfaction from the Russians or U Thant or Cuba tomorrow night, figure that Monday we're going to do something about the SAM sites."[123]

The President's decision not to retaliate was probably one of the most important of the entire crisis.[124] Khrushchev did accept the President's offer proposing a solution to the crisis and there were no further attacks on U.S. planes.

---

[123]   Executive Committee meeting of the National Security Council on the Cuban Missile Crisis on 27 October, time 9:00 PM transcript.

[124]   Joseph F. Bouchard. *Command In Crisis: Four Case Studies*, New York: Columbia University Press, 1991, p. 108.

Are the MRBM's Operational?

Senior U.S. officials were desperate to know the readiness status of the MRBM missiles. The longer it took to reach operational status the more time there was in which to decide a U.S. course of action. The members of ExComm were racing against the clock: as soon as the launching pads were ready, the threat of nuclear attack would be real and the Soviet position would be reinforced. According to Roger Hilsman, a surgical strike could be considered *only* if none of the missiles were operational. If any of the missiles were operational, some local Soviet commander might panic, assume that the big war was on with the Soviet Union itself under attack, and take matters into his own hands.[125]

Khrushchev pressed his forces in Cuba to make the missiles operational on a crash basis because he presumably thought he could improve the terms of an eventual bargain by increasing the stakes of any attack on the missiles, thereby increasing Kennedy's motivation for a deal. The danger of his strategy was that he was increasing pressure on the U.S. to attack the missiles before they became operational and that would likely been followed by an invasion, the event the missiles had been intended to forestall. On the other hand, the stronger his hand, the more likely that Kennedy might seek a diplomatic solution.[126]

Two intelligence sources contributed to answering the question of the readiness status of Soviet MRBM forces in Cuba: photographs from low-level reconnaissance missions and information provided by Colonel Oleg Penkovsky

---

[125] Hilsman, p. 99.

[126] Daniel Ellsberg. *The Doomsday Machine; Confessions of a Nuclear War Planner*, New York: Bloomsbury, 2017, p. 203.

of the GRU, a spy who worked as an agent for CIA and the British MI-6. One of Penkovsky's most important contributions was the secret Soviet manuals for the SS-4 MRBM that, at great personal risk, he secretly photographed and gave to Western intelligence. They contained the operational details of the liquid-fueled missiles that enabled analysts to interpret what they saw in the overhead photography.[127] In an interview of 8 December 1990, Richard Helms said he didn't know of any single instance where intelligence was more immediately valuable. Penkovsky's material had a direct application because it came right in the middle of the decision-making process.[128]

The analysts used Penkovsky's information to identify what they were seeing in the overhead images. But they also needed to understand what the position or status of an individual piece of equipment—say a missile fueling truck—meant in terms of the overall readiness to fire the missile. That piece of the puzzle was provided by interagency experts of USIB committees, the Joint Atomic Energy Intelligence Committee (JAEIC) and the Guided Missiles Astronautics Intelligence Committee (GMAIC). The experts provided criteria by which analysts could estimate the readiness and operational status of the Soviet missiles.

Penkovsky's information was helpful in identifying the missiles in Cuba as SS-4 MRBMs based on the similarity of the missile deployment patterns in Cuba to those shown in the missile manual. This intelligence supplanted what the U.S. already knew of Soviet missile deployments in the USSR because

---

[127] Jerrold L. Schecter and Peter Deriabin. *The Spy who Saved the World; How a Soviet Colonel Changed the Course of the Cold War,* New York: Charles Scribner's Sons, 1992, p. 334.

[128] Ibid, p. 335.

those patterns had been observed earlier on photographs taken by the CO-RONA reconnaissance satellite. Those photographs also enabled U.S. intelligence to identify pieces of equipment seen in Cuba as MRBM-related. CORONA images of the SS-4 in the USSR had been measured (a process called mensuration), and comparable measurements of photographs of the missile and its equipment in Cuba provided further proof that the MRBM's in Cuba were the Soviet SS-4 type.

Perhaps equally important to the technical intelligence on Soviet missiles that Penkovsky provided is that he shed light on the internal debate inside the USSR concerning nuclear war. His material made it clear that the USSR lacked the nuclear missile capability that Khrushchev claimed, thus enabling Kennedy to call Khrushchev's bluff. Penkovsky's reports and their insights were critical in forming Kennedy's view of Khrushchev and how to deal with him. It should be noted that Penkovsky never provided intelligence on the Soviet plans for the Cuban venture or concrete information as to military measures being undertaken in Cuba.[129]

No doubt Penkovsky contributed highly valuable intelligence to crisis decision-making, but Schecter and Deriabin overstate his contribution when they say, "During the Berlin crisis of 1961 and the Cuban Missile Crisis of 1962, Penkovsky was the spy who saved the world from nuclear war" and "This information, channeled directly to President Kennedy on a regular basis, was

---

[129] Kenneth Absher in his book, *Mind-sets and Missiles*, p. 30, claims that Penkovsky told his case officers about Soviet plans to send SAM's to Cuba. This is untrue, a misreading of *The Spy Who Saved the World*, p. 331. (Absher, *Mind-sets and Missiles: A First Hand Account of the Cuban Missile Crisis*, Carlisle, PA: Strategic Studies Institute, U.S. Army War College, September 2009. http://www.StrategicStudiesInstitute.army.mil.)

instrumental in assuring U.S. victory during the Cuban Missile Crisis."[130]

Colonel Oleg Penkovsky was arrested in the USSR on 22 October, coincidentally the same day that President Kennedy went on television and revealed to the world that the Soviets had deployed strategic nuclear missiles to the island of Cuba. On 17 May 1963, *Pravda* reported that O.V. Penkovsky had been sentenced to be shot for treason to the Motherland. "The sentence has been executed."[131]

There seems little reason to doubt that some nuclear missiles probably could have been launched during the critical week of 22-28 October. It is virtually certain that some missiles could have been launched at the U.S. from one or more sites by the time they were discovered and that some missiles could have been launched from all six sites by 28 October when the Soviet authorities announced their decision to withdraw the missiles.[132] This judgment was later proven to be accurate.

The actual operational status of the Soviet MRBM forces in Cuba at the time was revealed by the commander of the division that controlled the three regiments containing 24 launchers. Individual regiments reached full combat readiness on the dates of 20, 25 and 27 October, while the missile division reached full combat readiness and was able to deliver a strike from all 24 launchers on 27 October.[133]

---

[130]   Schecter and Deriabin, p. 3, and book jacket.
[131]   Ibid, pp. 353, 373.
[132]   CIA/ORR DD/I Staff Study, *Khrushchev's Miscalculated Risk*, pp. 60-4.
[133]   Statsenko, National Security Archive EBB No. 449.

How Is Moscow Reacting?

Following the President's speech, the U.S. military attachés of the American Embassy in Moscow made a concerted effort to observe firsthand the situation as the crisis unfolded: How was Moscow managing the crisis internally and were there any indictors of Soviet preparations for hostilities? The attachés put into operation a joint plan for comprehensive, around the clock intelligence observation in Moscow and environs, looking for anything out of the ordinary that might illuminate Soviet intentions and reaction to the situation, especially as concerned war preparations. Were government offices being evacuated? Were civil defense measures being taken? Were the number of trucks on the street day and night normal? The attachés of the three services pooled their efforts, sending daily a joint report to Washington.

Not surprisingly, Soviet leaders were very proficient at managing the news about the crisis: Soviet news sources did not report the blockade Kennedy announced on 22 October until some 48 hours later. Pravda carried a Soviet version of the president's speech distorted in such fashion that the Russian people would not know about the Soviet troops and missiles in Cuba. The first hint about Soviet missiles in Cuba was given to the Russians at 1900 hours, 27 October when Moscow radio argued that "...if the United States believes it has the right to demand removal from Cuba of missiles described by Washington as offensive, then it will be natural to recognize the USSR's right to demand the withdrawal of American destructive rocket weapons from Turkey, a country that is our next door neighbor."[134] The complete domination of the internal

---

[134] William F. Scott. "The Face of Moscow in the Missile Crisis; Observations of the attachés in the Soviet Union in the fall of 1962," *Studies in Intelligence*, Spring 1966.

information environment assured the Soviet leadership a high degree of flexibility in managing the crisis.

The Soviet government did issue a statement in response to President Kennedy's speech. A CIA assessment of the statement indicated that Soviet leaders desired to avoid any appearance of acquiescing to the measures announced by the President but, at the same time, to stay clear of specific countermeasures. The Soviet statement, warning that the U.S. is "recklessly playing with fire," appeared to be aimed at placing the U.S. on the defensive and generating worldwide opposition to U.S. policy in the Cuban Crisis. It sought to play down the USSR's role in the crisis by portraying the issue as one between Cuba and the U.S. Further, the statement said: "The U.S. is demanding that military equipment Cuba needs for self-defense be removed from Cuban territory, a demand which naturally no state which values its independence can meet."[135]

Throughout the entire period of the crisis, the attachés had seen nothing in Moscow that reflected the serious external tension. The only observable Soviet reaction was the ban on all travel in the Soviet Union, and this was not put into effect until after Kennedy's speech. Even with the benefit of hindsight, the attachés could not point to any unusual Soviet behavior during the month of October. That the crisis was fully ended became apparent on 1 November during a reception at the Japanese Embassy. An unusual number of senior Soviet air force officers was present, and their attitude toward the U.S. air attachés was more nearly appropriate to the days some seventeen years earlier

---

[135] Current Intelligence Memorandum, Subject: Comment on 23 October Soviet Government Statement on President Kennedy's Speech, dated 23 October. Central Intelligence Agency, Office of Current Intelligence, OCI No. 3555/62.

when the Russian and Americana allies met on the Elbe, than to the aftermath of a desperate hostile confrontation; the Soviet officers insisted on toasting and drinking with the U.S. airmen, offering toasts to peace and friendship.[136]

Though not apparent to the U.S. military attachés in Moscow, the Soviets had reacted to the deployment of their forces to Cuba and the crisis that followed by alerting their military forces. One of NSA's major jobs during the period was watching Soviet force readiness levels and it first saw an increase on 11 September when the Soviets suddenly went into their highest readiness stage since the beginning of the Cold War. Although the units at highest readiness were generally defense-related, the alert included some unprecedented activity among offensive forces. The alert may have been called because Moscow suspected that Kennedy had found out about the missiles. (Kennedy's public statement on 4 September had warned the Soviets.) The 11 September alert was canceled ten days later, but on 15 October Soviet forces went into a preliminary, perhaps precautionary, stage of alert. Once again, this readiness level was likely due to Khrushchev's supposition that the U.S. had discovered a missile site. He knew and expected that the U.S, would find out; the only question was when.

Following Kennedy's Oval Office speech on 22 October, Soviet forces again went into an extraordinarily high state of alert, similar to the September event. This time, however, with nuclear war threatening, defensive forces were primary. Offensive forces avoided assuming the highest readiness stage, as if to ensure that Kennedy understood that the USSR would not be the first to launch nuclear missiles. Long-range aviation units continued normal training,

---

[136]   Scott. "The Face of Moscow."

although some precautionary steps were taken, such as ensuring that the Arctic staging bases could be used. PVO (air defense) units went into the highest state of alert ever observed, as did Soviet tactical air forces.

NSA gave the White House the only timely information that it had about the Soviet reaction and military force alert posture prior to and during the crisis.[137] SIGINT data gave the U.S. decision makers some feel for Soviet responses to the statements of the U.S. positions during the crisis period. Also, it provided information on the reactions of other nations—friendly, uncommitted, and potential enemy.[138]

Will Khrushchev Run the Blockade?

The evening of 22 October, President Kennedy announced that a proclamation was to be signed the next day and would contain a period of grace, at the end of which a quarantine would be imposed. The following day, McNamara held a press conference where he stated: "The President thirty minutes ago at 7:00 PM signed the proclamation ordering the interdiction of offensive weapons moving into Cuba, and under the terms of that proclamation, I have taken the necessary steps to deploy our forces to be in a position to make effective the quarantine at 2:00 PM, tomorrow, Greenwich time. That will be the equivalent of 10:00 AM, Eastern Daylight Time." "Secondly, the Joint Chiefs of Staff have designated Admiral George Anderson, Chief of Naval Op-

---

[137] Thomas R. Johnson. *United States Cryptologic History; American Cryptology during the Cold War, 1945-1989, Book II: Centralization Wins, 1960-1972*, National Security Agency, p. 330.

[138] Donald C. Wigglesworth. "The Cuban Missile Crisis: A SIGINT Perspective," *Cryptologic Quarterly, Vol. 13, No. 1, Spring 1994*, p. 93.

erations, as their Executive Agent for the operation of the quarantine and the quarantine forces. In turn, Admiral Dennison, Commander in Chief, Atlantic, is the responsible Unified Commander. And, operating under him in direct charge of the quarantine task force will be Vice Admiral Alfred Ward, Commander of the Second Fleet. Admiral Ward's task force will be known as Task Force 136. It will be composed of major naval units, including carriers, cruisers, destroyers, and the associated logistical forces."[139]

Institution of the blockade presented the first test of will between the President and Premier Khrushchev. Khrushchev's first reaction to Kennedy's pronouncement came on 23 October and was followed by another on 24 October. In his first letter he mildly admonished the U.S. for what he regarded as undisguised interference in the internal affairs of the Republic of Cuba, the Soviet Union, and other states, and he reaffirmed that "the armaments which are in Cuba, regardless of the classification to which they may belong, are intended solely for defensive purposes in order to secure the Republic of Cuba against the attack of an aggressor." His second letter on 24 October took a more defiant position. "You, Mr. President, are not declaring a quarantine, but rather are setting forth an ultimatum and threatening that if we do not give in to your demands, you will use force." "No, Mr. President, I cannot agree to this." "You wish to compel us to renounce the rights that every sovereign state enjoys, you are trying to legislate in questions of international law, and you are violating the universally accepted norms of that law." "The Soviet government considers that the violation of the freedom to use international waters and international

---

[139] *The Naval Quarantine of Cuba, 1962: Quarantine, 22-26 October.* https://www.history.navy.mil/research/library/online-reading-room/title-list-alphabetically/n/the-naval-quarantine-of-cuba.html .

air space is an act of aggression which pushes mankind toward the abyss of a world nuclear-missile war. Therefore, the Soviet government cannot instruct the captains of Soviet vessels bound for Cuba to observe the orders of American naval forces blockading that island. Our instructions to Soviet mariners are to observe strictly the universally accepted norms of international waters and not to retreat one step from them." "Naturally we will not simply be bystanders with regard to puritanical acts by American ships on the high seas. We will then be forced on our part to take the measures we consider necessary and adequate in order to protect our rights. We have everything necessary to do so."[140, 141]

The morning the quarantine went into effect reports told of the Russian ships coming steadily on toward Cuba. Robert Kennedy wrote: "This Wednesday morning meeting, [ExComm 10:00 AM, 24 October] along with that of the following Saturday, 27 October, seemed the most trying, the most difficult, and the most filled with tension. I sat across from the President…the danger and concern that we all felt hung like a cloud over us all and particularly over the President." At that meeting Secretary McNamara announced that two Russian ships were within a few miles of the quarantine barrier. Then came the disturbing Navy report that a Russian submarine had moved into position between the two ships. "I think these few minutes were the time of gravest concern for the President."[142]

Then it was 10:25—a messenger brought in a note to John McCone who said. "Mr. President, we have a preliminary report which seems to indicate

---

[140] Pope, *Soviet Views, pp.* 32-6. Khrushchev's message was received in Washington at 9:24 PM, 24 October.

[141] In *Thirteen Days,* p. 62, the words attributed to Khrushchev's letter of 23 October were actually contained in his letter of 24 October.

[142] Kennedy, *Thirteen Days* pp. 52-3.

that some of the Russian ships have stopped dead in the water." Asked whether the report was true, McCone replied: "The report is accurate, Mr. President. Six ships previously on their way to Cuba at the edge of the quarantine line have stopped or have turned back toward the Soviet Union. A representative from the Office of Naval Intelligence is on his way over with the full report." A short time later, the report came that the twenty Russian ships closest to the barrier had stopped and were dead in the water or had turned around.[143]

The central nervous system for the Navy's planned blockade was located in Navy Flag Plot, room 6D624 in the Pentagon, where charts detailed the movements of every warship in the area. In command was Chief of Naval Operations Admiral George W. Anderson whose office was just down the hall from Flag Plot. The movements of Soviet ships were tracked by U.S. Navy, British and Canadian direction-finding (DF) stations located around the Atlantic periphery. Those stations continuously monitored every radio transmission from the Soviet merchant ships approaching the Cuban quarantine line.[144] By plotting the direction fixes on a chart, and seeing where the lines intersected, analysts could locate the source of the signal. By comparing those fixes over time, they could determine which direction and at what speed the ship was traveling.

On 24 October it became apparent from directional fixes that some of the Soviet ships enroute to Cuba had either slowed down or had altered or reversed their course. Initial indications of these facts were confirmed in Flag Plot and in the Navy Field Operational Intelligence Section in NSA at Fort

---

[143]   Ibid, p. 55.

[144]   David T. Spalding. *Naval Cryptology and the Cuban Missile Crisis,* Center for International Maritime Security, January 2016. https://cimsec.org/thirteen-days-the-naval-security-group-in-the-cuban-missile-crisis/ .

Meade. On 25 October, Kennedy issued an order not to intercept and board a Bloc vessel, in view of Khrushchev's apparent desire to avoid a direct U.S.-Russian confrontation as evidenced by the fact that of the 16 Soviet ships that had been located and determined to be enroute to Cuba, nine that were east of the line had reversed or altered course away from the quarantine area.[145]

In *Eyeball to Eyeball* Brugioni provides his version of the story: Late in the evening on 23 October, word was flashed from NSA to the CIA Watch Office that direction-finding indicated that the Soviet ships bound for Cuba had not only changed course but were probably on their way back to Russia. The CIA Watch officer, Harry Eisenbeiss, checked with the Office of Naval Intelligence (ONI). They were also in receipt of the NSA information but could not confirm the change of course. On the spot visual confirmation would have to wait until morning. The Navy felt that it might be a Soviet ploy. Eisenbeiss was convinced of the validity of the NSA information and in the wee hours of the morning of 24 October went to McCone's home where he told McCone that at least five of the Soviet ships had changed course and headed back to Russia, but that the Navy could not verify the NSA information. McCone said he would convey the information to the White House immediately.[146]

All morning long on Wednesday, 24 October, the Navy intelligence section at Fort Meade bombarded the Office of Naval Intelligence and Flag Plot with calls that their direction-finding efforts convinced them that a number of Russian ships had slowed, changed course, and that some might be on their way back to the Soviet Union. Later Wednesday, ONI and Flag Plot were con-

---

[145]   *The Naval Quarantine of Cuba.*
[146]   Brugioni, *Eyeball-to-Eyeball*, p. 391.

vinced the NSA information was valid and McNamara was informed. Later that afternoon, when McNamara found that the information had been available since early morning and he had not been told, he was furious. McNamara stormed into Flag Plot where a verbal confrontation between he and CNO Anderson ensued.[147] (Note that Brugioni's account of the Soviet ships having stopped or reversed direction is at odds with Robert Kennedy's depiction in *Thirteen Days*. Brugioni says McCone was told the night before the next day's ExComm meeting. Robert Kennedy says the president was informed at the morning's ExComm meeting by a note that was given him at the time. If McCone actually knew, or at least had strong indications about the ships' movements, he would have said so at the ExComm meeting. Note also that the depiction in *Thirteen Days* is backed up by an excerpt from a transcript of the ExComm meeting.[148]) Another account of Soviet ships redirecting course comes from an article in *Smithsonian* magazine. The team at NSA that had been monitoring the positions of Soviet ships was headed by Juanita Moody, chief of the Cuba desk. On learning in the middle of the night that at least one ship headed toward Cuba had stopped and changed direction, Moody felt the higher-ups needed to know about it right away. She made an urgent call to Adlai Stevenson, the U.S. ambassador to the UN, who was slated to address the Security Council about the crisis the next day. "I called New York and got him out of bed" she recalled. "I did what I felt was right, and I really didn't care about the politics."[149] (See the Vignette about Juanita Moody.)

---

[147]   Ibid, p. 399.

[148]   Excerpt from Meeting of the Executive Committee (ExComm) of the National Security Council, 10:00—11:15 AM, 24 October.

[149]   David Wolman. "The Once-Classified Tale of Juanita Moody," *Smithsonian Magazine*, March 2021.

The direction fixes on Soviet ships trickled in gradually, so there was no precise moment when the intelligence community determined that Khrushchev had "blinked" as was commonly reported. And yet the mistaken notion that the Soviet ships had turned around in a tense battle of wills lingered for decades. The "eyeball to eyeball" imagery served the political interests of the Kennedy brothers, emphasizing their courage and coolness at a decisive moment in history but misrepresents history. The myth was fed by popular books and the movie *Thirteen Days*.[150,151]

(The only ship to have been interdicted was the *Marucla*, a Lebanese flagged vessel. On 26 October it was boarded and, after inspection revealed it held no questionable material, was released to proceed to Havana. The *Marucla* had carefully and personally been selected by Kennedy to be the first ship stopped and boarded. It would demonstrate to Khrushchev that the quarantine would be enforced, and yet because it was not a Soviet-owned vessel, did not represent a direct affront to the Soviets, giving them more time, but simultaneously demonstrating that the U.S. meant business.)

---

[150] Dobbs, *One Minute to Midnight*, p. 88.

[151] *Thirteen Days* and the movie of the same name were harshly criticized by Sheldon Stern, the first professional historian to have listened to the secret White House tape recordings that were made during the crisis. The verbatim record provided by the recordings reveals what was actually said by the participants in the ExComm meetings, leading Stern to expose Robert Kennedy's reflections in *Thirteen days* as not just selective or slanted history, but rather as the capstone of an effort to manipulate the history of the crisis to RFK's political advantage. "RFK's *Thirteen Days* cannot be taken seriously as a historical account of the ExComm meetings." See Sheldon M. Stern. *The Cuban Missile Crisis in American Memory; Myths versus Reality*, Stanford, CA; Stanford University Press, 2012, pp. 34, viii.

Can We Prove There Are Missiles in Cuba?

U-2 missions were designed to provided photographic coverage of large areas of Cuba searching for evidence of Soviet nuclear missiles, and in that they succeeded brilliantly. What U-2 photographs could not do was to show the details of what was found in those photographs. A U-2 photo could show that a medium-range ballistic missile was present, but it could not provide the detail that would enable experts to determine their operational status and readiness for action. This could only be done from higher quality photography that could be obtained by reconnaissance aircraft flying at very low level, i.e., tactical reconnaissance. DCI McCone saw the value in low-level reconnaissance flights and in late August of 1962 in his absence he urged DDCI Carter to propose low-level reconnaissance missions, but McNamara was unreceptive to the idea. On 10 September, Carter sent a memorandum to the Secretary of Defense explaining the need for tactical reconnaissance and as justification he cited the need to establish the exact function and operational characteristics of the Banes facility that had been identified as a possible surface-to-surface missile site.[152] McNamara delayed a decision "until the results of CIA high-level reconnaissance became available." The author of *Blue Moon Over Cuba* suggests that McNamara's repeated refusal to allow low-level reconnaissance flights was most likely based on his belief that the U-2 flights were undetected. The same would not be the case for low-level flights and he did not want to reveal American knowledge of Soviet secrets until the time was right.[153]

The same day (16 October) that President Kennedy was told of the finding

---

[152] Memorandum for SecDef by Marshall S. Carter, Acting Director, dated 10 September 1962, subject: Tactical Reconnaissance of Cuba. CIA archives.

[153] Ecker and Jack. *Blue Moon Over Cuba,* p. 59.

of missiles in Cuba, McNamara held a meeting to formulate plans for stepped up U-2 reconnaissance that the President had directed. In attendance were DDCI Carter, NPIC's Arthur Lundahl and Air Force officers. The feasibility of low-altitude reconnaissance missions was also discussed. It was no secret in Washington that the Navy, which had devoted considerable time and effort to developing an effective reconnaissance capability, had the best totally integrated low-altitude reconnaissance capabilities. Lundahl specifically recommended the Navy's Light Photographic Squadron No. 62 (VFP-62)[154]. The squadron flew unarmed supersonic RF-8A Crusaders.

On Thursday, 18 October, Lundahl[155] was briefing the President on the latest U-2 photography that revealed that at least sixteen MRBM missiles were deployed in Western Cuba at two launch sites. The President questioned Lundahl if the uninitiated could be persuaded that the U-2 photographs showed offensive MRBM facilities. Lundahl stated "probably not; we must have low-level photography for public consumption." The president agreed, but those missions were delayed for several days so that the Soviets would not be tipped off that the U.S. government knew their secrets, thus causing them to expedite construction on the missile sites. President Kennedy was playing for time while strategies and options were being debated and developed.[156]

On 19 October, Captain Ecker (author of *Blue Moon Over Cuba*) received his orders to stage to Naval Air Station Boca Chica, Key West, Florida, but he and his VFP-62 reconnaissance squadron would have to wait until the President's address on 22 October broke the news that Russian missiles had been

---

[154] Brugioni, *Eyeball to Eyeball*, pp. 234-5.
[155] See Vignette on Lundahl, The President's Briefer.
[156] Ecker and Jack. *Blue Moon Over Cuba*, pp. 74-5.

discovered before they could fly. On 23 October during a meeting of the JCS, the chiefs were told the White House had approved VFP-62 sorties, and on the same day six VFP-62 pilots took off on missions codenamed *Blue Moon* to obtain photographs of the MRBM site at San Cristóbal and other high priority targets.[157] Eckert's photography of the San Cristóbal site showed the missile assembly equipment, the fuel-tank trailers, the missile erector sites and the launchers themselves. (These were the pictures that Ambassador Stevenson used on 25 October when he confronted Soviet Ambassador Zorin at the UN Security Council.) Photos from missions flown on October 25 of four MRBM sites showed that the Soviets were working overtime to make the MRBM's operational, and it was estimated that the San Cristóbal site No 2 would probably be operational by 26 October.

Photos from Blue Moon missions on 25 October revealed a class of Soviet weapons not previously discovered. As noted by Michael Dobbs, what the NPIC photo interpreters found was recognized by Lundahl as a FROG (Free Rocket Over Ground—Soviet name: "Luna") missile. It was well known to U.S. intelligence that FROG missiles could be armed with either a conventional or a nuclear weapon, but there was no way of determining which it was from the overhead photography.[158]

The Air Force was anxious to get in on the act and on 24 October, pilots of the Tactical Air Command (TAC) flew their first missions. The Air Force, however, lacked a satisfactory low-level reconnaissance system and the photography from those first missions was unusable. As Brugioni wrote in *Eyeball*

---

[157]   Ibid pp. 94-101, 143.
[158]   Dobbs, *One Minute to Midnight*, pp. 137-8.

to Eyeball, the Air Force had not developed cameras and procedures for high-speed low-altitude photography.[159] The Navy came to the rescue by providing cameras for Air Force planes after which Air Force missions provided high quality photography.

During the crisis, Navy and Air Force pilots flew many missions over Cuba, flying at near-supersonic speed a few hundred feet above the ground under intense enemy ground fire. The Cuban gunners were inexperienced and that may have saved U.S. pilots from being shot down. A quote is attributed to Fidel Castro in which he describes his attempts to shoot down the low-level reconnaissance planes: "The inexperience of our artillerymen, who had recently learned to operate these pieces, probably made them miss as they fired on the low-flying aircraft."[160]

The author of *Blue Moon* writes that there is a widely written account that one of the low-flying jets was hit by anti-aircraft fire but managed to limp back to base. "This is almost certainly a false report. There is no documented evidence that RF-8As were ever hit and it is undetermined if an RF-101 was."[161]

Authors James Blight and Janet Lang write about how the low-level reconnaissance flights affected the Cuban people and the humiliation they experienced. "Every hour, two U.S. low-flying, high-speed reconnaissance planes fly overhead at near-supersonic velocity…There follows a momentary but ex-

---

159   A history of Air Force involvement in the Cuban Missile Crisis noted that "TAC [Tactical Air Command] possessed inadequate photographic intelligence of potential Cuban targets and lacked high-resolution aerial cameras and efficient photo-processing equipment which limited its ability to produce quality target photography in a timely manner." *The Air Force Response to The Cuban Missile Crisis*, prepared by USAF Historical Division Liaison Office, Headquarters USAF, Tab B-3.

160   Ecker and Jack. *Blue Moon Over Cuba*, p. 153.

161   Ibid, p. 154. The USAF history of the crisis makes no mention of Air Force aircraft being hit.

cruciatingly loud roar, well after the planes have passed overhead… Fidel does not fear these planes, nor do his troops. What he and they feel is anger: the U.S. planes violate Cuban sovereignty at will." "And now, they assert their right to fly into our airspace whenever they feel like it, the sonic booms breaking windows, terrorizing and angering the population."[162] If the Cubans had shot down one or more of the U.S. reconnaissance planes, the U.S. would likely have attacked the island of Cuba. Kennedy had held his fire after the shoot down of Major Anderson; a second loss would have forced his hand as the military would have demanded a U.S. response. A Russian response would likely have been forthcoming, and that response would probably have included, among other actions, nuking the base at Guantanamo Bay. Armageddon would have followed in short order.[163]

What Are Those Submarines Doing?

As part of Operation Anadyr, the Soviets in early October deployed multiple submarines to Cuba from Northern Fleet waters. The deployment was unusual and assumed additional significance because, in the past, the USSR had seldom deployed even a single submarine in the Western Atlantic. The Navy began detecting signs of increased Soviet submarine activity in the Atlantic as early as 13 October, and began increasing the readiness of its anti-submarine warfare (ASW) forces. By 24 October, the Soviet subs were well on their way to Cuba and would reach the quarantine zone a few days later.[164]

---

[162] James G. Blight and Janet M. Lang. *Dark Beyond Darkness,* pp. 82-3.
[163] Ibid, p. 12.
[164] Bouchard. *Command in Crisis,* p.117.

The Soviet submarines were identified as Foxtrot (NATO classification) diesel-electric attack boats, but the mission of the naval part of Operation Anadyr, named Kama, was unclear to U.S. intelligence: would they bring nuclear warheads to Cuba; would they establish a submarine base in Cuba; were they to protect the Soviet merchant ships and attack U.S. ships enforcing the quarantine. Because of concerns over possibly bringing nuclear warheads to Cuba the Kennedy administration would include Soviet submarines in the quarantine.[165]

CIA clandestine reports received before the crisis had suggested the Soviets were establishing a submarine base in Cuba possibly at Banes or Mariel. However, CIA had stated that there is no conclusive evidence that the Soviet authorities intended to use Cuban ports as bases for either submarines or logistical support.[166] Later it would be learned that CIA's assessment was incorrect.

Had the Foxtrot subs been deployed to protect the ships that were delivering offensive missiles to Cuba? Huchthausen writes that the U.S. Navy assumed the worst case, that the Soviets would not possibly undertake this vast movement of arms and troops without at least some armed escort. In the absence of surface or long-range air assets, protection would be provided by the most advanced submarines in the Soviet naval arsenal.[167] But what Bouchard has written contradicts Huchthausen's thesis: "The other three confirmed Soviet submarines (hull numbers C-18, C-19, and C-20/26) operated in the Atlantic east and north-east of the Bahamas. They were detected moving toward

---

[165] Ibid, p. 118.
[166] *Khrushchev's Miscalculated Risk,* pp. 46-7.
[167] Peter A. Huchthausen. *October Fury,* Hoboken, NJ: John Wiley & Sons, Inc., 2002, p. 31.

the quarantine zone shortly before the quarantine went into effect. Although these three submarines are often described as escorting the merchant ships carrying offensive arms to Cuba, their locations and movements were unrelated to those of the merchant ships."[168]

It is now known that the real purpose of the Foxtrot deployment was to prepare for the establishment of a permanent ballistic missile submarine base at Mariel. The four subs were to proceed undetected to Mariel as an advanced reconnaissance and preparatory move for the ballistic missile subs, which would follow later according to Russian documents that the National Security Archive published in 2012 and to Huchthausen, who writes about orders given by Admiral Rybalko, the operational commander of the mission: "Your assignment is to get to Mariel undetected by 20 October and to prepare for the subsequent deployment of seven ballistic missile submarines, which will follow with their support ships. You are to reconnoiter the waters surrounding Mariel and ensure they are free of American anti-submarine forces, fixed acoustic arrays, and to survey and report the hydroacoustic conditions of the area."[169]

At the time of the ExComm meeting on the morning of 24 October Russian merchant ships were proceeding and were nearing the five-hundred-mile quarantine barrier. McNamara announced that two Russian ships, the *Gagarin* and the *Kimovsk* were within a few miles of the barrier. The interception of both ships would probably be before noon Washington time. Then came the disturbing Navy report that a Russian submarine had moved into position be-

---

[168] Bouchard, *Command in Crisis*, p. 124.
[169] *The Underwater Cuban Missile Crisis: Soviet Submarines and the Risk of Nuclear War*; National Security Archive Electronic Briefing Book No. 399, posted October 24, 2012; Huchthausen, p. 17.

tween the two ships causing President Kennedy to express alarm "If this submarine should sink our destroyer, then what is our proposed reply." General Taylor responded to the President's concern saying the submarine is going to be "covered by our anti-submarine warfare patrols and that we have a signaling arrangement with that submarine." Alexis Johnson interjected that he had sent a message to Moscow the night before saying that in accordance with the President's proclamation, the Secretary of Defense had issued the procedures for identification of submarines. McNamara added that the procedures included the use of practice depth charges as a warning signal. "When our forces come upon an unidentified submarine, we will ask it to come to the surface for inspection by transmitting the following signals…which they may not be able to accept and interpret. Therefore, it is the depth charge that is the warning notice and the instruction to surface."[170]

Robert Kennedy later wrote: "I think these few minutes were the time of gravest concern for the President. Was the world on the brink of a holocaust? Was it our error? A mistake? Was there something further that should have been done? Or not done? His hands went up to his face and covered his mouth. He opened and closed his fist. His face seemed drawn, his eyes pained, almost gray. We stared at each other across the table."[171]

McNamara, aware that the President had directed a maximum ASW effort, was concerned that lack of a standard means of signaling Soviet submarines to surface could lead to weapons unnecessarily being used against a Soviet submarine. After the evening ExComm meeting on 23 October he went to

---

[170] Meeting of the Executive Committee (ExComm) of the National Security Council. 10:00-1:15 AM, 24 October
[171] Kennedy, *Thirteen Days*, p. 53.

the CNO's office and met with Vice Admiral Griffin, Deputy for Fleet Operations and together they devised a unique set of signals that could be used to signal Soviet submarines to surface. McNamara immediately approved the special signals. The special "Submarine Surfacing and Identification Procedures" were transmitted to the fleet five hours before the quarantine went into effect on 24 October. The next day they were broadcast to the world, including the Soviet Union, in a Notice to Mariners, the standard message used by all nations to send warnings of navigation hazards.

To ensure the Soviets understood the intent of the notice Assistant Secretary of Defense for Public Affairs Arthur Sylvester told reporters on 24 October that "action will be taken to interdict" any submarine that did not surface when ordered, and the next day a Department of Defense spokesman told the press that "should a submarine refuse to cooperate, it would be subject to the same orders applied to other vessels, calling for the minimum amount of force necessary—sinking if necessary—to require the vessel to permit itself to be searched."[172]

The purpose of the warning signals had been described in a Pentagon message transmitted to the Soviet government via the U.S. Embassy in Moscow on 24 October. "Submerged submarines, on hearing this signal, should surface on an easterly course." Both Kennedy and McNamara assumed that the Soviet submarine captains had been informed about the new procedure and understood the meaning of the new signals. According to Michael Dobbs they were mistaken. The Soviet government never acknowledged receipt of the message about the underwater signals, and never relayed the contents to

---

[172] Bouchard, *Command in Crisis*, pp. 120-1.

the commanders of the Foxtrot submarines.[173]

In *The Doomsday Machine* Daniel Ellsberg discusses the surfacing and interception procedures from the morning ExComm meeting on 24 October. He writes: "They presumed, they said, that the Soviets had received the message and passed it on, but they couldn't be sure." (A reading of the transcript fails to find those exact words, but the transcript is confusing at best.) Ellsberg then says that the four sub commanders all denied that they had received any such message.[174] The surfacing and identification procedures were used on Soviet submarines (C-19 and C-21 and possibly C-18 and C-20/26) during the crisis, but there are no reported instances of a Soviet submarine immediately surfacing on hearing the signals. They surfaced because they needed to replenish air, recharge batteries or because they had a mechanical problem.[175]

There are indications that the Soviet government may have directed its submarines to comply with the U.S. procedures. At least three of the submarines had surfaced on an easterly course as specified in the Notice to Mariners. Although this suggests the subs were directed to comply, it is not conclusive: the three subs had been on an easterly heading before surfacing anyway. There are no clear cases of Soviet subs making a large course change specifically to surface on an easterly heading. What is more revealing is that they surfaced at all. Normally, a sub need only expose its snorkel to recharge batteries and replenish air. It was unusual that all of the Soviet subs fully surfaced, sometimes repeatedly rather than just snorkeling. The Soviet government thus appears to have directed its subs to comply with U.S. instructions. Bouchard does not

---

[173] Dobbs, *One Minute to Midnight*, pp. 299-300.
[174] Ellsberg, *The Doomsday Machine*, p. 212.
[175] Bouchard, *Command in Crisis*, pp. 120-3.

go as far as to say that, therefore, the submarine commanders surfaced in response to instructions, but that logically follows.[176]

Huchthausen believes the Soviets received the Notice to Mariners and sent it to the submarine commandeers. On 25 October at the Headquarters, Main Navy Staff, Moscow, Admiral Rybalko[177] was handed the American Notice to Mariners. He and Admiral Fokin[178] disagreed about sending the notice. Rybalko said the notice must be sent to the submarine commanders so they know what's going on. Fokin responded that Gorshkov[179] is dead set against sending extraneous material on the schedules because he believes the traffic analysis will give away the operation. Rybalko ordered the message to be sent to all units in the Atlantic and took responsibility for his action.[180]

After their return from the deployment, the Soviet submarine commanders gathered together and spoke of Rybalko and the hardships of their deployment. They all knew Rybalko had tried hard to help them and probably would soon disappear from the scene. He would no doubt be relieved of his command for his unauthorized transmission of the U.S. Notice to Mariners on 25 October, against the specific orders of the commander in chief, Fleet Admiral Gorshkov.[181]

Huchthausen writes that the Foxtrot commanders had, in fact, received the Notice to Mariners. The commander of B-59, Captain Vitali Savitsky, re-

---

[176] Ibid, p. 123.

[177] Rear Admiral Leonid F. Rybalko, commander of the Fourth Red Banner, Order of Ushakov submarine Squadron.

[178] Admiral Vitali Fokin was overall coordinator of Operation *Kama* responsible for preparing all naval forces participating in the operation.

[179] Admiral of the Fleet Sergei Georgevich Gorshkov was known as the father of the modern Soviet Navy.

[180] Huchthausen, *October Fury,* p. 152.

[181] Ibid, p. 256.

ceived the notice on October 5; Captain Aleksei Dubivko, commander of B-36 had received the warning notice repeatedly indicating that whoever was sending it was eager for them to receive it; and Captain Nikolai Shumkov, commander of B-130, also had the Notice to Mariners.[182]

The National Security Archive, in its posting of 24 October 2012, noted that the Soviet submarine commanders, in a series of interviews in recent years, reported they never received the message conveying the Notice to Mariners. The Foxtrot commanders had been instructed in the strongest terms that their transits were to remain secret and to avoid detection by U.S. ASW forces. "We were constantly reminded of the need for secrecy in all operation documents and by those who came to our departure."[183] It would not be surprising then that the commanders would deny receiving the notice even if they had. Of interest in this regard is Dubivko's comments after returning home and being interviewed by a commission that was aimed at uncovering violations of orders, documents, or instructions by the commander or the crew. "We were accused of violating the secrecy…while trying to avoid the anti-submarine aircraft of the United States and the anti-submarine ships…However, they did not take into account the fact that if the commander abided by NIS-58 [instructions], then the submarine would never have been able to arrive at the final destination…"[184]

Of the four Foxtrot subs that secretly left for Cuba on 1 October, the U.S. Navy detected and closely tracked three: B-36, commanded by Dubivko, and

---

[182] Ibid, pp. 168, 183, 208.

[183] A.F. Dubivko, First Captain (retired). "In the Depths of the Sargasso Sea," *On the Edge of the Nuclear Precipice*, Moscow: Gregory Page, 1998, p. 4. (Translated by Svetlana Savranskaya). The National Security Archive Electronic Briefing Book No.75, Document 32. In Operation Anadyr Dubivko was commander of submarine B-36 of the Northern Fleet.

[184] Ibid, p. 16.

identified by the U.S. Navy as C-26 and also as C-20/26; B-59, commanded by Savitsky, and identified as C-19; and B-130, commanded by Shumkov, and identified as C-18. Only submarine B-4, commanded by Captain Rurik Ketov, escaped intensive U.S. surveillance.[185]

With the exception of submarine B-4, the U.S. detected and located the Foxtrot submarines early, and generally kept them under near constant surveillance. In reports that the Russians have released, they indicate that the Americans seemed to have had some advance knowledge of their position. In recollections of his experience on B-59, Senior Lieutenant Vadim Orlov who was assigned as the onboard head of the Radio Intercept Group, wrote that the ASW forces of the opponent were ready for an encounter with us from the very beginning of our sail to the Cuban shores. "In the beginning, the Norwegian hydroplanes were searching for us, then at the Farer line—the British 'Shackleton's.' Then it was the turn of the American 'Neptune's.'"[186]

Huchthausen writes about the experience of Captain Aleksei Dubivko, Commander of Soviet submarine B-36. "Dubivko knew a little about the U.S. underwater passive hydrophones called the Caesar System.[187] But he didn't know that they had been as accurate as apparently they were. Many times, the long-range anti-submarine aircraft came right over their track and dropped

---

[185]   B-36 was identified by the U.S. Navy as C-26 and later found to be identical with another identified submarine C-20, thus the designation C-20/26.

[186]   Recollections of Vadim Orlov (USSR Submarine B-59). The National Security Archive Electronic Briefing Book No. 399, Document 7.

[187]   The Caesar System was the unclassified name for the Sound Surveillance System (SOSUS), the Navy's formerly secret underwater network of passive hydrophones deployed on the ocean floor to detect and track Soviet submarines. SOSUS was deployed at major natural choke points, and sensor data was transmitted by undersea cables to on-shore receiving stations. With the end of the Cold War and new technology, SOSUS was substantially reduced and today supports civilian and scientific applications. SOSUS was officially declassified in 1998.

sonobuoy patterns almost directly ahead. He felt they must be using other information, yet he had been careful not to radiate their radar, except in low power and only for single sweeps when visibility dictated and safety was an overriding issue."[188] Orlov and Dubivko, of course, had no way of knowing that what they had speculated was in fact true; the U.S. had indeed been aware of the presence of their submarines. The U.S. Navy had been monitoring the Foxtrot submarines ever since they slipped out of the Soviet submarine base on the night of 1 October. Electronic eavesdroppers followed the flotilla as it rounded the coast of Norway and moved down the Atlantic, between Iceland and the Western Coast of Scotland. Whenever one of the Foxtrots communicated with Moscow—which it was required to do at least once a day—it risked giving away its general location. The bursts of data were intercepted by listening posts scattered across the Atlantic, from Scotland to New England. By getting multiple fixes on the source of the signal, the submarine hunters could get a rough idea of the subs' locations.[189]

The methods used by the U.S. to obtain such highly important intelligence were at the time extremely sensitive and highly compartmented. Chief of Naval Operations Admiral George W. Anderson managed U.S. naval operations from Flag Plot where the positions of Soviet merchant ships and submarines were monitored. McNamara made frequent evening visits to Flag Plot, and on one occasion he had an encounter with Admiral Anderson. McNamara asked why a destroyer was out of position. The reason was that it was tracking a Soviet submarine, but Anderson could not reveal that sensitive

---

[188] Huchthausen, p. 177.
[189] Dobbs, *One Minute to Midnight*, pp. 91-2.

information because few in the room were permitted access to such highly classified intelligence. Anderson invited McNamara to an inner sanctuary and explained the sensitive source to the Secretary of Defense.[190]

Years before the Cuban Missile Crisis Soviet submarines had been communicating with fleet headquarters using manual Morse transmissions. The U.S. Navy used these communications to locate the submarines by direction-finding techniques to triangulate on the source of the transmission. In December 1958 those transmissions stopped, leaving no way for the U.S. Navy to locate Soviet submarines. A research activity called Project Clarinet Bullseye was initiated in December 1958 to investigate the loss of Soviet submarine communications and in 1959 it was discovered that the Soviets had begun to communicate using High Frequency (HF) microbursts to make themselves more difficult to pinpoint. Microburst signals lasted only about seven tenths of a second. Prior to that, the Naval Research Laboratory (NRL) in Washington, D.C. had developed Project Boresight, key to which was a system that allowed operators to record signals and analyze them "after the fact" to determine the bearing to the submarine, the source of the transmission. This retrospective direction-finding capability was one of NRL's most significant achievements. The capability became critically important after 1958 when Soviet subs ceased their Morse code transmissions and effectively went silent.

By 1960, Boresight[191] stations of the Naval Security Group[192] in the At-

---

[190]   Anderson reminiscences as told by A. Dennis Clift. "Ringside at the Missile Crisis," *Proceedings*, U.S. Naval Institute, updated 2013. https://www.usni.org/magazines/proceedings/2012/october/ringside-missile-crisis .

[191]   Boresight is the subject of *Red November; Inside the Secret U.S.- Soviet War* by W. Craig Reed, published 2010. An extremely critical review of the book and a related in-

lantic (Homestead, Florida; Galeta Island, Panama; Bermuda; the Azores; Edzell, Scotland; and Hafnir, Iceland) were fully operational. During the Cuban Missile Crisis in October 1962, Boresight HFDF (High Frequency Direction Finding) stations were able to track nearly all Soviet submarines at sea by monitoring their burst transmissions. Boresight and its successor Clarinet Bullseye and Classic Bullseye were all closely guarded, secret compartmentalized programs.[193]

At NSA the organization responsible for the production of intelligence on the Soviet Navy was the office of A2 where A21 was responsible for Merchant Shipping, and A22 for Out of Area Soviet Submarines. The Navy Field Operational Intelligence Office (NFOIO) at NSA was heavily involved with A22 that was exploiting the data from Boresight. (One of the analysts in NFOIO at the time was Lt. Bobby Ray Inman, who would become the Director of NSA [DIRNSA] in 1977 and in 1981 CIA's Deputy Director.)[194]

One of the Navy personnel in A22 was Capt. Norman Klar. He wrote that there were many supposed sightings of Soviet submarines headed for Cuba at the time of the Cuban Missile Crisis, but we proved the exact, much smaller number was "more than three and less than five." "The so-called Cuban Missile Crisis was more of the threat of the Soviets building a Soviet submarine base at Cienfuegos than it was about land-based missiles. I truly believe that

___

ternet manuscript is posted under Project Boresight. The reviewers' comments provide more information on the Boresight and Bullseye programs. http://jproc.ca/rrp/rrp2/boresight.html .

[192] The Naval Security Group was an organization within the United States Navy, tasked with signals intelligence gathering, cryptology and information assurance.

[193] Station HYPO. "Early Direction Finding: From WW1 Through the Cold War." https://stationhypo.com/2019/01/05/early-direction-finding-part-1-of-2/.

[194] Norman Klar. *Confessions of a Code Breaker: Tales from Decrypt,* Charlestown, SC: BookSurge Publishing, 2004, p. 130.

A22 and A21were the two most valuable sources of intelligence in the entire government during the missile crisis."[195]

The man at NRL credited with devising the means to locate Soviet submarines was Howard O. Lorenzen,[196] known as the father of electronic warfare. In 2010, the U.S. Navy named the USNS Lorenzen after him. At NRL, Howard Lorenzen pioneered another breakthrough—America's first reconnaissance satellite—in the history of American electronic intelligence. Known under the cover name GRAB (Galactic Radiation and Background), it was first conceived by NRL in early 1958 and combined the laboratory's long experience in electronic intercept systems with its interest in satellites. On 22 June 1960, the first U.S. SIGINT satellite was launched from Cape Canaveral. It and its successor satellites, known as POPPY, collected signals from air defense radars in the Soviet Union that could not otherwise be observed by U.S. intelligence.[197]

---

[195] Ibid, p. 138.

[196] After five years of designing commercial radios and components for Colonial Radio and Zenith Radio, Iowa State University alumnus Howard O. Lorenzen became an electrical engineer at the Naval Research Laboratory (NRL) in 1940. During his career, Lorenzen helped with developments in radar, electronic countermeasures systems, and intelligence satellite designs. https://www.ece.iastate.edu/profiles/howard-o-lorenzen/ .

[197] The second launch of a GRAB satellite occurred on 30 November 1960. Unfortunately, the booster did not perform properly and was destroyed by the range safety officer. Fragments landed in Cuba and killed a cow in a farmer's field. The incident, memorialized as the "herd shot round the world," resulted in the prohibition of any launches that passed over Cuba. (*The SIGINT Satellite Story*, published by NRO in 1994 and released, heavily redacted, in 2016, pp. 45-7. https://www.nro.gov/Freedom-of-Information-Act-FOIA/Declassified-Records/Selected-Historically-Significant-Documents-of-Public-Interest/sigint/ .)

THE POST-CRISIS PERIOD

By 28 October, Khrushchev had evidently had had enough of his high-risk, low-profit adventure and in his letter to President Kennedy of that date said: "In order to eliminate as rapidly as possible a conflict which endangers the cause of peace, to give confidence to all peoples of the Soviet Union, the Soviet government, in addition to previously issued instructions for the cessation of further work at the weapons construction sites, has issued a new order to dismantle the weapons, which you describe as offensive, and to crate and return them to the Soviet Union." "I regard with respect and trust the statement you made in your message of October 27, 1962, that no attack would be made on Cuba and that no invasion would take place—not only on the part of the United States, but also on the part of other countries of the Western Hemisphere, as your same message pointed out. In view of this, the motives which prompted us to give aid of this nature to Cuba no longer prevail."[198]

On 1 November the Soviets began dismantling the long-range missile sites and withdrawing the MRBM's and their associated equipment. The question for U.S. intelligence was then ensuring the missiles were gone. The with-

---

[198] The message was delivered to the American Embassy at Moscow at 5:10 PM on October 28 and broadcast over Moscow radio in Russian and English beginning at 5 PM Moscow time on the same date. CIA's Foreign Broadcast Information Service (FBIS) had been monitoring Radio Moscow throughout the crisis and provided President Kennedy the first news of the Soviet decision to withdraw missiles from Cuba.

drawal operation was notable for its rapidity and its overtness, especially in comparison to the ultra-secret Anadyr operation.

Because none of the large-hatch ships in which the missiles had been brought to Cuba as hold cargo were near Cuban waters on the first of November, Soviet authorities chose to use shipping immediately available in Cuba and return the missiles as deck cargo. On 2 November, missiles and equipment began appearing at the port of Mariel. On 5 November, missile equipment was noted moving into the port of La Isabella. By 10 November all 42 missiles had been loaded and were at sea enroute back to the USSR.

Although the use of immediately available shipping required deck loading of the missiles and thus contributed to the overtness of the withdrawal, there are some indications of a deliberate effort by the Soviet authorities to demonstrate as plainly as possible, short of on-site inspection, that the offending offensive missiles and bases were gone: they made no attempt to shelter the missiles and equipment while in port awaiting shipment; IRBM sites were simply bulldozed over; and the Soviet authorities generally cooperated in drawing back tarpaulins from the missiles when challenged at sea by U.S. inspection parties.

In contrast to the expeditious withdrawal of the MRBM's the 42 IL-28 bombers in Cuba were not removed until early December and then only after Anastas Mikoyan had spent some uncomfortable days and nights exercising his powers of persuasion convincing Castro to have them removed. In fact, assembly of the IL-28's went on slowly but steadily after 28 October until about mid-November, following which no change was observed in the status of the aircraft. After Khrushchev's announcement on 20 November that the IL-28's would be withdrawn, all of the aircraft were moved from airfields to the ports where they were loaded on the decks of vessels that departed by 7 December. The fact that they were not withdrawn sooner, together with the apparent disarray between Moscow and Havana provides evidence that these aircraft were intended from the outset to be turned over to Castro's forces.[199]

---

[199] *Khrushchev's Miscalculated Risk,* pp. 78-80.

Throughout the crisis, President Kennedy held firm to his objective—the removal by one means or another of the Soviet strategic missiles. American intelligence did its part in supporting Kennedy in meeting his objective. Former DCI Helms was noted at the beginning of this story as saying the Cuban Missile Crisis was about discovering the missiles and confirming that they left. In this, American intelligence did its job well. It is fair to say that intelligence made a difference, perhaps *the* difference in bringing the crisis to a successful closure.

At the same time, U.S. intelligence missed and misjudged important aspects of the Soviet venture in Cuba. Those errors did not materially affect the peaceful resolution of the crisis that was accomplished through diplomatic means. But options of a military nature were very seriously considered by Ex-Comm and were initially favored, especially, though not exclusively, by the military. The military options included an air strike, which the JCS never stopped promoting, and an air strike followed by an invasion, the expulsion of Castro, and the installation of an American-friendly government. General Anatoli I. Gribkov discussed what might have happened if U.S. air strikes and an invasion had been launched. "Under combat conditions, in the terrible disorder of the battlefield, there is an outside possibility that an enterprising Soviet commander could have put a low-yield atomic warhead on a short-range cruise missile. If such an officer had also found a target for that weapon, it is hard to believe he would have waited long for approval from higher authority before firing. It is impossible to know what the U.S. response to such an act would have been."[200]

A review U.S. intelligence performance during the crisis reveals: The size, composition and organization of Soviet forces on the island was seriously underestimated; intelligence and U.S. ASW forces hunting Soviet submarines didn't know, and possibly could not have known, that those submarines were equipped with nuclear-armed torpedoes in addition to conventionally-armed ones; and most significantly, intelligence did not confirm the presence of tactical nuclear weapons on the island, and may have under-played the possibility of their existence. One may argue, as some observers of the crisis have, that these errors contributed to the successful resolution of the crisis; had the U.S. known that Soviet forces on the island were combat ready and armed with nuclear weapons, it would have created a problem, at least a political problem, for the administration. How could the U.S. have made its non-invasion pledge in exchange for the Soviets agreeing to remove the missiles knowing that such a dangerous military force could be left in Cuba?

Soviet Troops in Cuba

On 6 February 1963 in response to the many conflicting rumors and reports, DCI McCone made a statement that represented the agreed views of the United States Intelligence Board based on what the U.S. knew at the time.

---

[200] Gribkov and Smith, *Operation Anadyr*, pp. 67-8.

The statement rested on the most up-to-date and reliable data available to the United States Government and was derived from all of the intelligence gathering resources at its disposal including daily aerial surveillance. In it he said "From a few hundred military technicians in the summer of 1962, the Soviet armed forces in Cuba grew by 24 October to include regular troops manning the tanks and other weapons of mobile armored groups, specialists in charge of an extensive surface to air missile system, and a large number of other air force, naval, and army personnel. Our current evaluation, based on all sources including known tables of organization of Soviet units, is that a total of about 22,000 Soviet troops were in Cuba during September and October. Since then, about 5,000 troops associated with offensive missile systems have left. Some 17,000 Soviet military personnel now remain in Cuba."[201]

It came as a shock to U.S. intelligence experts when they learned that the actual strength of Soviet troops on Cuba was more than twice the number that they had long thought. The actual number was given by General Anatoli Gribkov in his book published in 1994: "Actual Soviet troop strength on Cuba when John Kennedy imposed the naval blockade on 24 October was 41,902."[202] A similar number was disclosed at the Cambridge Conference[203] of October 1987 in a statement by Sergo Mikoyan who said that Khrushchev

[201] Statement on Cuba by Director of Central Intelligence, 6 February 1963. CIA archives.

[202] Gribkov and Smith, *Operation Anadyr*, p. 28.

[203] The Cambridge Conference brought together Soviet political commentator Fyodor Berlatsky; Sergo Mikoyan, son of Anastas Mikoyan, who accompanied his father on his delicate mission to Cuba at the conclusion of the crisis; and Georgi Shaknazarov, personal aide to General Secretary Gorbachev. American participants included McGeorge Bundy, Robert McNamara, and Theodore Sorenson among others; Sorenson was special counsel to the President during the crisis. (See Conferences on the Cuban Missile Crisis.)

sent forty-two thousand men to Cuba to deter a U.S. Invasion.[204] Mikoyan's figure is very close to Castro's later recollection of 40,000.[205]

The disclosure of the actual numbers of Soviet troops was shocking, but even more shocking was learning that the deployment constituted a large organized combat force comprising Soviet air force, air defense, coastal defense, and ground force elements. The CIA believed there were 20,000 Soviet "technicians and advisers" on the island. In fact, there were more than forty thousand Soviet soldiers on Cuba, including at least ten thousand highly trained combat troops.[206]

Historians have never satisfactorily explained the reason(s) for the gross underestimation by American intelligence. According to Blight and Welch, CIA operatives believed the number of Soviet troops was much greater than Agency analysts estimated, and they ask: "why did U.S. analysts ignore the estimate of the size of the Soviet force in Cuba provided by the operational branch of the CIA? Samuel Halpern, Task Force W executive officer, testified that Task Force W concluded in September 1962 that there were 45,000-50,000 Soviet military personnel in Cuba." As we now know, the operations people had it just about right. Halpern is certain that CIA analysts received the Task Force W estimate in September, but does not know what happened to it. Why did the estimators dismiss it? "The only defensible reason would be that they had some contrary evidence to suggest that the estimate must have been off by about an order of magnitude. If so, this evidence has never been

---

204 James G. Blight and David A. Welch. *On The Brink; Americans and Soviets Reexamine the Cuban Missile Crisis*, New York: Hill and Wang, 1989, p. 241.
205 Ibid, footnote p. 356.
206 Dobbs, *One Minute*, p. 352.

made public." Blight and Welch offer other possibilities but lean toward what they refer to as a cognitive explanation: the estimators may simply have seen what they expected to see; the CIA's presumption that the Soviet mission was to train Cuban troops. The CIA did not believe at the time that the Soviets intended to deploy to Cuba a substantial nuclear deterrent and a full battle-capable conventional force to defend the island from American attack.[207]

Nuclear Torpedoes

On 30 September 1962 four Foxtrot submarines sat moored at Sayda Bay's wooden fishing piers where, to mask their departure, they had moved under cover of darkness three days earlier from their usual berths in Polyarny. The silent move had been made so that last-minute loading of the "special" [nuclear] torpedoes could be done in total secrecy.[208]

Just prior to the launch of the Foxtrot boats Fleet Admiral Sergei Gorshkov met with Admiral Rybalko, commander of the submarine squadron, and told him: "you are in no way to allow American ASW forces to discover your subs during your transit. Your assignment is to get to Mariel undetected and to reconnoiter the waters surrounding Mariel and ensure they are free of American ASW forces. You will load one special torpedo on each of your boats. You will use these weapons if American forces attack you submerged or force your units to surface and then attack, or upon receipt of orders from Moscow."[209]

---

[207] Blight and Welch, *Intelligence and the Cuban Missile Crisis*, pp. 180-1.
[208] Huchthausen, *October Fury*, p. 46.
[209] Ibid, p. 17.

At sea the sub commanders opened a secret package that contained the rules of engagement: (1) Weapons in transit will be in combat readiness for use; (2) Conventional weapons to be used as directed by the Main Navy Staff except may be used in case of attack against the sub; (3) Torpedoes with atomic weapons may be used only as directed in instructions from the Ministry of Defense or the Main Navy Staff. These words were considerably at odds with what they had been earlier told at the send-off briefing at the pier.[210]

No one on the U.S. side knew that the Soviet submarines were armed with nuclear torpedoes even as they dropped the practice depth charges attempting to force the submarines to the surface. No one knew at the time that conditions in the Soviet submarines were so physically difficult and unstable that commanding officers, fearing they were under attack by U.S. forces, may have briefly considered arming the nuclear torpedoes.[211]

Tactical Nuclear Weapons

The revelation of the previously unknown fact about the Cuban Missile Crisis occurred in a conference room in Havana, Cuba in early January 1992. It was there that Russian general Anatoly Gribkov disclosed that which the Americans had believed was unlikely, if not impossible, but turned out to be real—the Soviets had tactical nuclear weapons, including warheads, in Cuba during the crisis. Gribkov was a member of a Soviet delegation to the Havana conference on 9-12 January 1992 that also included key U.S. and Cuban figures

---

[210] Ibid, p. 65.

[211] The National Security Archive; *The Submarines of October*, National Security Archive Electronic Briefing Book No. 75, 2002.

who were involved in the actual crisis. They included Robert McNamara and Fidel Castro.

Gribkov would later write about his experience at the conference. "My disclosure that battlefield nuclear weapons had been part of the Soviet arsenal on Cuba in October 1962 caused a sensation among the conference participants, and later in the Western press." "…I actually spoke in Havana about six Luna (NATO designation FROG) launchers and nine missiles with nuclear warheads, when the actual number of warheads was twelve. Because I was not certain about what information was still to be kept secret, I did not mention the eighty small cruise missiles or the six atomic bombs for the IL-28's."[212]

"The Luna missiles…and the other tactical nuclear systems were installed to repel a direct landing of the enemy on the coast of Cuba." "…the truth is that any strike by U.S. forces against Cuba and its Soviet defenders would have heightened the risk of nuclear war, no matter whether the first response was with conventional or battlefield nuclear arms. That was the terrible danger that both John Kennedy and Nikita Khrushchev wisely recognized and acted to contain in 1962."[213]

The Soviet decision to include short-range nuclear weapons in the deployment to Cuba had been carefully weighed in Moscow. Although the Lunas, FKR's and specially fitted IL-28 bombers were not among the standard armaments then assigned to Soviet forces stationed outside the USSR, it was felt that the Soviet commander on the island, General Issa Pliyev, being so far from reinforcements, might need the added battlefield strength that such tac-

---

[212] Gribkov and Smith, *Operation Anadyr*, pp. 165-6.
[213] Ibid, p. 166.

tical arms could provide. The battlefield nuclear weapons were put on the island in case deterrence failed. Targeted on the approaches an invading fleet was thought most likely to use, and on the beaches where U.S. troops seemed most likely to come ashore, the low-yield Luna and FKR warheads were weapons Soviet planners classed as a kind of powerful artillery shell.[214]

U.S. intelligence was aware of the Luna and FKR weapons having photographed them on low-level reconnaissance missions and identified them as such. U.S. intelligence also knew from other earlier intelligence that each was capable of carrying either a nuclear or conventional weapon. An item in the President's Intelligence Checklist of 27 October said: "Photography has also turned up a launcher for the 'FROG' missile. This is a short-range (50,000 yards) tactical unguided rocket similar to our Honest John. It can carry either a *nuclear* [italics added] or conventional warhead."[215]

According to General William Y. Smith, who at the time was assistant to General Maxwell Taylor in the White House and at the Joint Chiefs of Staff, the U.S. JCS assumed that nuclear warheads for the Luna rockets might be available and adopted contingency plans to what they saw as the unlikely possibility that the Soviets would use such nuclear arms. "The Chiefs did not know that the tactical nuclear arsenal on Cuba totaled ninety-eight weapons as General Gribkov has stated."[216]

Faced with a possibility that invading American troops could face an onslaught of tactical nuclear weapons, U.S. decision makers seemed unsure how

---

[214] Ibid, p. 28.

[215] *The President's Intelligence Checklist*, issued by the Central Intelligence Agency, 27 October 1962.

[216] Gribkov and Smith, *Operation Anadyr*, p. 172.

to respond to the contingency judging how it was described by Roger Hilsman. "Because the American Army expected to be met with battlefield nuclear weapons, its contingency plan for a possible invasion also called for tactical nuclear weapons." Hilsman further says: "McGeorge Bundy later wrote that he did not realize at the time that the Army planned to include battlefield nuclear weapons in their equipment and that if an invasion had actually been ordered, McNamara, or Maxwell Taylor would have made sure that the tactical nuclear weapons were left behind. I have no doubt at all that the Army would have been ordered to keep any tactical nuclear weapons well to the rear and that they would not have been permitted to use them unless President Kennedy gave his express permission. I also have no doubt that Kennedy would have given that permission only if the Soviets had used their battlefield nuclear weapons first. But since we *knew* [emphasis added] the Soviet troops defending the missiles were armed with battlefield nuclear weapons it would have been unduly risky not to give the American forces the same capability."[217]

In the view of Blight and Welch, "American officials did not presume that Soviet forces in Cuba would be equipped with tactical nuclear weapons, and had Kennedy sent American forces into Cuba, they would have not have been equipped with similar weapons themselves."[218] "While the potential nuclear role of the IL-28 aircraft and Luna rockets had been known, few if any in Washington really believed there were tactical nuclear warheads in Cuba"[219]

In a memorandum of 2 November 1962, JCS Chairman Maxwell Taylor advised the President that the Joint Chiefs of Staff had concluded that since

---

[217] Roger Hilsman, *The Cuban Missile Crisis*, p. 117.
[218] Blight and Welch, *Intelligence and the Cuban Missile Crisis*, pp. 198-9.
[219] Ibid, p. 29.

there are nuclear-capable delivery system in Cuba, we must accept the possibility that the enemy may use nuclear weapons to repel invasion. He further said: "however, if the *Cuban* [emphasis added] leaders took this foolhardy step, we would respond at once in overwhelming nuclear force against military targets." Taylor goes on to advise Kennedy that in the more likely case that atomic weapons would not be used by either side, our present plan of invasion is adequate and feasible. Coming back to nuclear weapons he tells Kennedy that if such weapons were used, certainly, we might expect to lose very heavily at the outset if caught by surprise, but our retaliation would be rapid and devastating and thus would bring to a sudden close the period of heavy losses.[220]

Naftali and Fursenko write about the effects of the use of tactical nuclear weapons by the Soviets in Cuba. With twelve of the Lunas at his disposal the Soviet commander in Cuba could easily destroy any beachhead established by U.S. Marines in an invasion of Cuba and obliterate the U.S. base in Guantanamo. The cruise missiles, the FKR, if used, would not have as dramatic an effect on the battlefield but, as predicted by Soviet military journals, could inflict heavy costs on the U.S. Navy task force participating in an attack. One FKR cruise missile carried enough power to blow a U.S. aircraft carrier group apart.[221]

Soviet military doctrine in October 1962 provided for the use of nuclear weapons on the battlefield. Malinovsky's predecessor as defense minister predicted in 1957, "Atomic weapons will be widely employed as organic weapons

---

[220] Memorandum for the President; Evaluation of the Effect on U.S. Operational Plans of Soviet Army equipment Introduced into Cuba, 2 November 1962, by Maxwell D. Taylor, Chairman Joint Chiefs of Staff.

[221] Aleksandr Fursenko and Timothy Naftali. *One Hell of a Gamble; Khrushchev, Castro & Kennedy 1958-1964,* New York: W.W. Norton, 1997. pp. 242-3.

in the armies." Articles in Soviet military publications argued that tactical nuclear weapons would make amphibious landings difficult, if not impossible. Naftali and Fursenko ask: And what would be the U.S. reaction to the first use of nuclear weapons by the Soviet Union? A look at the blast effect of these weapons left little doubt that if Pliyev used his battlefield weapons there would be enormous pressure on President Kennedy to destroy Cuba, at the very least.[222]

Many years after the crisis, the head of the Soviet nuclear arsenal in Cuba, Lt. General Nikolai Beloborodov, observed: "It was clear that in the conditions of the existing balance of forces in conventional arms, which was ten to one against us, there was only one way we could repel a massive assault—by using tactical nuclear weapons against the invaders. In principle, this action would be consistent with international law on the protection of sovereignty and freedom."[223]

Nuclear warheads for the battlefield weapons were delivered to Cuba incrementally. On 4 October, the *Indigirka* brought 36 warheads for the FKR, 12 warheads for the Lunas, and six nuclear bombs for the IL-28's; On 23 October, the *Aleksandrovsk* brought 44 warheads for the FKR's in addition to strategic missile warheads. On 26-28 October it was "partially" unloaded with warheads for FKR's being sent to units. It then departed still carrying the R-14 (IRBM) warheads (that had never been unloaded) and probably 36 R-12 (MRBM) warheads.[224]

---

[222] Ibid.

[223] Report of Lieutenant General Nikolai Beloborodov, head of the Soviet nuclear arsenal in Cuba, The National Security Archive Electronic Briefing Book No. 449, Document 2, p. 10.

[224] The National Security Archive Briefing Book No. 449, *The Last Nuclear Weapons Left Cuba in December 1962*; Brief Chronology of Soviet Tactical Nuclear Weapons in Cuba. https://nsarchive2.gwu.edu/NSAEBB/NSAEBB449/ .

The Cubans had pressured the Soviets to have the tactical battlefield nuclear weapons remain in Cuba, and Anastas Mikoyan who was conducting negotiations with Castro, had at one point suggested transferring "all remaining weapons" to the Cubans after special training. But being acutely aware of the fanatical tendencies of the Cuban leadership, Khrushchev decided it would be foolhardy to leave nuclear weapons in Cuba, and on 1 December, all tactical nuclear warheads left Cuba on the *Arkhangelsk*.[225]

In his Foreword to Robert Kennedy's book *Thirteen Days*, that was written in April 1999, Arthur Schlesinger, Jr. made an astounding statement: "No one in Washington dreamed that the Soviet soldiers might be equipped with tactical nukes"[226] As noted above, the CIA had written in the President's Checklist on 27 October that the FROG missile could carry a nuclear warhead. In doing so it was simply stating a fact. But was there a failure of imagination by the CIA? Should the Agency have highlighted the *possibility* of a nuclear warhead? Should they have inserted something like: While we have no evidence that the Luna missile could be equipped with a nuclear warhead, we cannot completely discount the possibility that it could. Perhaps the reason that "No one in Washington dreamed that Soviet soldiers might be equipped with tactical nukes" is because the CIA had given it insufficient credence. And given that, one wonders how seriously the possibility was regarded in DOD's invasion operations planning.

At the 1992 Havana conference, McNamara said that the planned invasion force "would *not* [his emphasis] have been equipped with tactical nuclear

---

225 Ibid.
226 Kennedy, *Thirteen Days,* p. 8.

weapons, although its commander had requested authority to carry them." McNamara declined, however, to rule out the likelihood that an atomic attack on the landing force would have canceled the restriction. McNamara further said the presence of Soviet tactical weapons in Cuba created an added element of danger, which *some of us had not anticipated*. [emphasis added] "It horrifies me to think what would have happened in the event of an invasion of Cuba!"[227]

On the morning of Friday 26 October President Kennedy ordered the State Department to proceed with preparations for a crash program on a Cuban civil government to be established after the invasion and occupation of that country. Secretary McNamara reported the conclusion of the military that we should expect very heavy casualties in an invasion. McCone added that everyone should understand that an invasion was going to be a much more serious undertaking than most people had previously realized.[228] McNamara and McCone were certainly right in their warning, but they didn't know why or just how right, they were. They did not know that an invading American force would face, not only the Cuban army, but a large, organized Soviet force equipped with battlefield nuclear weapons. The presence in Cuba of tactical nuclear weapons remained a closely held Kremlin secret for more than three decades as was the presence of 42,000 Soviet troops.

Blight and Lang excuse the failure of U.S. intelligence to discover the tactical nuclear weapons. "While this was certainly a lacuna, it is unclear that the CIA should have been expected to discover that the Soviet Union had equipped its forces with tactical nuclear weapons, and it is possible to

---

[227] Gribkov and Smith, *Operation Anadyr*, p. 68.
[228] Kennedy, *Thirteen Days*, pp. 65-6.

argue that the CIA had furnished Kennedy with ample information on the basis of which to conclude that an invasion carried with it unacceptable risks in any case."[229]

---

229   Blight and Welch, *Intelligence and the Cuban Missile Crisis,* pp. 198-9.

Final Thoughts

The Ending

In his private letter to Kennedy of 27 October Khrushchev outlined a path to resolve the crisis that the White House saw as a positive step. But that private message was shortly followed by a public message of 28 October in which Khrushchev sought the removal of the Jupiter missiles in exchange for his in Cuba. President Kennedy viewed the trade as not unreasonable; the Jupiters were obsolete and had little military utility. Importantly, Kennedy saw the trade as *the* way to end the crisis. He also saw that not being willing to give up the missiles in exchange for a peaceful ending to the crisis was an indefensible position for the United States, and he argued his point of view strongly with ExComm. But the members almost universally disagreed. In their view, an abrupt removal of the missiles would send a grave message to the European allies and threaten the NATO pact.

Following the ExComm meeting on the night of 27 October, Kennedy called together his closest advisors. Together, they agreed that the President would respond to the earlier conciliatory Khrushchev letter while ignoring the second public letter, and that Robert Kennedy would be dispatched to meet Ambassador Dobrynin. The junior Kennedy told Dobrynin that in due course the U.S. would remove the missiles from Turkey, but only on condition that the deal not be revealed even in the highest American and Kremlin political councils. The secret pact remained so for many years.

Immediately prior to Khrushchev's 27 October letter calling for a reciprocal Soviet-U.S. withdrawal of offensive weapons from Cuba and Turkey, the USSR reportedly attempted to bring pressure to bear on the Turkish government to forswear unilaterally the use of the missiles. The Soviet ambassador, in emphasizing the horrors of nuclear war, asked the Turkish Foreign Minister on the night of 26 October for assurances that missiles in Turkey would not be used in any war in which Turkey was not involved.[230]

The Soviet offer to dismantle the Soviet bases in Cuba under UN supervision was a clear backdown with the only quid pro quo exacted a U.S. promise not to invade Cuba. This action appears to have been motivated almost entirely by fear that U.S. military action against Cuba was imminent. The Soviet leadership saw that the USSR would either have to swallow this embarrassment, with enormous damage to its world position, or make a response which, given the state of mind they believed existed in the U.S., would carry risks of escalation to general war that they could not accept.[231]

Answering the "Why" Question

Why did Khrushchev take the gamble that ended so badly? Most scholars cite three motivating factors: first, he felt a strong need to support the Communist cause in Cuba and feared the country was threatened by the Americans; second, he sought to correct the imbalance in strategic nuclear armaments, and

---

[230] "A Reaction to Khrushchev's Announcement," a stray document, dated 29 October, 1962. CIA archive.

[231] Implications of Khrushchev's message of 28 October. Central Intelligence Agency *Memorandum*, 29 October.

putting Soviet missiles in Cuba promised a cheap and quick, even if temporary, way of accomplishing that; and third, he sought to improve the political position of the Soviet Union, strengthening the Communist cause, particularly with respect to China. While there is broad agreement about these motivations, experts disagree on which were the most important in Khrushchev's calculations. The truth is we may never know since Khrushchev has been ambiguous, but most likely he had all of those considerations in mind in the spring of 1962. Some students of the crisis have cited the U.S. Jupiter missiles in Turkey as a factor but it more than likely was not. While the missiles factored into the final resolution of the crisis, their removal was not an objective motivating Khrushchev to take the action that he did. It is true that Khrushchev thought it only right that America should live with missiles in its backyard just as the Soviet Union had and he frequently said so. But the Jupiter missiles were more of an after the fact *justification for* than a *cause of* his decisions and actions. As Graham Allison and Philip Zelikow wrote in their classic work on the Cuban Missile Crisis, *Essence of Decision*, "The Jupiters were not the reason Khrushchev took the extraordinary step of ordering missiles to Cuba, but they provided a ready rationale for it."[232]

Why then did Khrushchev take the gamble he did? Why did he deploy strategic nuclear missiles and attempt to establish a base for Soviet strategic nuclear missile submarines? Why did he pull out? And why did the Soviets not even attempt to conceal the deployed missiles from U.S. reconnaissance? Every other aspect of Operation Anadyr was executed under extreme secrecy, and the Soviets certainly knew about U.S. overhead reconnaissance given what

---

[232] Allison and Zelikow, *Essence of Decision,* p. 98.

they had learned from Gary Powers' U-2. Yet they seemingly ignored this vulnerability in their planning.

Allison and Zelikow attempt to answer these questions.[233] They do so by delving into the ways that governments make decisions on the gravest matters of national security. As for answering the question of why the Soviets deployed strategic missiles to Cuba, they posit three possible hypotheses. They then examine each from several vantage points: Was it the action of a rational decision maker? Was it the Soviet government responding to established policy? Or was it due to the influence exerted by Kremlin politicians.[234]

The hypotheses that Allison and Zelikow examine are the "Cuban Defense" hypothesis where the objective was to defend against or defer American aggression in Cuba; the "Cold War Politics" hypothesis where the objective was to demonstrate that the world balance of forces has shifted in their favor away from the U.S., strengthening the Soviet position in the Communist world; and "The Missile Power" hypothesis where the objective was to achieve a measure of parity with the U.S. on strategic nuclear weapons.

On the "Cuban Defense" hypothesis, Allison and Zelikow write that it does not stand up to careful examination. If defense or deterrence was the ob-

---

[233] Ibid.

[234] Allison and Zelikow refer to these vantage points as models through which to understand government behavior: Model I is the Rational Actor Model where governments make decisions after a rational weighing of alternatives, essentially a cost-benefit calculation much like the process a consumer might use in buying a car. Model II is the Organizational Behavior Model where decisions are made according to the standard organization playbook; actions take place, not because they are necessarily rational or sensible, but because that is just the way things are done, a following of standard operating procedures. Model III is the Governmental Politics Model where individuals or organizational units within the larger organization, the "players," engage in bargaining as they vie for power, status or influence, or perhaps vie to avoid influence and its associated risks.

jective, there was no need for ballistic missiles as there were other options: a sizable contingent of Soviet troops or conceivably a public defense treaty. And even if strategic missiles were thought necessary, why wouldn't MRBM's suffice? Why were the expensive IRBM's needed? As Allison and Zelikow point out, another problem with the "Cuban Defense" hypothesis is that the missiles made Cuba's position more, not less, perilous. Indeed, the U.S. came close to a massive air attack and possible invasion of the island in response to the Soviet missiles. According to Allison and Zelikow, there is no evidence that Khrushchev seriously analyzed possible options for Cuba's defense (though options were apparently considered in the first early decisions to send Cuba conventional arms.)

Arguments in favor of the "Cold War Politics" hypothesis to explain sending nuclear missiles to Cuba are that doing so would bring Russia and China closer together again, helping to heal a split that had widened since 1959. It would also deal the United States a tremendous political blow and show that Russia was capable of bold action in support of the Communist cause. But if the objective was political in nature, why did it require a massive military force with a large contingent of nuclear weapons. A few MRBM's would threaten the entire southeastern United States; what would longer range IRBM's add to the achievement of this objective?

Allison and Zelikow discuss the "Missile Power" hypothesis in some detail and one may conclude that they embrace it as the objective of the missile deployment, although they never explicitly say so. There is a strong argument to be made in support of the "Missile Power" hypothesis. Despite Khrushchev's earlier bravado (comparing missile production to sausage production), the Soviet strategic nuclear position in 1962 was extremely weak: a few dozen soft ICBM's, a small, very vulnerable bomber force, and a ragtag assortment of missile submarines that the U.S. Navy had under constant surveillance. The bulk of the Soviet nuclear capability consisted not of long-range threats to the U.S. but rather medium and intermediate range missiles that could hit American allies, but not America. In contrast, the U.S. had a vast arsenal of nuclear weapons. Until the CORONA satellite photographs had proved otherwise, there was a supposed "missile gap" between the Soviets and the U.S. where the Soviets were far ahead. The myth of the missile gap was exploded in a speech by Deputy Secretary of Defense Roswell L. Gilpatric at Hot Springs on 21 October 1961. The Soviets faced a near future of strategic vulnerability. They had to do something. They could have deployed new ICBMs that could reach the U.S. when launched from the Soviet heartland but that would take several years. In the meantime, they were vulnerable to a U.S. nuclear strike. They knew it and knew we knew it. Installing medium and intermediate range nuclear missiles in Cuba that could reach the U.S. was a cheap and quick solution to the problem. The ability to launch more than 40 missiles against the United States from Cuba would increase Soviet missile striking power against the United States by at least 50 percent. A nuclear submarine base that the Soviets tried to establish in Cuba would have improved their strategic capability even further.

The decision of the Soviets to improve their strategic position in this way would appear to be consistent with the "Rational Actor Model," yet not fully so. Faced with a choice of essentially doing nothing until their ICBM's were operational or locating their shorter-range missiles in Cuba, they choose the later but had they done a rational calculation, they would have clearly seen the benefits, but they would also have seen the potential risk. They apparently did not. Indeed, it appears that Khrushchev didn't even ask his experts to assess how the Americans would likely react to Soviet missiles in their backyard. Nor did they consult their experts on the likelihood that the missiles would remain undiscovered until they were operational.

Allison and Zelikow cite two major objections to the "Missile Power" hypothesis. First, why did Khrushchev feel such extraordinary urgency to redress the strategic balance? Why did he feel he could not wait two or three years for his ICBM force? Second, why was Khrushchev willing to run such extraordinary risks in order to solve his problem? But Allison and Zelikow seem later to answer their own question when they describe Khrushchev's decision-making as a product of a leader who had little appreciation of the situation, whose judgments were bereft of any attribute of high quality deliberations, and who relied on haphazard and often incorrect information.[235]

Allison's first edition of *Essence of Decision*, published in 1971, was reviewed by Fritz Ermarth, a noted CIA Soviet Kremlinologist. While Ermarth's review lacks the benefit of Allison's later 1999 edition, it nevertheless offers a useful perspective from one familiar with the inner workings of Soviet leadership.[236] Ermarth writes that Allison's analysis falls short in explaining Soviet behavior.

---

[235]   Allison and Zelikow, *Essence of Decision*, pp. 86-99.
[236]   Review by Fritz W. Ermarth: *"Essence of Decision; Explaining the Cuban Missile Crisis by Graham Allison (Little, Brown, and Company, Boston, 1971)," Studies in Intelligence*, Vol. 18, Number 1, 1974, p. 61.

He believes that Allison resisted the "Rational Actor" model explanation and force-fitted Models II and III to help him do so. Ermarth comes down solidly on the "Rational Actor" model to explain the missile deployment and that to him "the strategic power approach ["Missile Power" hypothesis] offers as good an explanation of Allison's key question—why they started and stopped the missile gambit—as any available." (Interestingly, Allison writes in his second edition that with more information then available "The Cuban Defense hypothesis becomes less plausible and the Missile Power hypothesis more."[237])

When the U.S. finally made it clear it would not stand for the missiles in Cuba, the Soviets had no choice but to back off, for the very same reasons they initiated the missile venture: they were too vulnerable. The remaining mystery in this is if Khrushchev was so impressed by U.S. strategic strength that he would try such a desperate move, how could he believe the U.S. would let him get away with it?

Operation Anadyr failed not because the plan leaked, or because communications security was lax, or because of an espionage breach. It failed because it allowed the missiles to be discovered too early, before the *"fait"* had been *"accompli."* Why did the Soviets think they could keep it secret from the U.S. for so long, especially considering the domestic political pressure on Kennedy? Anadyr planners apparently gave little thought to concealing or camouflaging the missiles and other telltale indicators of the deployment (camouflage was introduced after the Soviets learned they had been discovered, apparently in an effort to hide them from an American air attack). Here Allison and Ermarth seem to agree that that decision (or lack of a decision) can be un-

---

237   Allison and Zelikow, *Essence of Decision*, p. 380.

derstood by Model II. The causes of the failure to conceal the missiles were rooted in established routines designed for settings in which concealment had never been required. The Soviet authorities in charge, namely the Strategic Rocket Forces (SRF), set about deploying the missiles as they always had, in nice identifiable sites, mindless of the need to maintain secrecy until it was too late for the Americans to take action against them.[238] At the Cambridge Conference, Harvard University professor Joseph Nye, one of the participants asked "How could the Soviets believe they could keep this [the missiles] secret from the Americans, given the satellites and the reconnaissance planes? The construction of the missile sites…looked exactly like the missile sites we knew very well in the Soviet Union. It's hard to reconcile all of this with a desire to maintain secrecy." Participant Fyodor Burlatsky replied "It is very simple. You know, we are a planned society, but not a real planning society. [laughter] It is very typical." Nye responded "Were the organizations involved merely following their standard operating procedures?" to which Anastas Mikoyan replied "Yes, the organizations involved were simply following their routines. It was not thought through."[239]

Assessing U.S. Intelligence

Operation Anadyr proved to be an especially difficult target for U.S. intelligence. Extreme security measures permeated every aspect of Soviet plans that for the most part were brilliantly executed. The Soviets successfully moved

---

[238] An interesting, if farfetched, alternative cited by Ermarth is that the Kennedy administration had somehow signaled its willingness to let the missiles be deployed in Cuba, from which the Soviets may have concluded that the U.S. would acquiesce in the missile move as long as the Soviets kept it from public view, as would the U.S.

[239] Blight and Welch, *On the Brink,* p. 251.

vast numbers of personnel and equipment thousands of miles from home to a foreign land without their true intentions being known. Where Anadyr failed was that the Soviets did not prevent the U.S. from discovering the missiles once they were installed in Cuba.

So how well did U.S. intelligence perform as it sought to penetrate the secrets of Anadyr? By one measure it performed exceedingly well: practically every critical decision or action by President Kennedy was made based on, or related in some way, to information derived from intelligence, and since the U.S. successfully ended the crisis, it is reasonable to conclude that intelligence did its job well. But the reader need not look far to find references to U.S. intelligence failures and near failures, and without a doubt, U.S. intelligence committed errors. Some were significant though not consequential, while others could have been, but through good fortune did not have grave consequences. U.S. intelligence succeeded where it most mattered; the missiles were discovered in time such that negotiations could be conducted without them falling under the threat of nuclear war. Throughout the crisis the intelligence community provided crucial, highly timely information to support policy decisions by President Kennedy and the ExComm. Intelligence failed where it didn't matter because even though it came close to doing so, the U.S. never invaded Cuba. But as one imagines how horrific the battle of a Cuban invasion would have been, one is left to question that judgment.

It is often said that in the business of intelligence a failure can be traced to an error in the interpretation of information, not to an absence of information; the information that was needed to answer the intelligence question had been obtained by the appropriate means, but the analysis of that information was flawed for a variety of reasons—cognitive bias, lack of imagination, mirror imaging, unchallenged assumptions and the fallacy of the "rational actor model," among others. Such an analytic failure can be seen in the intelligence estimate (SNIE 85-3-62) that incorrectly assessed that the Soviets were unlikely to deploy nuclear missiles to Cuba. But the aforementioned wisdom may unduly let intelligence collectors off the hook while placing too much blame for failure on analysts. While the analysts responsible for the incorrect estimate can be faulted, a lack of critical information that could have contributed to a more informed estimate and less reliance on what proved to be faulty assumptions did not exist. Collection shortfalls compounded the analytical failure and were thus a contributing factor. U.S. intelligence had no insights into Soviet intentions and plans for Anadyr since at the time CIA lacked clandestine access to the most senior Kremlin leadership. Clearly, access to such extremely closely held information requires a degree of good fortune; former DCI Helms once said, the occasional Penkovsky is a windfall—a pure golden apple, but a windfall nonetheless.[240]

Klaus Knorr, a former consultant to CIA's Office of National Estimates (the office that produced the estimate), argues that the estimative failure occurred due to a lack of intelligence: "we do not know the information on which an opponent acts, or because we simply assume that he acts on approximately the same information we have and that he will not make any technical mistakes in his calculations."[241] Citing a similar lack of high-level intelligence, Jack

---

[240] Richard Helms. "Intelligence in American Society."

[241] Francis Rico C. Domingo, "Intelligence Successes and Failures: Revisiting the Cuban Missile Crisis," *OSS Digest* 1st Quarter 2010, p.41,

Davis writing in Sherman Kent Center for Intelligence Analysis Occasional Papers says "U.S. analysts, for example, did not know the extent to which Khrushchev, as dominant decision maker, was misinformed about the seriousness of U.S. warnings against the introduction into Cuba of offensive nuclear weapons."[242]

Kent himself acknowledged a scarcity of evidence; "there was of course no information that the Soviets had decided to deploy nuclear missiles to Cuba and indeed no indication suggesting such a decision. Moreover, months after that decision had been reached, and during the period when the estimate was being drafted and discussed, there was still no evidence that the missiles were in fact moving to their emplacements." In the absence of direct evidence, the estimators used other methods—analogy, extrapolation, logic, and judgment—in producing the estimate. Kent admits that in doing so it is inevitable that an estimate will on occasion end up with the wrong conclusion, and he argued that a lack of evidence is not an excuse for simply saying this or that may happen, which is of little use to policymakers.[243]

A lack of intelligence from SIGINT sources contributed to the U.S. lack of understanding Soviet plans and intentions for Anadyr, and the conditions that could have affected the decision to deploy offensive missile to Cuba. SIGINT largely failed by not having intercepted communications of senior military and other officials that would have provided indications of preparations for and the movement of Soviet nuclear forces from home bases in the Soviet

---

242   Jack Davis, "Strategic Warning: If Surprise is inevitable, What Role for Analysis?" Sherman Kent Center for Intelligence Analysis Occasional Papers: Volume 2, Number 1, Central Intelligence Agency, 2003, p. 8.
243   Kent, "A Crucial Estimate Relived." *Studies in Intelligence*, Vol. 8, No. 2, Spring 1964.

Union to Cuba. SIGINT did not pick up any indication whatsoever that nuclear missiles were bound for or in Cuba before the U-2 found them. Thomas R. Johnson, NSA veteran and author of the exhaustive "American Cryptology during the Cold War, 1945-1989," rendered a harsh verdict: "It [the Cuban Missile Crisis] marked the most significant failure of SIGINT to warn national leaders since World War II."[244]

Although SIGINT failed in its job to warn, in other respects, it did perform admirably in the period just prior to and during the crucial days of White House decision-making. It was notable for the intelligence it collected in conjunction with its intelligence community partners regarding Soviet maritime activities and correctly alerted key leaders to the Soviet buildup in Cuba as it was happening. But while it did provide excellent coverage of maritime activities, and knew from inaccurate cargo manifests and other indicators that something unusual was being transported, it was unable to know that cargoes included nuclear missiles.

NSA's ELINT collection by the *Oxford* spy ship, together with the Air Force's RB-47H ELINT aircraft provided immediate insights into the operational status of surface to air missiles that threatened U-2 overflights of Cuba. SIGINT also gave the White House the only timely information that it had about the Soviet reaction to the crisis, particularly the changes in the military alert posture of Soviet forces in the USSR prior to and during the crisis. Unfortunately, due to extremely tight communications security by the Soviets, it had no information with which to assess the operational status of Soviet nuclear forces in Cuba.

---

[244] Thomas R. Johnson, *American Cryptology during the Cold War, 1945-1989 Book II: Centralization Wins, 1960-1972*, National Security Agency, p. 317.

While a lack of HUMINT and SIGINT intelligence concerning the intentions of Soviet leaders and their plans for Anadyr constituted a strategic intelligence failure, *tactical* level intelligence was very effective at discovering what the Soviets were doing in Cuba. That intelligence came from Cuban refugees, who were interrogated at the Opa Locka Caribbean Admissions Center and from CIA agents in Cuba. While CIA analysts had serious doubts about the reliability of the massive amount of information provided by Cuban refugees, some reports were corroborated by clandestine agent reports leading CIA and DIA analysts to a most important piece of information—the location of a suspect MRBM site in the San Cristóbal area of Cuba. That intelligence led to the area being targeted for collection by the U-2 and to the mission of 14 October where the evidence of MRBM's was discovered. The CIA analytic apparatus recognized and correlated the first authentic reports of MRBM equipment ever to be received in Washington and together with DIA took action on them. In this regard, U.S. intelligence analysts did a remarkable job of putting the pieces of the puzzle together, as Richard Lehman recognized in his post-crisis investigation: "a considerable technical achievement."[245]

The information from the U-2 photography provided the irrefutable evidence that was crucial to President Kennedy establishing the blockade to interdict Soviet ships. And without such evidence international pressures for mutual accommodation might have led to greater U.S. concessions or to reluctant acquiescence in the existing Soviet deployment.

The strategic failure to warn of Soviet plans for its Cuban missile deployment had no direct adverse consequences; the nuclear missiles were discovered

---

[245] Lehman in McAuliffe, p. 99

before they became operational, a critical issue for US decisionmakers, some of whom believed that the operational status of the missiles would determine when a decision to destroy them had to be made. The failure to warn, however, cannot be dismissed so readily; had the Kennedy administration had good intelligence of Soviet intentions early enough, it could have made it abundantly clear to the Soviets that such action was unacceptable to the U.S., thereby possibly nipping Operation Anadyr in the bud.

U.S. intelligence was able to determine with considerable accuracy the operational status of the deployed Soviet SS-4 (MRBM) missiles using photographs collected by Navy and Air Force tactical reconnaissance aircraft. CIA analysts and NPIC photo interpreters used the photos together with what was known of the operational details of those missiles from the secret manuals that Penkovsky had copied and given to the West to estimate their operational status.

The most potentially consequential failure of the crisis is that U.S. intelligence did not know that the Soviets had brought to Cuba nuclear-capable battlefield weapons. The U.S. had studied such weapons that had been observed in the USSR and knew that they could be fitted with either a conventional or a nuclear warhead. Knowing that the tactical battlefield weapons were dual-capable, U.S. intelligence should have asked itself and administration officials should likewise have asked, is it likely that FROG and FKR weapons in Cuba are fitted with nuclear warheads? The answer would most likely not have been found in reconnaissance photography and it isn't at all clear that any of the other intelligence sources in Cuba or the Soviet Union could have contributed to answering the question. Even still, it appears that an answer to the question was not sought. The only known reporting related to the question was the statement in the President's Intelligence Checklist of 27 October that said, "It can carry either a *nuclear* [italics added] or conventional warhead." Late in October 1962, Robert McNamara believed implicitly that it was virtually *impossible* that the Russians would have deployed tactical nuclear weapons to Cuba, prepared for their use against a U.S. invading force, and given the Russian troops in Cuba authorization to use those weapons. It was thought to be impossible because the use of those weapons in Cuba would have elicited a devastating U.S. response, destroying vast areas of Cuba. Blight and Lang write that McNamara erred in believing it *impossible*. The threat, perhaps highly improbable, was hardly impossible and they attribute McNamara's *impossibility* to an inability to imagine what it felt like to face a choice between guaranteed total destruction for no redeeming purpose, and guaranteed total destruction, but destruction with a purpose, which was the martyrdom of Cuba for the cause of world socialism.[246,247]

Noted scholar Raymond Garthoff believes that the intelligence *failure* (emphasis added) to estimate that the Soviets had tactical nuclear weapons in Cuba was proper because there was no evidence to support any other judgment. "The possibility of Soviet tactical nuclear weapons in Cuba was recog-

---

[246] Blight and Lang, *Dark Beyond Darkness*, p. 71.

[247] Blight and Lang use a quotation from Arthur Conan Doyle's *The Sign of Four* to make the point: Sherlock Holmes says to his colleague Watson "How often have I said to you that when you have eliminated the impossible whatever remains, *however improbable,* must be the truth.?" Holmes believes Watson needs to carefully distinguish between what is improbable (but still possible), and what is, for whatever reason, simply impossible. What Holmes knows, and what he preaches incessantly to Watson, is how little is really *impossible*.

nized. There was no evidence or reason to do more than that."[248] He also argues that sometimes it is better that senior leadership not know: "What if U.S. intelligence in October-November 1962 had had *complete* information on Soviet military forces in Cuba? Paradoxically, as I have suggested earlier, full intelligence information could have made the resolution of the crisis much more difficult." "The danger posed by tactical nuclear weapons would have made more difficult a decision to invade, but countervailing pressure would have been strong to invade in order to ensure elimination of all nuclear weapons on the island." "There would also have been strong pressures on President Kennedy to demand withdrawal of all Soviet forces from Cuba, and although I believe Khrushchev would probably have acceded to that demand, the negotiation would certainly have been more difficult."[249]

Garthoff summarizes his assessments of U.S. intelligences: "In sum, judged on the basis of what could reasonably have been expected of the contribution of U.S. intelligence in the Cuban Missile Crisis, performance was reasonably good, in some respects outstanding, albeit with a few shortcomings. More useful than assigning any grade to performance, however, is reflection on the potentialities and natural limitations of intelligence" He also essentially suggests, as above, that a failure need not be a failure: "…more complete information at the time may sometimes make political and diplomatic decisions and conflict resolution more, rather than less, difficult." [250]

---

[248] Garthoff, *Intelligence and the Cuban Missile Crisis,* p. 53.
[249] Ibid, pp. 53-4.
[250] Ibid, p. 55.

Khrushchev's Miscalculation

Khrushchev is to blame for the Cuban Missile Crisis, even though a predicate had been laid by U.S. actions that were viewed by the Cubans and Soviets alike as seriously threatening the island nation. And while he was responsible for the crisis, he at least had the good sense to end it on what were essentially U.S. terms. He did so because he, like President Kennedy, greatly feared the horrific power of nuclear weapons. Both men fought to end the crisis before it spun out of control into a war that neither could win.

But Khrushchev's miscalculation had cost him heavily. He had been shown to be a liar, as being willing to sacrifice an ally, and as a much less cool and capable man in a crisis than his principal adversary. He had not changed the balance of strategic military power, even temporarily, and the inferior Soviet position was now plain for all to see. The attempt to redress the imbalance in a political sense had also failed, and Khrushchev had weakened his bargaining position in world affairs. He had lost ground with the underdeveloped countries, had exposed himself to Chinese ridicule and strengthened the Chinese case against his leadership. He had broken even in only one respect: he still had his "socialist" Cuba, his foothold in the Western Hemisphere; and even here it was made clear that his foothold could be maintained only on American sufferance.[251]

On 14 October 1964, after a palace coup orchestrated by his "loyal" protégé and deputy, Leonid Brezhnev, the Central Committee forced Khrushchev to retire from his position as the party's First Secretary and Chairman of the

---

[251] "The Soviet Missile Base Venture in Cuba," CIA/RSS, DDI Staff Study/RS, Spring 1964, p. xiii.

Council of Ministers of the Soviet Union because of his "advanced age and poor health." The Communist Party subsequently accused Khrushchev of mishandling the Cuban Missile Crisis among other political mistakes. Following his ouster, Khrushchev spent seven years under house arrest. He died at his home in Moscow on 11 September 1971.

The story of intelligence in the Cuban Missile Crisis is an all-source story. Virtually all intelligence disciplines contributed important information, but the principal sources were clandestine human intelligence, signals intelligence, photographic interpretation, and overhead reconnaissance. The vignettes here, stories within the main story, highlight the role that each played in understanding what the Soviets were doing in Cuba. The last vignette tells the story of the mysterious ABC Newsman – KGB backchannel where the author tries to answer the questions of what really happened; was it an important factor in resolving the crisis, or not, or something else?

Operation Cobra

Operation Cobra was run out of CIA's Miami station (JMWAVE) and had been the idea of Tom Hewitt, one of hundreds of Agency employees and contractors at the CIA station. Hewitt devised a plan to infiltrate two agents into Cuba to establish an effective espionage network whose mission was to gather intelligence, and, if necessary, to foment counterrevolution against the Castro regime.

Hewitt's principal agent in the operation was Esteban Marquez Novo whom Hewitt recruited and provided extensive training in clandestine operational procedures. Marquez Novo's cryptonym for use in all communications was AM-BANTY (The AM digraph preceded all CIA Cuba-related codenames.)

The infiltration of Marquez Novo and his communicator was a complicated affair requiring a round trip of at least 1,400 miles; A World War II landing craft would depart for a three-day voyage from Key West towing a much smaller boat around the western end of Cuba to within 10 miles of the Cuban coast. The smaller boat, a 30-foot Forest Johnson Prowler, came to within a mile of the shore on the night of 11 March 1962 where the crew put a canoe loaded with supplies into the water.

CIA station in Miami known as JMWAVE. It was the headquarters for espionage and covert actions against Cuba. (Source: McCone history)

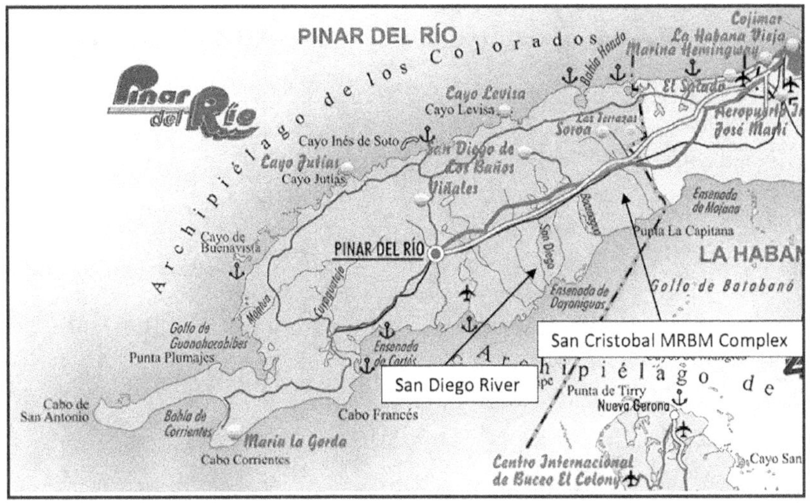

CIA agents came ashore from San Diego River. The Map also Show the location of the San Cristobal missile complex where Soviet MRBM missiles were first discovered. (Source: https://www.lahistoriaconmapas.com.)

Once on shore, Marquez Novo and his radio operator went to work contacting existing underground organizations, establishing radio contact with the Miami base, developing a maritime channel for infiltration/ exfiltration operations, and gathering intelligence on the local situation. In the months following his infiltration, Marquez Novo steadily built up his network, which he named the Frente Unido Occidental (FUO), or United Western Front. The network developed into an extensive resistance/ intelligence complex extending throughout Pinar del Rio, with branches covering Havana and the Isle of Pines.

Beginning in August of 1962, intelligence developed by AMBANTY would be key to uncovering the Soviet Cuban venture. On 1 August an agent reported very unusual events at the port of Mariel; the arrival and unloading of a Soviet ship was done under extraordinary secrecy, trucks from the ship were driven off under guard of Soviet personnel. The agent added: "It is probable that the trucks were loaded with rockets, nose cones for rockets, or most probably atomic bombs."

The initial stages of the Soviet buildup were reported by Hewitt's AM-BANTY network in western Cuba, by agents in Las Villas and Matanzas provinces, reporting to another JMWAVE case officer, and by newly arrived Cuban refugees who were cycled through the Opa Locka Interrogation Center.

An AMBANTY agent report, which the CIA circulated on 18 September, said that a large area in central Pinar del Rio province "is heavily guarded by Soviets..." In particular, the report noted heavy security "where very secret and important work is in progress, believed to be concerned with missiles." The report gave the grid locations for the four small towns that marked the boundaries of the area in what became known as the trapezoid area and used in targeting the 14 October U-2 flight.

The AMBANTY network continued its operations after the end of the Cuban Missile Crisis. But due to a combination of lax security by the network and an increase in Cuban security forces, by the spring of 1964 the Castro regime had rolled up AMBANTY and Marquez Novo was dead.

In January 2005, a gathering was held in a conference room of the old headquarters building in Langley to posthumously honor Hewitt. Jack Downing, former CIA deputy director of operations, presented Hewitt's wife with the Agency's Distinguished Intelligence Medal. The citation read:

"In January 1961, Mr. Hewitt joined the Miami Station as a paramilitary Officer in the Cuban program. Shortly thereafter he developed and ran one of the most successful operations in the history of the organization. Mr. Hewitt spotted, developed, recruited, and

provided extensive paramilitary training to a team that was infiltrated into Cuba. It was this team that reported on the presence of nuclear equipment in the Pinar del Rio province of Cuba. Based upon the reporting from Mr. Hewitt's team, U-2 aircraft were dispatched to the region. Their photographs confirmed the presence of nuclear capable missile equipment. The rest is history, known today as the Cuban Missile Crisis. Public credit for the discovery of the missiles in Cuba was given to the U-2 reconnaissance aircraft in order to preserve the security of the team that Mr. Hewitt created, trained, managed, and motivated through one of the darkest periods of the cold war..."

———-

Source: "Operation Cobra: The untold Story of how a CIA officer trained a network of agents who found the Soviet missiles in Cuba," published by *Yahoo News*, 23 January 2019.

Cuba Chief – An NSA Pioneer

Juanita Moody had worked for most of her NSA career almost entirely dedicated to the Soviet target as had the majority of the NSA workforce. According to her: "I'd say leading up to the approximate time of the Bay of Pigs, that effort [rest of world signals intelligence] was just sparse, and the whole area of Cuba was just nothing." Moody would later say that the Agency [NSA] had not done very much anywhere except the Soviet Union; "I think I figured out one time there might have been the equivalent of two people on the problem [Cuba] at that point. Well, then all of a sudden it becomes a high priority and USIB starts rearranging its requirements and NSA decides that we're going to have to redistribute some of our resources and we're going to have to get new resources, and things were going to happen, so here comes the reorganization."

NSA was reorganized in 1961 and Moody was assigned as chief of G Group charged with overseeing NSA's collection and processing operations nearly everywhere except China and the Soviet Union. As Cuba became a national priority and NSA was shifting resources accordingly, Moody was in command of NSA's collection and processing operations against Cuba.

Juanita Moody was the key figure at NSA Overseeing all SIGNIT collection and Reporting during the Cuban Missile Crisis. (Source: NSA.)

In November of 1961, General Lansdale, the chief of the MONGOOSE operation, wanted to know what intelligence NSA had on Cuba and he sought out Juanita Moody. On telling him what NSA was finding—Russian technicians and money moving into Cuba, greatly increased Soviet shipping to the island among other indications of "a lot of Russian activity"—Lansdale asked her to document the findings in a single document, a product that would integrate all of the individual items of raw signals intelligence. After she and her team worked over a three-day weekend to produce what was called a "serialized report," she was told by NSA management that such a report would get NSA in trouble for having exceeded its mandate. Moody protested that "there isn't anything in it except SIGINT" and sent it to Lansdale.

By February of 1962, Moody and her team were seeing so much evidence of Soviet activity in Cuba that she sought NSA management approval to publish serialized reports on Cuba, and again was told by NSA Deputy Director Louis Tordella that it couldn't be done "We can't do that, it will get us in trouble because it would be considered outside of our charter." Moody responded that she was more worried about the trouble NSA would be in if they didn't publish than if they did: "And so we went with the publication in February '62."

As Moody and her team focused their effort on the Cuban target, one of the first things they discovered was that soon after the Bay of Pigs, Cuban authorities had increased the security of their communications systems. They introduced a microwave system across the island that complicated NSA's ability to spy on Cuban communications because intercept stations had to be within line-of-sight of microwave towers. By the early summer of 1962 Moody and her team had made major improvements in collection capabilities: using surveys, NSA found suitable locations for intercepting Cuban communications and established and augmented facilities in Florida, Vint Hill,[252] and still-secret locations; the Oxford spy ship was operating off the Cuban coast to intercept those and other signals including those from radars associated with air defense systems; and the Air Force increased its collection by the RB-47H ELINT aircraft.

To translate the enormous amount of material NSA was collecting, Moody pushed an unconventional approach despite caution urged by the NSA security guardians. People undergoing processing for security clearances could be used as linguists with little risk to the security of NSA operations she argued. She also brought in linguists from NSA's sister cryptologic organizations. As the crisis heated up, NSA Director Gordon Blake established an around the clock team to produce daily SIGINT summary reports and he assigned Moody, who frequently spent nights in her office, to make it happen.

The USS *Oxford* spy ship was the principal SIGINT asset collecting communications and electronic intelligence during the crisis. (Source: NSA archives)

With Moody in charge of the Cuban "desk," NSA with its sister cryptologic agencies that operated

---

[252] Vint Hill Farms Station, known as Vint Hill, was a field station of the Army Security Agency, a subordinate of the NSA that conducted signal intelligence operations. Located near Warrenton, Virginia it closed in 1997. The Cold War Museum is currently located on the property.

under NSA oversight achieved major successes before the crisis and as it unfolded: it closely monitored Soviet shipping to the island and reported on the large number of ships and the Soviet efforts to conceal the nature of their cargo; it reported on the massive buildup of Soviet military equipment and personnel on the island; it discovered and monitored radar signals associated with the SA-2 surface to air missile, although that vital information could not have saved Major Anderson from the SA-2 that shot down his U-2 because of a disconnect with SAC; it reported that shortly following the quarantine imposition, Soviet ships had turned around and were headed back to the USSR, a report that the White House was eager to receive.

While NSA contributed significantly to understanding what the Soviets were doing in Cuba, it had provided no specific warning that Moscow was sending nuclear missiles to the island. SIGINT can capture only what is transmitted or emitted and because Soviet communications security was nearly perfect, there was little for U.S. intelligence to capture.

Moody had pioneered the idea of serialized SIGINT reports. NSA moved more and more to producing reports by combining information and putting it in a consolidated, summary form as opposed to raw intercepts.

———

Sources: Moody Interview 16 June 1994 by David Hatch, et al. in NSA archives; David Alvarez, "American Signals Intelligence and the Cuban Missile Crisis" in *Intelligence and National Security*, Vol. 15, No.1, p. 169-176. See also David Wolman, "The Once-Classified Tale of Juanita Moody," *Smithsonian Magazine*, March 2021.

The President's Briefer

Arthur Lundahl joined the CIA after having been chief of the Navy's Photographic Interpretation Center. His job at CIA was to establish an organization to exploit photography of the Soviet Union to be acquired by U-2 overflights that would begin in mid-1956. One of Lundahl's first tasks was to find a home for his organization. The nondescript Steuart Motor Car Co. building in a crime-ridden area of Washington at Fifth and K Streets, NW. was selected. The four upper floors of the building would be occupied by Lundahl's organization, while the three lower floors would be occupied by the motor car company, along with the Steuart Real Estate Office. Broken bottles, abandoned autos, and trash littered the area.

Photo-interpretation had traditionally been the private preserve of the military, especially the Air Force, which was extremely sensitive to the Agency's encroachment on its territory. (SAC commander General Curtis LeMay was particularly incensed that the Agency was becoming involved with photo-interpretation.) Lundahl believed that photo-interpretation elements of the military services should be included in his new organization and CIA leadership agreed to do so in creating the National Photographic Interpretation Center, or NPIC as it was known.

Arthur Lundahl, Director of the National Photographic Interpretation Center (NPIC), led the team that on 15 October 1962 found the evidence of Soviet nuclear missiles in Cuba. (Source: National Geospatial Intelligence Agency.)

The National Photographic Interpretation Center under Lundahl was responsible for the evolution of photographic interpretation. Lundahl fused the skills of diverse disciplines: photo-interpretation, collateral information, data processing, photogrammetry, and technical analysis. The result was a team of experienced personnel that inspired great confidence from other intelligence and government officials.

Lundahl's leadership was reinforced by an unusual level of talent. CIA Director Allen Dulles and his deputy, Lieutenant General Charles F. Cabell, US Army, extended Lundahl a free-hand in selecting personnel to staff the Center. Although the Steuart Building left much to be desired in physical amenities, Lundahl would frequently remark: "Where a choice be necessary, give me good men in poor ships than the converse."

NPIC was a unique interdepartmental national-level organization. The formal structure was controlled, staffed, and funded by the CIA, but the informal organizational structure also included special detachments from the Army, Air Force and Navy. They were under the administrative control of "service chiefs," who contributed personnel for photo-interpretation projects of national interest such as the exploitation of photography acquired over Cuba. After its founding, interpreters from the Defense Intelligence Agency were also assigned.

When the U-2 was flying missions over the Soviet Union, Lundahl would brief President Eisenhower on the intelligence significance of each photograph as the president listened intently. Lundahl remembered that the president "asked questions about targets of great national interest. He was impressed with the quality of the photography and asked questions about the resolution and the altitude the pictures were made from." A warm and friendly relationship developed between the two men.

Lundahl's combination of energy, memory, intelligence, knowledge, and especially his articulateness, was making quite a name for him and the art of photo-interpretation. He was a superb photo interpreter and photogrammetrist, and this ability, combined with a warm enthusiasm and a strong empathy with his audiences, was proving daily the value of photo-intelligence in the intelligence assessment process.

The task of educating the new President Kennedy on photo-interpretation fell to Lundahl who established a close working relationship with him and the assistant to the president for national security affairs, McGeorge Bundy. Lundahl's articu-

late and succinct explanations of what was seen on aerial photography were always welcome at the White House. The president wanted technical information presented in a straightforward manner, free of military jargon, so it would be comprehensible not only to him but also the average person.

Lundahl would frequently update Kennedy on the latest finds from both the U-2 and satellite photography. Lundahl would be seated on the sofa to the right of the president, and the director of the CIA would frequently be seated on the president's left. Lundahl would arrange his briefing materials and using a magnifying glass the President would study the latest photography as Lundahl briefed.

The U-2 had been flying over Cuba collecting intelligence since before the Bay of Pigs disaster in 1961 and had continued afterward. The first finding in Cuba of something particularly unusual and alarming occurred with the U-2 mission of 29 August. Within minutes after the film was placed on the light table, an NPIC photo interpreter assigned to the mission scan team shouted, "I've got a SAM site." When McCone was briefed on the finding, his reaction reflected his belief in the reason the Soviets had installed the missiles: "They're not putting them [the SA-2 missiles] in to protect the cane cutters. They're putting them in to blind our reconnaissance eye."

The U-2 missions that followed found evidence of more SAM sites, but not offensive weapons until mission 3101 on 14 October. Film from the mission was processed under stringent quality and security controls, carefully edited and titled, and the duplicate positives from the processors spooled and packaged in film cans. This particular day had all the appearances of being routine. Lundahl happened to glance out his office window overlooking Fifth Street and noted that a U.S. Navy truck was parked in front of the building. Two armed Marines had dismounted and taken positions immediately behind the truck. An armed Navy officer and an enlisted man entered the truck from the rear, lifted a box off the truck, and carried it into the Steuart Building.

Lundahl smiled, shook his head, and noted how good intentions often become counter-productive. Every effort had been made to keep the Steuart Building looking as innocuous as possible. Yet the regulations for transporting U-2 film specified that movement of the film be made under armed guard. But in doing so, it was revealing that personnel in the Steuart Building were undoubtedly engaged in some extremely classified and sensitive work.

The Steuart Motor Car Company Building, 5th Street and New York Ave., NW, Washington, D.C. was NPIC's first home. NPIC occupied the top four floors. (Source: McCone History).

Earl Shoemaker had his photo-interpretation teams ready. The interpreters began cranking the reels of duplicate positives onto the light tables. Normally, six photo-interpretation stations were employed in scanning, three teams of two interpreters each representing the CIA, Army, Air Force and Navy. As they examined the film, the interpreters wrote their observations on the worksheets provided and passed them to their team leaders for review.

The two cans of film covering the trapezoidal area near San Cristóbal that the U-2 mission had targeted were scanned by the interpretation team who concluded: "We've got MRBMs in Cuba." Lundahl was alerted to the finding and joined the interpreters. He turned from the table and looked at them and said, "I think I know what you guys think they are, and if I think they are the same thing and we both are right, we are sitting on the biggest story of our time." "If there was ever a time I want to be right in my life, this is it." Lundahl pointed to each of the team members and asked if they agreed the missiles in question were MRBMs. Each reply was affirmative. The director then said: "Gentlemen. I am convinced. Because of the grave responsibility of this find, I want to personally sign the cable."

Lundahl then arranged to brief his boss, CIA deputy director of intelligence Ray Cline who asked: "Are you fellows sure?" Lundahl replied, "Yes, we are sure." Cline said, "I'll get hold of Carter. I want you to be in my office with the evidence by seven-thirty tomorrow morning."

Lundahl arrived at the Steuart Building at 6 AM on 16 October and carefully reviewed the briefing boards and notes. Frank Beck, the courier, was waiting. Lundahl closed the large, black briefing board case and said, "Let's go." About the same time, Walter Elder, special assistant to the DCI, called McCone in Seattle and cryptically reported, "That which you always expected has occurred."

Lundahl, Cline, and Beck left CIA headquarters for the White House shortly before 8 AM. There they went directly to McGeorge Bundy's office. Cline summarized the photo-intelligence findings and asked Lundahl to explain what had been found. Bundy made a telephone call and took the elevator to the president's private quarters. The president, sitting on his bed and still in his pajamas, was looking at the morning newspapers. Bundy told the president about the missiles being in Cuba and together they decided to schedule a meeting of all principals for 11:45 that morning.

At 9:30 AM General Carter arrived at Bundy's office. Cline felt that Carter, as Acting DCI, should handle the scheduled 11:45 meeting. Cline advised him that Lundahl would handle the briefing but that he would be sending over Sydney Graybeal, the Agency's offensive missile expert, to provide analytical backup if needed.

After all the principals were seated in the Cabinet Room, General Carter read a prepared statement that MRBM missiles had been discovered at two locations in Cuba and that

Lundahl would brief the group. The president was seated at the center of the long conference table in the Cabinet Room, with his back to the windows. Lundahl had placed the briefing boards on an easel at the far end of the room near the fireplace. He gave a brief description of the MRBM sites and then asked permission of the president to come to the table and show him the evidence at close range. The president replied, "By all means." Lundahl approached the conference table and stood between the president and Secretary Rusk. Handing the president a large magnifying glass, he placed the briefing boards on the table in front of the president and proceeded to point out details of the three MRBM sites.

Lundahl was acutely aware that photo interpreters can recognize and point out things that the untrained eye would easily miss. He therefore dwelled on the enlargements of the missile equipment. The President after asking a few questions looked Lundahl straight in the eye and asked, "Are you sure?" Lundahl replied, "Mr. President, I am as sure of this as a photo interpreter can be sure of anything. Yes, I am convinced they are missiles." The briefing left a particularly somber mood in the room. The worst fears had come to pass. The president turned to the group and said he wanted the whole island covered – he didn't care how many missions it took. "I want the photography interpreted and the finds from the readouts as soon as possible."

Lundahl held a prolonged staff meeting at the Center the following morning to structure operational changes for the duration of the crisis. Center personnel were equally divided into two twelve-hour shifts. Photography acquired by U-2 missions flown in the morning would be processed in the afternoon, then analyzed in the late afternoon and nightly at NPIC. Teams of photo interpreters working with missile and nuclear experts from other components of the intelligence community produced situation summaries that were then disseminated the following morning. After being briefed each morning at the Center on the information generated the previous evening, Lundahl would depart for a briefing of the United States Intelligence Board, which met each morning at 8 AM at the Agency East Building, 2430 E St., NW.

On 23 October, Navy low-level reconnaissance aircraft landed at the naval air station at Jacksonville after overflying Cuba for the first time. When the aircraft stopped, there was an immediate flurry of activity as film magazines were unloaded and rushed to the nearby Fleet Air Photo Laboratory. The film was placed in the processors and within minutes the first negatives were finished: "Run the duplicate positives and let's get them to Washington." The low-altitude photography added a new dimension to NPIC's mission.

Of all the awards and honors Lundahl received, one is particularly noteworthy: an autographed photograph of Allen Dulles and himself which reads: "Art Lundahl has done as much to protect the security of this nation as any man I know. Allen W. Dulles."

———

Source: Brugioni, *Eyeball to Eyeball.*

The U-2C Reconnaissance Aircraft

The loss of Francis Gary Powers' U-2 over the Soviet Union on 1May 1960 from a Soviet SA-2 surface to air missile marked the end of the aircraft's use over the Soviet Bloc. Soon after the May Day incident, President Eisenhower ordered an end to overflights. His successor, John Kennedy, told a 25 January 1961 press conference, "I have ordered that the flights not be resumed, which is a continuation of the order given by President Eisenhower." While serious thought was never given to a resumption of overflights of the Soviet Union, CIA sought ways to improve the aircraft's survivability against the surface to air missile threat. One of those was to re-engine the U-2 with the more powerful Pratt and Whitney J-75. With a J-75 engine, the U-2 would achieve a 3,000-foot higher maximum operat-

ing altitude compared to the original J-57 engine, permitting it to attain a cruise altitude of 74,600 feet. And with its higher power the U-2 could reach its operational altitude more quickly, reducing the time spent climbing through 45-55,000 feet where telltale contrails formed. CIA's U-2's were refitted with J-75 engines late in 1958 and early 1959 and carried the model designator U-2C. (The Air Force never equipped its original U-2's with J-75 engines.)

The U-2 was very effective at searching the island of Cuba for evidence of Soviet offensive weapons. (Image source: The National Security Archive.)

CIA had first flown reconnaissance missions over Cuba in preparation for the ill-fated Bay of Pigs invasion. Cuba remained a high priority target thereafter with Agency U-2's flying monthly missions over Cuba in a program known as Project Nimbus. By the spring of 1962, having received reports of increased Soviet activity in Cuba, CIA increased the number of Cuban overflights. By early August 1962, CIA analysts had noted a substantial increase in Soviet arms deliveries to Cuba, and a U-2 mission on August 29 discovered SA-2 surface to air missile sites. The discovery of SA-2's made the Kennedy administration much more cautious using the U-2 over Cuba in search of Soviet nuclear missiles.

On 9 October 1962 the White House Special Group met to discuss a CIA-proposed U-2 flight over a "suspect" MRBM site. At the conclusion of the meeting, Deputy Secretary of Defense Gilpatric and the Air Force representative questioned the adequacy of the Agency's cover story for its Cuban missions, which was that its pilots were Lockheed employees on a ferry flight to Puerto Rico. The Air Force and DOD argued that it would be better to use Air Force pilots, and that in the event of a mishap to state the overflight was a routine peripheral surveillance mission that had gone off course. CIA agreed that the Air Force cover story was better but noted that SAC U-2's were more vulnerable than CIA's U-2C's because of their lower maximum altitude and suggested that Air Force pilots fly Agency aircraft after receiving familiarization training. McCone and Gilpatric then met with President Kennedy who approved the use of Air Force pilots. Air Force control of Cuban overflights became official on 12 October when President Kennedy transferred "responsibility, to include command and control and operational decisions with regard to U-2 reconnaissance overflights of Cuba" from the CIA to the Department of Defense. The Air Force then asked to borrow two of CIA's U-2s.

Acting DCI Marshall Carter reacted strongly to the Air Force takeover of a major CIA operation. At one point he remarked, "I think it's a hell of a way to run a railroad. It's perfectly obviously a geared operation to get SAC in the act." In a series of conversations with high-ranking Air Force and administration officials, Carter argued against changing command and control at such a crucial time. The Agency operation, Carter pointed out, was already in place and working well, whereas the Air Force lacked experience in controlling U-2 overflights, particularly with the U-2C which was not in the Air Force inventory. Carter told Gilpatric, ''To put in a brand-new green pilot just because he happens to have on a blue suit and to completely disrupt the command and control and communication and ground support system on 72 hours' notice to me doesn't

make a God damn bit of sense, Mr. Secretary." Carter 's efforts were in vain. The Air Force insisted on immediate control of the operation, and administration officials were unwilling to become involved in what they perceived as a jurisdictional dispute. Carter was clearly disappointed and concerned, and he told McCone that the immediate turnover was "a hell of a way to run a railroad." McCone then told Carter: "If that's the way they're going to run the railroad, let them run the goddamn thing." [253]

It was a bitter pill to swallow. The U-2 was CIA's baby; the Agency had spawned it, nurtured it and had an abiding faith in the airplane and the

---

[253] David Robarge. *John McCone as Director of Central Intelligence, 1961-1965,* Center for the Study of Intelligence, Central Intelligence Agency, 2005. P.110

pilots that flew it. CIA had had seven years of experience with the U-2 during which it performed 327 overflights of denied territory. In Cuba alone, CIA had flown 61 successful missions. The Agency U-2 pilot group averaged at least six years flying the U-2, the majority of it with the J-75, U-2C, model. Strategic Air Command leaders had made numerous attempts over the years to get the Agency out of the business of overhead reconnaissance. There can be no doubt that SAC leaders were pleased with the decision to transfer responsibility for the Cuban missions.

SAC pilot Mal. Richard Heyser flew the 14 October mission in a "borrowed" CIA U-2C. (Source: This Day in Aviation" Important Dates in Aviation History.")

Once the decision was made, the Agency loaned J-75 configured U-2's to SAC. Agency detachment personnel at Edwards Air Force Base (AFB) supervised the training of SAC pilots. SAC launched Major Heyser in his "borrowed" U-2C on the 14 October

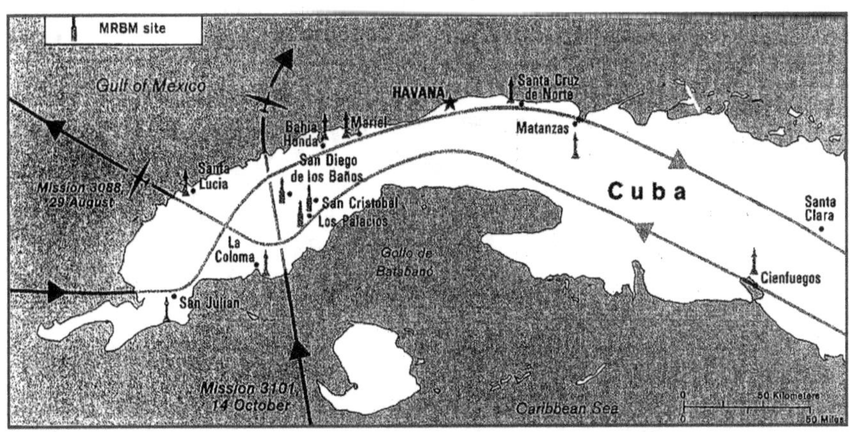

Tracks of U-2 flights. The August 29 flight showed the first evidence of Soviet surface to air (SA-2) missiles; the flight on October 14 provided the first evidence of offensive MRBM missiles. (Image source: McCone history, CIA archive.)

mission which would discover Soviet MRBM installations.

On 27 October SAC pilot Major Rudolf Anderson was on what was his sixth mission over Cuba in the U-2C. He had taken off from McCoy AFB that morning, and as he flew over the Banes naval base, a salvo of SA-2's was fired. One of the missiles exploded above and behind his aircraft tragically killing him. Even with the higher altitude capability of the U-2C, the aircraft was not invulnerable to the SA-2 as senior officials well knew.

Air Force U-2's with J-75 engines are frequently referred to as U-2F versions, seemingly the Air Force designation for the CIA's U-2C.

SAC pilot Maj. Rudolf Anderson was killed when his U-2 was shot down by a SA-2 missile during a reconnaissance mission over Cuba October 27, 1962, a day known as "Black Saturday." Anderson was the sole casualty of the Cuban Missile Crisis. (image source: National Geospatial-Intelligence Agency.)

—————

Sources: Pedlow and Welzenbach, *The Central Intelligence Agency and Overhead Reconnaissance; the U-2 and Oxcart Programs, 1954-1974*; Robarge, *John McCone as Director of Central Intelligence.*

**The Mysterious ABC Newsman –
KGB Backchannel:
Was It an Important Factor, or
not, or Something Else?**

The mysterious communications channel was a well-kept secret until ABC News television correspondent John Scali revealed in 1964 that he and his contact, a Soviet KGB official, had served as intermediaries between the U.S. and Soviet governments at the height of the Cuban Missile Crisis.[254] The Soviet official, Aleksandr Feklisov, revealed the details of his involvement at a conference of scholars and former officials in Moscow in January 1989 (see Conferences on the Cuban Missile Crisis).

ABC newsman John Scali and KGB *Rezident* Aleksandr Feklisov. (Source: Russia Beyond.)

A resolution of the Cuban Missile Crisis had remained out of reach, and the latest exchange of letters between Khrushchev and Kennedy on 24 and 25 October had done nothing to calm the crisis or to offer a way out. Meaningful communications between the two governments had ground to a halt at the most dangerous period of the crisis; the U.S. was on the verge of going to war in Cuba, while the Soviets were continuing construction of their ballistic missile launch sites making them ready to launch a nuclear attack against the U.S. The chances for a peaceful resolution appeared dim while the possibility of war accelerated.

Aleksandr Feklisov (alias Fomin) had a long and very successful career as a KGB officer working for the Chief Directorate charged with foreign espionage. He had been the case

---

254   ABC News special of 13 August 1964, and a 25 October 1964 edition of *Family Weekly* published Scali's "I was the Secret Go-Between in the Cuban Crisis."

officer handling the secret Rosenberg intelligence network in New York and also the case officer in London of Manhattan project spy Klaus Fuchs. At the time of the Cuban Missile Crisis, he was one of the KGB's top agents in the United States and served as the KGB *Rezident* running the KGB's principal station in Washington, D.C. Feklisov, officially the Soviet Embassy public affairs counselor, had been closely following the crisis as it deepened. Worried that the situation was deteriorating by the hour he sought information from his sources concerning how the Kennedy White House was handling the crisis.

Feklisov had had only limited success in penetrating the Washington power centers, but he did develop a number of useful journalistic sources, one of whom was John Scali, the moderator of ABC's Issues and Answers program whom Feklisov had met on several occasions. Feklisov knew that Scali was well connected with Secretary of State Dean Rusk and Roger Hilsman, head of intelligence at the State Department.

Feklisov had reason to worry that the deepening crisis could easily lead to war. He had been given information by Anatoli Gorsky, a subordinate of his at the *Rezidentura*. Ostensibly a TASS correspondent, Gorsky was a member of the National Press Club and late on the night of 24-25 October he had visited the Press Club's Tap Room where the bartender, Johnny Prokov, shared information he had overheard earlier that evening. What the bartender overheard was a conversation between Robert Donovan and Warren Rogers, celebrated correspondents of the *New York Herald Tribune*. Rogers and Donovan had been discussing a planned American military invasion of Cuba and apparently Donovan was on the Pentagon's list of reporters to fly south that very night to cover the action. This was the first solid indication that Gorsky had that Kennedy had decided on war and he rushed back to the Embassy that night to make his report. Shortly after 8:30 AM in Moscow on Friday, 26 October, KGB chief Vladimir Semichastny received Gorsky's report that would command Khrushchev's full attention that day since the information squared with Khrushchev's fear that Kennedy was going to invade.[255,256] At about the same time as the KGB was gathering intelligence about the U.S. military plans for war, Russian military intelligence, the GRU, intercepted an order from the U.S. Joint Chiefs of Staff to the Strategic Air Command placing SAC on a nuclear alert. In the 15 years of intercepting U.S. military messages, Soviet military intelligence had never seen anything like that.

Sequence of Scali-Feklisov Meetings

The story of the Scali-Feklisov communications channel begins with their first meeting on Friday, October 26, 1962. The days that followed were a time of extreme anxiety in Washington. Senior officials were desperate to find a way out and saw the Scali-Feklisov backchannel as offering hope.

Friday October 26 — 1:30 PM. The threatening signals he was receiving and believing that the situation was deteriorating by the hour led Feklisov

---

[255] Fursenko and Naftali, *Soviet Intelligence and the Cuban Missile Crisis*, pp. 78-9, 83. Also Fursenko and Naftali, *One Hell of a Gamble*, pp. 257-62.

[256] Curiously, Feklisov makes no mention in his memoir of Anatoli Gorsky, his coworker in the *Rezidentura* with whom he worked to gather intelligence during the crisis. The sole reference to the "Gorsky scoop" is that by Fursenko and Naftali. Allison, pp. 349-50, refers to a KGB agent's conversation with Warren Rogers citing Fursenko and Naftali as the source.

to phone John Scali to request an urgent meeting. Scali, who knew from the FBI that Feklisov was the KGB *Rezident*, or chief of station in Washington, agreed to meet Feklisov at the Occidental Restaurant. According to Feklisov's recollection of the meeting Scali told Feklisov "The ExComm members are more and more inclined to accept the military option and invade Cuba without further delay. The Pentagon is telling the President that if he agrees, he can be free of both the missiles and the Castro regime in 48 hours." Feklisov then told Scali that an American landing in Cuba would untie Khrushchev's hands completely and that it was highly probable that West Berlin would be invaded within 24 hours of a U.S. invasion. Feklisov wrote on reflection that he had clearly gone beyond his mission. A diplomat would never have spoken for his country without having been authorized to do so. "Yet it was not just a bluff on my part. I firmly believed it, and I knew that, should the situation worsen, it was one way events might evolve."[257]

After their meeting, Feklisov returned to his office unsure of what had actually transpired. Scali, thinking that Feklisov had made a tentative offer rushed to see his State Department contact and reported that Feklisov had asked if State would be interested in a settlement of the Cuban crisis along these lines: missile bases would be dismantled under United Nations supervision and Castro would pledge not to accept offensive weapons of any kind, ever, in return for a U.S. pledge not to invade Cuba. Feklisov asked that Scali check with state and let him know. Scali has Feklisov also saying that if Stevenson pursued this line, Zorin [Valerian A. Zorin, Soviet Ambassador to the UN

---

257   Feklisov, p. 378-9.

Security Council] would be interested.[258] What is peculiar about Scali's note is that it has Castro, not Khrushchev, pledging to keep Cuba free of offensive weapons.

In his book, *The Cuban Missile Crisis: The Struggle over Policy*, Roger Hilsman wrote of the Scali/Feklisov meeting: "Scali told Fomin [Feklisov] that if the message was genuine and if it had indeed originated at the highest levels of the Soviet government, then he believed that I, as the head of the State Department's intelligence bureau, would be willing to convey it to the secretary of state and the president. Fomin repeatedly assured Scali that the message came from Khrushchev himself. Scali took it to me, and after hearing of Fomin's assurances that the message came from Khrushchev himself, I took it to Rusk and Kennedy."[259] There is reason to doubt Hilsman here. In everything that Feklisov has said he consistently and strongly has denied that he was acting on instructions from Khrushchev. Second, why did Scali not include such an important piece of information in his notes; Scali's note says nothing about Feklisov's repeated assurances that Hilsman attributes to him, nor is there any indication in the notes that Feklisov is acting as Khrushchev's messenger. Scali's notes do not conflict with what Feklisov has long maintained; he was not under instructions and that he was merely thinking out loud about possibilities.

Friday, October 26 — 6:00 PM. The State Department begins receiving a message from the U.S. Embassy in Moscow containing a private letter

---

258   Editors Laurence Chang and Peter Kornbluh. *The Cuban Missile Crisis, 1962*, New York: New Press, 1992, p. 184. Document 43 shows a copy of Scali's actual notes. Also, Pierre Salinger, *With Kennedy*, Garden City; Doubleday, 1966, p. 274.

259   Hilsman, p. 121.

from Premier Khrushchev. The message arrives in Washington in four sections between 6 and 9 PM. Washington time.[260] Khrushchev's message, almost certainly composed by Khrushchev himself, was a long, personal, rambling letter that showed unmistakable signs of alarm and suggested the terms of a settlement: If the United States would promise not to invade Cuba, the "necessity for the presence of our military specialists would disappear… Mr. President you and I should not pull on the ends of the rope in which you have tied a knot of war, because the harder you and I pull, the tighter this knot will become. And a time may come when this knot is tied so tight that the person who tied it is no longer capable of untying it, and the knot will have to be cut. What that would mean I need not explain to you, because you yourself understand perfectly what dread forces our two countries possess."[261]

Friday, October 26 — 6:45 PM. Scali tells Dean Rusk and Roger Hilsman what Scali described as the Soviet proposal. Hilsman believed his friendship with Scali was known to the Soviets, and that Moscow had decided to use Scali to open a new channel. Rusk considered this to be the first concrete offer from the Soviet leadership for ending the crisis. Rusk could not authorize Scali to accept the Soviet "proposal," but he asked Scali to arrange a second meeting quickly so that Moscow would know that U.S. officials saw promise in the negotiating formula. Rusk prepared

---

[260] Text received by the American Embassy at Moscow from the Soviet Foreign Ministry at 4:43 pm Moscow time on 26 October and transmitted to the Department of State at 7 PM Moscow time, being received in Washington in four sections between 6 and 9 PM, 26 October Washington time. Ronald R. Pope (editor and commentator). *Soviet Views on the Cuban Missile Crisis; Myth and Reality in Foreign Policy Analysis,* Lanham, Md and London; University Press of America, 1982. p.37.

[261] Pope, pp. 37-49.

notes for Scali to use in his later meeting with Feklisov.[262,263]

As Secretary Rusk had asked, Scali called Feklisov for a second meeting. The two met at the Statler Hotel, a symbolic location, halfway between the White House and the Soviet Embassy. As told by Feklisov, Scali said: "Okay Al, the highest authority has asked me to give you the conditions to solve this crisis. One: the USSR dismantles and ships back its missiles under UN Control. Two: the US lifts the quarantine. Three: the US will officially agree not to invade Cuba. This agreement could be reached within the United Nations." Scali said highest authority meant the president. Feklisov wrote "I went as fast as I could and composed a cable and handed it to Dobrynin for his signature. But he wouldn't sign it and

said: 'The MID [Ministry of Foreign Affairs] has not authorized the embassy to conduct this type of negotiation.' I had assured Scali that the proposal would go to Moscow immediately not knowing that this would be a problem."[264] Still later that day Feklisov sent a long cable to Moscow detailing both of his conversations with Scali.

In *With Kennedy*, Pierre Salinger provides summaries of the notes that Scali prepared after each of his meetings with Feklisov. Scali's notes from their meeting on the evening of 26 October offer his version of what transpired: Scali told Feklisov "I have real reason to believe that the Unites States government sees real possibilities in this [referring to Feklisov's earlier "proposal"] and supposes that the representatives of the USSR and

---

[262] Fursenko and Naftali, pp. 269-71.
[263] According to Brugioni, Scali retained the note he used in his discussion with Feklisov and displayed it to reporters on August 4, 1964.
[264] Feklisov, pp. 380-2.

the United States in New York can work this out with U Thant and with each other. It is my definite impression that time is very urgent." Scali's notes also say that he told Feklisov of his understanding of the arrangement: "That the offensive Cuban missile sites would be dismantled under United Nations supervision, that Castro would publicly pledge never to receive offensive weapons again, that the Soviet Union would also promise not to ship them again, and that in return the United States would publicly promise not to invade Cuba. He [Feklisov] agreed that this was precisely what he had mentioned."[265] Their different interpretations (one having to do with removing the quarantine, and another with Castro's pledge) of what was said show that Scali and Feklisov misunderstood what happened between them.

Friday, October 26, 1962 — 10:00 PM. The ExComm reconvened in an extraordinary session to consider Khrushchev's private letter that had suggested a possible solution to the crisis. The decision was made to treat it as a bona fide proposal, meriting a serious reply. Hilsman set his Soviet affairs experts to analyze the letter alongside what they considered to be a proposal from Feklisov. "They worked through the night. The rest of us went to bed…with a vast sense of relief"[266]

U.S. officials greeted the Scali information with great interest. They assumed that Feklisov's message had been initiated by the Kremlin, and they interpreted Khrushchev's newly arrived letter in light of what they saw as Feklisov's offer that the Soviet Union remove its missiles under

---

265   Pierre Salinger, *With Kennedy*, p. 275.
266   Elie Abel, *The Missile Crisis*, Philadelphia & New York; Lippincott, 1966, pp. 183-4.

U.N. inspection in return for a U.S. non-invasion pledge.

Hilsman writes that Khrushchev's private cable communicated a willingness to negotiate but gave no specifics; the Fomin [Feklisov] message gave the specifics. "...it became even more clear to us [State Department Soviet experts] that Fomin's approach through Scali and the Khrushchev cable were really a single package. We pictured the Politburo in continuous session...with Khrushchev in the chair. A decision is reached—a vague but encouraging cable from Khrushchev and an unofficial approach through Fomin that offered specifics." "Many years later, high Soviet officials confirmed that our speculations about the Politburo meeting and Khrushchev himself dictating the cable were, in fact, correct." "It was apparently Fomin's assign- ment to stimulate the U.S. govern- ments interest in Khrushchev's imprecise formulation by adding specifics."[267]

Salinger also seems to support such a connection between the private letter and the Feklisov "proposal" when he writes "...the *first* communication from Khrushchev the night before, stipulating terms for a settlement, was almost identical to Fomin's [Feklisov's] proposal."[268]

Saturday, October 27, 1962 — 10:00 AM. The ExComm meets at the White House. During the meeting, Khrushchev's latest message begins to be received having been broadcast by Moscow Radio at 5 PM Moscow time. The full text of Khrushchev's message came across a FBIS (Foreign Broadcast Information Service) ticker in the White House at 11:03 AM. In

---

267　Hilsman, pp. 122-3.
268　Salinger, p. 277.

contrast to the private conciliatorily message of the day before, the new public message calls for the dismantling of U.S. missile bases in Turkey in return for the removal of the Soviet missiles in Cuba.

Saturday, October 27, 1962 — afternoon.[269] Wanting to get back to the more promising proposals put forth Friday, Rusk called Scali and suggested he see Feklisov again and ask what was happening in Moscow. After Khrushchev's public message Scali felt with some justification that the Russians had been using him to buy time and he had good reason to believe Feklisov had not dealt with him in good faith. Scali called Feklisov for an urgent meeting and within five minutes the two met in a bar.

Feklisov had not had a response from Moscow on Scali's proposal of the previous evening and he had nothing to offer to Scali. Feklisov states that Khrushchev's new message had been drafted before his report on the favorable U.S. reaction to the October 26 proposal had arrived. Scali asks Feklisov why the October 26 proposal had been scrapped and the Jupiters[270] introduced into the deal and he accused Feklisov of trying to trick him by being underhanded, to try to gain time by dragging out the negotiations.[271]

Scali reported on the Saturday meeting in a memo to Rusk in which he wrote: "I told him I found it exceedingly difficult to believe; that, as a reporter, I had no alternative but to conclude it was a stinking double-cross." "The formula mentioned by Radio Moscow had no connection

---

[269]   Feklisov implies the meeting happened early Saturday afternoon; Chang and Kornbluh, citing Hilsman and Bundy and Salinger say the meeting occurred at 4:15.

[270]   Jupiters were American 1,500-mile medium-range ballistic missiles with a 1.4 megaton warhead that had been deployed in Italy and Turkey in 1958 and 1959.

[271]   Feklisov, pp. 387-8.

whatever with what he and I discussed last night." "He agreed and reiterated again that the message had not been received by Moscow in time." Scali told Feklisov that "it was completely, totally, utterly and perpetually unacceptable. It was unacceptable in the past, I told him, is unacceptable today, would be unacceptable tomorrow and into infinity—that the American government just wouldn't consider it.". Feklisov insisted he still expected a reply from Moscow and would get in touch with me immediately when it came.[272,273]

Saturday October 27, 1962 — 7:45 PM. President Kennedy, greatly troubled over the prospect of war and wanting to make sure he had done everything in his power to prevent such a catastrophe, decided with Secretary Rusk that Robert Kennedy should meet with Ambassador Dobrynin to personally convey the Presidents great concern. Robert Kennedy phoned Dobrynin about 7:15 PM and asked him to come to the Department of Justice where they met at 7:45. In *Thirteen Days* Kennedy writes "We had to have a commitment by tomorrow that those bases would be removed. I was not giving them an ultimatum but a statement of fact. He should understand that if they did not remove those bases, we would remove

---

[272]   Salinger, p.277.

[273]   Feklisov in his memoir writes about a meeting that supposedly took place in the afternoon of 27 October between Robert Kennedy and Dobrynin at the Soviet Embassy at which he was present. He writes that when he returned to the embassy from his meeting with Scali, Dobrynin called him into a meeting that Dobrynin was having with Robert Kennedy. Feklisov said that he was there because Robert Kennedy had wanted to meet him. "I had the impression that he [Robert Kennedy] had come to the embassy just to make sure that counselor Feklisov, on whom his brother had placed such a large bet, did in fact exist and had given the President's message to the Soviet ambassador." (See Feklisov, p. 388.) Evidence of such a meeting is lacking; RFK makes no mention of such a meeting in *Thirteen Days,* although he writes about other key meetings with Dobrynin.

them." Dobrynin raised the question of the U.S. removing the missiles from Turkey and Kennedy responded that President Kennedy had been anxious to remove them from Turkey and Italy for a long time; within a short time after the crisis was over, those missiles would be gone. He also told Dobrynin "Time is running out. We have only a few more hours—we needed an answer immediately from the Soviet Union. I said we must have it the next day." [274] Dobrynin has contradicted Kennedy's account. According to him, Kennedy did not in fact threaten military action against the missile sites if the Soviet government did not remove them.[275] Dobrynin's record of the meeting that was cabled to the USSR Foreign Ministry includes the following: "R. Kennedy said in conclusion, 'The president also asked N.S. Khrushchev to give him an answer (through the Soviet ambassador and R. Kennedy) if possible, within the next day… The request for a reply tomorrow, 'stressed R. Kennedy,' 'is just that—a request, and not an ultimatum.'"[276]

Saturday, October 27, 1962, 8:05 PM. President Kennedy's letter to Khrushchev drafted earlier in the day is transmitted to Moscow and released to the press to avoid any communication delays. In the letter, Kennedy is responding to Khrushchev's private letter of 26 October while ignoring Khrushchev's Jupiter missile demand in his October 27 broadcast message. "As I read your letter, the key elements of your pro-

---

[274] *Thirteen Days*, p. 82-3.

[275] Chang and Kornbluh, p. 378.

[276] Dobrynin's Top Secret cable is from Russian Foreign Ministry archives, in Richard Ned Lebow and Janice Gross Stein, *We All Lost the Cold War* (Princeton, N.J: Princeton University Press, 1994), appendix, pp. 523-26; also printed in the Cold War International History Project Bulletin No. 5, with minor revisions.

posal—which seem generally acceptable as I understand them—are as follows: 1) You would agree to remove these weapons systems from Cuba under appropriate United Nations observation and supervision; and undertake, with suitable safeguards, to halt the further introduction of such weapons systems into Cuba. 2) We, on our part, would agree—upon the establishment of adequate arrangements through the United Nations to ensure the carrying out and continuation of these commitments—(a) to remove promptly the quarantine measures now in effect and (b) to give assurances against an invasion of Cuba."[277]

Sunday October 28, 1962 9:00 AM.

A new message from Khrushchev, which effectively terminates the missile crisis, was broadcast on Radio Moscow in Russian and English beginning at 5 PM, 28 October Moscow time. Washington received the message at 9 AM, Sunday 28 October.

Mysteries of the Backchannel

The true story of what happened between Scali and Feklisov remains elusive. Was Feklisov a message carrier for the Soviet government who sought a way out of the crisis on 26 October? Did Feklisov act on his own? Did Feklisov believe that what Scali suggested as the conditions for a settlement at the Statler Hilton meeting constituted an American proposal? What effect, if any, did the Scali-Feklisov channel have on the resolution of the crisis?

In Washington it had generally been assumed that the Kremlin had

---

[277] Pope, p. 56-7. Text transmitted to the American Embassy at Moscow at 8:05 PM, Washington time, October 27; delivered to the Soviet Foreign Ministry at 10:30 AM Moscow time, October 28. Text also delivered to the Soviet Embassy at Washington during the evening of October 27 and released to the press.

used Feklisov at the most dangerous moment of the crisis to float a trial balloon. CIA regarded Feklisov's "proposal" as probably genuine and the Agency's Russian expert, Sherman Kent, thought that Feklisov was obviously acting on instruction from the Kremlin. DCI McCone was convinced that no Soviet official of that rank could make such a suggestion without the expressed approval of Khrushchev. The Agency knew that Feklisov's KGB position gave him a separate secure channel of communications with KGB headquarters, independent of Ambassador Dobrynin and Foreign Minister Gromyko.[278]

As earlier noted, Hilsman believed that Feklisov was acting on Khrushchev's personal instructions as did Pierre Salinger who observed "There can be no question that Fomin [Feklisov] was acting on orders from Ambassador Dobrynin and was speaking directly for Khrushchev. The eventual settlement was on almost precisely the terms Fomin presented to Scali at their first meeting."[279]

Many years after the crisis Hilsman continued to assert that Feklisov was under instructions. At the Cambridge Conference on October 11-13, 1987 Hilsman reiterated that "Fomin [Feklisov] asked Scali if he would ask me to get a message to the president himself. Scali said that he thought I would do it if I was convinced that the message did indeed come from Khrushchev. Fomin, had stressed from the beginning that the message came directly from Khrushchev and that he Fomin, was acting on Khrushchev's personal instructions. And Fomin repeated these statements several times. Without

---

278 Brugioni, p. 445.
279 Salinger, p.276.

those assurances, I would not have taken the message to the secretary of state and the president.". "I have been told by a Soviet official who was a personal aid to Gromyko that the approach had indeed been instituted by Khrushchev." The Soviet representative at the same conference had asserted that the approach by Feklisov was his own idea, prompting Hilsman's rebuttal.[280]

Fursenko and Naftali challenge the traditional story that Feklisov had a proposal that his government wanted Scali to convey to the White House. They note that if indeed Feklisov was a message carrier for Khrushchev, why did the Kremlin not wait for the Kennedy administration to respond to this trial balloon before issuing a new, and more exacting set of terms on 27 October?[281]

Graham Allison subscribes to the theory that Feklisov was acting alone. He writes that the Americans saw confirmation of Khrushchev's readiness to negotiate when Feklisov approached Scali echoing similar terms. But he says the convergence of Feklisov's message with Khrushchev's wishes was a coincidence. "The KGB man apparently acted on his own, without instructions from Moscow, perhaps prompted by his own fears of nuclear war."[282]

Dobrynin's refusal to sign the cable that Feklisov prepared after his second meeting with Scali supports Feklisov's claim that he was not under instructions from the Kremlin. Had he been, Dobrynin would not have hesitated to send Feklisov's message.

Soviet records of the time are consistent with Feklisov's version of

---

[280] Hilsman, pp. 140-1.
[281] Fursenko and Naftali, *Intelligence and the Cuban Missile Crisis*, p.80.
[282] Allison and Zelikow, *Essence of Decision* pg. 350. In *Essence of revision* p. 156 Allyn, Blight and Welch write that Feklisov was apparently acting on his own initiative.

what happened. There apparently is no record of an instruction from the Presidium to the Foreign Ministry or the KGB on 25 October to seek a diplomatic settlement. The Foreign Intelligence Service of the Russian Federation (SVR), the successor to the KGB's FCD, told Fursenko and Naftali that it could not find any separate instruction to Feklisov during the crisis. Information concerning the handling of Feklisov's 26 October cable provides additional evidence that whatever happened at the Occidental Restaurant meeting was not authorized by the Kremlin. Feklisov's cable distribution was not expedited for transmission and delivery as one would expect if it was a response to the KGB having been tasked to pursue an approach to President Kennedy.[283]

As a further indication that Moscow was uninvolved, Fursenko and Naftali write that in his cable of 26 October Feklisov had to introduce Scali to the KGB: "We have been meeting for over a year." This statement, of course, would not have been necessary had Moscow already considered Scali a channel to the U.S. government. According to Fursenko and Naftali, the KGB had no warning that its representative in Washington had established, albeit unwittingly, a channel of communication to President Kennedy.[284]

A KGB Scheme?

Fursenko and Naftali pose the speculative idea of a KGB operation given the similarity between the formula presented by Khrushchev and the deal discussed only a few hours later

---

[283] Fursenko and Naftali, *Intelligence and the Cuban Missile Crisis*, p. 81.

[284] Alexander Fursenko and Timothy Naftali, "Using KGB Documents: The Scali-Feklisov Channel in the Cuban Missile Crisis," *Cold War International History Project Bulletin* No. 5 (Spring 1995), pp. 58, 60-2, p.62 footnote 1.

by Feklisov with Scali. They write that although KGB Chairman Semichastny and Feklisov both deny that Moscow sent any instructions to meet Scali, Semichastny credits Feklisov with having engaged in private diplomacy of his own, a charge that Feklisov rejects. Feklisov has come to believe that the KGB mounted a little deception campaign against him. Feklisov's feelings of betrayal lend some credence to the possibility that Aleksandr Shelepin (former chairman of the KGB) and Semichastny schemed to use Fomin to present Khrushchev with an "American proposal" that would make retreat less humiliating.[285]

Fursenko and Naftali believe that the Scali-Feklisov meetings were irrelevant to resolving the crisis; "For a generation it was thought that the meetings between Scali and Feklisov had played a role in the Kennedy-Khrushchev negotiations ending the crisis. They did not."[286] Their analysis supports the conclusion that Khrushchev's messages of 26 and 27 October could not have been influenced by Feklisov's reporting; Khrushchev's private letter of 26 October was sent nearly a day before Feklisov's first cable to Moscow. Concerning Khrushchev's about-face on 27 October, Fursenko and Naftali note that because the Feklisov cable was not expected, it was not given priority treatment. It had been delayed and by the time the Ministry of Foreign Affairs received a copy, Khrushchev's new message referring to the Jupiter missiles had already been broadcast over Radio Moscow.

Following their meeting on Saturday October 27 at which Scali was irate at Feklisov for what he saw as a

---

[285] Fursenko and Naftali, pp.81-2.
[286] Fursenko and Naftali, p. 291.

delaying tactic, Feklisov cabled a short report that arrived in the Foreign Ministry office at 7 PM, 28 October. By then, Radio Moscow had broadcast that Khrushchev had accepted Kennedy's terms for ending the crisis.

While Fursenko and Naftali write above that the Scali-Fomin connection did not influence Khrushchev's decisions, Feklisov's version of Khrushchev's ultimate decision to end the crisis (see later) indicates that his report(s) had been received by Khrushchev which raises the possibly that the connection did matter after all. Feklisov doesn't elaborate, but his late 26 October cable of his discussion with Scali of the grave consequences of war would have alarmed Khrushchev.

Differing Theories

From what is known, President Kennedy did not use the Scali-Feklisov channel as a mechanism to settle the crisis. Instead, he took two separate actions in an effort to affect a settlement. One was his response to Khrushchev's letter of October 26 that ignored Khrushchev's missile swap message broadcast of the 27th. Kennedy was doubtful that his letter would help to end the crisis, but he agreed to it largely to placate Ex-Comm members who were almost universally opposed to the swap. In his letter Kennedy wrote of "a permanent solution to the Cuban problem along the lines suggested in your letter of October 26." This was dubbed the "Trollope ploy" after the recurrent scene in Anthony Trollope's novels in which the girl interprets a squeeze of the hand as a proposal of marriage.[287]

Kennedy's second action, unbeknownst to most of ExComm, was to

---

[287] Hilsman, p. 128. Also, Sheldon M. Stern. *The Cuban Missile Crisis in American Memory; Myths versus Reality*, Stanford, CA; Stanford University Press, 2012, pp. 134-7.

send his brother on the night of October 27 to meet with Dobrynin and offer the face-saving deal of removing, at some later time, the Jupiter missiles from Turkey. Between the time Dobrynin took his leave of Robert Kennedy on October 27 and the time the ExComm met again at 9:00 Sunday morning, Khrushchev had decided to bring the confrontation to an end.

Khrushchev had suggested a way out of the crisis in his 26 October message, reversed himself shortly thereafter in demanding the missile swap, then reversed again by offering to concede on 28 October. What led Khrushchev to the abrupt course changes? All we know are the theories that have attempted to explain it. Allyn, Blight and Welch attribute it to the shifting intelligence that Khrushchev received. During the night of 25-26 October, Soviet intelligence apparently reported persuasive evidence of an American attack leading Khrushchev to propose conciliatory terms in his Friday letter. Later in the day on 26 October, Soviet intelligence reversed its earlier estimate, possibly encouraging Khrushchev to toughen the terms by demanding the Turkey/Cuban missile swap. But some time still later on 26 or 27 October Soviet and Cuban intelligence appeared once again to have concluded that an American attack could be expected momentarily. If this indeed was their assessment, it may have weighed heavily in Khrushchev's decision to capitulate.[288]

Hilsman and his staff had studied the earlier private Khrushchev message and the Moscow broadcast and concluded that the former was pure Khrushchev, while the public broadcast was pure Soviet bureaucratize. "It was a typical case of the bureaucratic

---

[288] Allyn, Blight and Welch, p. 166.

left hand of a government not knowing that the leadership right hand had developed an entirely different policy. The broadcast had all the earmarks of a *low-level, bureaucratic initiative* [emphasis added] to take advantage of Lippmann's piece." (An article by syndicated columnist Walter Lippmann on Wednesday, 24 October linked the missiles in Turkey to those in Cuba.)[289]

Fursenko and Naftali write that many of Kennedy's advisors were convinced the two messages were written by different groups in the Soviet government. The second letter, in their view, had to be the product of the Kremlin militarists who wanted to present Washington with an unacceptable, or at least humiliating proposal. If Kennedy could find a way to address himself directly to Khrushchev, they believed, the trade might be unnecessary. "No one in the room stopped to think that Khrushchev might have changed his mind, that something might have encouraged him to extract a higher price for dismantling his missiles."[290] In another of their writings Fursenko and Naftali say it was Khrushchev acting alone, that he had decided that he could up the ante for a diplomatic settlement. Over the concerns of his Kremlin colleagues, he decided to propose the additional demand that the United States remove its Jupiter missiles from Turkey as part of the price for Moscow dismantling its Cuban sites. Khrushchev's dramatic policy shift was apparently not caused by the information he received from his intelligence services; "It was not the information that changed but Khrushchev's understanding of the crisis."[291]

Saturday, 27 October, was the tensest day of the crisis. In the U.S. it

---

[289] Hilsman, pp. 126-7.
[290] Fursenko and Naftali, pp. 279-80.
[291] Fursenko and Naftali *Intelligence and the Cuban Missile Crisis,* pp.83-4.

became known as "Black Saturday," and in Moscow it seemed that events were spinning out of control. Many worrisome factors combined that day leading Khrushchev to decide to end the crisis: The U-2 that was shot down over Cuba on 27 October by a Soviet missile commander angered Khrushchev and signified his loss of control; not only did he have no control over American forces, he lacked control over his own; the violation of Soviet airspace by an American U-2, also on 27 October, alarmed Khrushchev over the possibility of a provocation leading to war. It also appears that Khrushchev was influenced by a communication on 27 October from Castro through Soviet Ambassador to Cuba Alekseev, the precise meaning of which is uncertain, but which may have been interpreted by Khrushchev as Castro urging a preemptive attack against the U.S. Feklisov noted in his memoir: "Alexeyev, with whom I was friendly, told me later he was convinced that this alarming message persuaded Khrushchev to accept a compromise solution." [292] Dobrynin's report of his meeting with RFK on 27 October had also to have worried Khrushchev. In that report Dobrynin cabled "The Cuban crisis, R. Kennedy began, continues to quickly worsen." "The current serious situation, unfortunately, is such that there is very little time to resolve this whole issue. Unfortunately, events are developing too quickly." [293]

Feklisov provides his version of Khrushchev's decision to end the crisis early in the morning of 28 October: "The First Secretary summoned his advisers to his residence outside Moscow. He [Khru-

---

[292] Feklisov, p. 385.
[293] Dobrynin cable.

shchev] had received all our reports, mine included, and was aware that peace was hanging by a thread. An alarming bit of news was announced at the beginning of the meeting: President Kennedy would address the American people at 5 PM. It could be the announcement of an attack on the island. It was now up to the Soviets to show that they didn't want war. The decision came immediately."[294]

The question that remains as one of the enduring mysteries of the Cuban Missile Crisis is what was Scali's role in the drama and what was Feklisov's, and what exactly happened between them? What is clear is that both men feared the worst, a nuclear disaster, and both worked to avert it. Scali and Feklisov each have their contradictory versions and have steadfastly clung to them. Feklisov is adamant that he was neither a message carrier for Khrushchev nor a lone rogue operator. He maintains that in his meeting with Scali he was merely thinking about a scenario for how the crisis might be brought to an end. He believes it was Scali who brought forward a solution that the American's were offering. It seems clear that Scali did not offer a proposed settlement at their first meeting. If he had, Feklisov would certainly have reported it to Moscow. But he did not. Instead Feklisov's only report of that day came after the second meeting later on the 26th where Feklisov seems to have interpreted Scali's response to their earlier meeting as an American offer.

Scali and Feklisov had at least one meeting following the end of the crisis. Hilsman writes about one such meeting where he says Scali and Feklisov met on Sunday, 28 October where Feklisov told Scali "I have been instructed to thank you and to tell you

---

[294]   Feklisov, p. 390.

that the information you supplied was very valuable to the chairman in making up his mind quickly." And, "he added with a smile, that includes your 'explosion' Saturday."[295] There are reasons to doubt this account of Khrushchev thanking John Scali. Based on what is known from Fursenko and Naftali's analysis of Russian archival records, a report of Scali's "explosion" at that Saturday meeting would, as earlier noted, likely have been too late to have influenced Khrushchev's concession decision. A further reason to doubt this story is the absence of notes by Scali from such a meeting. Following each of his meetings with Feklisov (26 October afternoon, 26 October evening, 27 October, 29 October, 3 November) Scali dutifully recorded what happened in memoranda that he prepared for Secretary Rusk. In *Why Kennedy*, Salinger provides quotations from Scali's notes for each of those meetings, but there are no notes for a 28 October meeting. Finally, Feklisov does not mention a 28 October meeting with Scali when he writes: "I was in such a state of mind on October 29 when Scali called me. He wanted to celebrate the happy ending. On November 3 he invited me to dinner a second time. It's possible but I remember only one meal and I remember it perfectly well: it was at Rive Gauche, famous for its cuisine. Scali told me that he was inviting me at President Kennedy's request because he considered our backchannel as very important to the resolution of the crisis and wished to express his thanks. As he ordered the best dishes on the menu and some rare wines, Scali repeated with a smile: 'We deserve it!'"[296]

There are some indications that John Scali's backchannel was valued

---

[295] Hilsman, p. 131; Salinger, p. 278. Also, Chang and Kornbluh, who cite as the source "John Scali, ABC News," 8/13/64.

[296] Feklisov, p.391.

by the Kennedy White House. Salinger wrote: "At the President's suggestion, Scali met again with Fomin on October 29 and November 3 and his memos to Rusk were extremely valuable in assessing Moscow's post-crisis positions."[297] Brugioni wrote that the president was so pleased with Scali's performance that he planned public recognition for Scali, but due to Kennedy's assassination, that never happened.[298] And Hilsman wrote that "when we asked Scali not to make his role public in the immediate aftermath of the crisis, we promised that in due time one or another high official would give him our public thanks."[299] Was President Kennedy really pleased with Scali's performance? Kennedy's letter of 14 December 1962 in response to Khrushchev's 11 December letter seems to indicate otherwise. In the letter Kennedy expresses hope that a final settlement to the Cuban question could be found quickly and he discusses communications between the two leaders during the missile crisis: he suggests that the use of reporters such as John Scali is not a satisfactory method of transmitting messages.[300]

John Scali has clung to his story that Feklisov was acting on Moscow's behalf, and dismissed him as a liar, "no one can convince me that Feklisov was acting without instructions."[301]

Feklisov tells his side of the story:

"The Americans tried to promote the idea that the proposals that were to end the conflict didn't come from President Kennedy, but from the Soviet side, through embassy counselor Fomin [Feklisov]. This is the position taken by all the

[297]   Salinger, p. 278.
[298]   Brugioni, p.444.
[299]   Hilsman, pp. 141-2.
[300]   Chang and Kornbluh, p.393.
[301]   Fursenko and Naftali, p. 80, citing telephone interview with John Scali, 8 July 1994.

American sources I was able to consult, starting with the books by Pierre Salinger and Arthur Schlesinger who, as assistants to Kennedy, were aware of the truth. I can understand that people may not believe what I am saying. But it is more difficult to reject logical explanations indicating Kennedy was the first one to open his hand to Khrushchev. Clearly, neither Scali not I had the necessary stature to submit our own proposals to the heads of state, especially while facing a nuclear threat. I only drew the attention of my counterpart to a possible scenario as to how events might unfold in case of aggression against Cuba. The mistake the Americans made was to overestimate my own authority; I was speaking as a mere analyst while they saw me as a Kremlin spokesman. Only one possibility remains: the man in the White House took my scenario as a warning from the Soviet leader; should you attack Cuba, we will invade West Berlin. JFK put a compromise on the table having Scali transmit the proposal that Scali attributed to the highest authority." [302] *"John Kennedy, who deserves the credit, didn't want it because it could have been interpreted as a sign of weakness. To maintain that image, and perhaps to avoid being seen as JFK's letter carrier, Scali doggedly refused to tell the truth. Had I really carried the proposals of the head of the Soviet government, I would certainly have asked for my reward. I am the only one who knows the truth today."* [303]

Conclusion

Answers to questions about this curious chapter of the Cuban Missile Crisis remain a mystery to this day. The participants are deceased, Scali in 1995 and Feklisov in 2007, and so we are left with what they have earlier revealed about their relationship. Of

---

[302] Feklisov, pp.395-6.
[303] Ibid, p. 401.

the two, Feklisov has been much more forthcoming than Scali, who has revealed little over the years as is seen by the paucity of information about his role in this writing. Scali's reticence about his role may be attributed, at least in part, to the fact that the Kennedy administration had requested him to be silent. Feklisov wrote extensively about his interaction with Scali in his book, *The Man Behind the Rosenbergs*. There Feklisov explains his version of what happened when both men attended the January 1989 Cuban Missile Crisis in Moscow. At the conference, Scali, according to Feklisov, said: "I have listened carefully to the statement by Alexander Fomin regarding our conversations in October 1962. I think highly of Mr. Fomin and agree that we both played a significant role on that occasion. Yet I must say that some facts he mentioned do not match those that, as an experienced and professional newsman, I remember perfectly well. I don't wish to start an argument with him, but, for the record, I wish to say that my recollections differ from those of Mr. Fomin."

Feklisov's version of events is supported by evidence, while. Scali's version is largely limited to an interview he gave to Fursenko and Naftali, his ABC News special, and an edition of *Family Weekly* which published "I was the Secret Go-Between in the Cuban Crisis." The source for much of what the Kennedy administration thought about the Scali-Feklisov backchannel comes from Roger Hilsman in his book *The Cuban Missile Crisis; The Struggle over Policy*. Yet the accuracy of much of what he writes is questionable and doesn't stand up to scrutiny as, for example, when he describes Feklisov telling Scali that

Khrushchev wished to thank him for the valuable information he provided. The available evidence is such that this almost certainly did not happen.

Feklisov has claimed that he was neither a messenger for Khrushchev nor a diplomat that had exceeded his authority by advancing his own proposal. As to the first point, it is easy to see how Scali could have interpreted what Feklisov said at their meeting at the Occidental as a Soviet proposal. Yet there is no evidence in Russian archives of any instructions given to Feklisov, and the routine handling of his cables in Moscow is strongly suggestive that he was not under instructions. The second point is less easily dispended with. According to Fursenko and Naftali, even KGB Chairman Semichastny credits Feklisov with having engaged in private diplomacy of his own. Feklisov strongly rejects that charge and insists

he was merely talking out loud with Scali about possibilities, not making a proposal. DCI McCone was apparently convinced that no Soviet official of Feklisov's rank could make such a suggestion without the expressed approval of Khrushchev. Finally, it should be noted that Feklisov was a highly experienced KGB officer with a stellar record, and it seems unlikely that he would have gone off the reservation to make an unsanctioned proposal.

The most important question remaining is whether the mysterious channel made a difference. Within the Kennedy administration, the first Scali-Feklisov meeting was viewed very positively as potentially offered a negotiating formula to which it quickly responded favorably. That response was received by Feklisov at their second meeting and was understandably seen by him as an American proposal. Washington expected a response to what Feklisov saw as a proposal but were disappointed when it was not quickly forthcoming. There are no indications that Washington's other actions to end the crisis were influenced by the Scali-Feklisov communications.

In Moscow, were the Kremlin's actions during the crisis influenced by the Scali- Feklisov connection? Noted experts Fursenko and Naftali maintain that the meetings between Scali and Feklisov played no role in the Kennedy-Khrushchev negotiations ending the crisis, thus seeming to answer the question, but for one nagging detail. With Khrushchev on the verge of his final decision Feklisov wrote: "Early in the morning of October 28, the First Secretary summoned his advisors to his residence outside Moscow. He had received all our reports, *mine included* [emphasis added], and was aware that peace was hanging by a thread...The decision came immediately."

CONFERENCES ON THE CUBAN MISSILE CRISIS

A series of international conferences brought together scholars and government participants from the U.S., the USSR (later Russia) and Cuba and produced extraordinarily startling personal recollections by those present. The more significant of those are cited below.

5-8 March 1987; Hawks Cay, Florida. The conference was attended by surviving ExComm members Robert McNamara, C. Douglas Dillon, George Ball, McGeorge Bundy, Theodore Sorenson, and Arthur Schlesinger, Jr., as well as the most prominent crisis scholars, among them Graham T. Allison, Ernest May, Joseph Nye, Richard Neustadt, and Thomas Schelling. A number of significant revelations emerged at the conference—most notably that President Kennedy had secretly asked Secretary of State Dean Rusk to initiate a UN proposal on trading missiles in Turkey for Soviet missiles in Cuba if negotiations broke down between the superpowers. See David A. Welch, ed., *Proceedings of the Hawk's Cay Conference on the Cuban Missile Crisis, March 5-8, 1987,* CSIA Working Paper 89-1, Center for Science and International Affairs, Harvard University.

11-13 October 1987; Cambridge, Massachusetts. Sponsored by the Center for Science and International Affairs at Harvard University, the key participants at the Cambridge Conference were, on the Soviet side: Fyodor Burlatsky, political commentator and chief of the philosophy department, Social Sciences Institute, Moscow, as well as political adviser for socialist countries of Eastern Europe and speech-writer for Chairman Khrushchev and General Secretary Mikhail Gorbachev; Sergo Mikoyan formerly personal secretary to his father (Soviet First Deputy Premier Anastas Mikoyan, close associate of Khrushchev, and special envoy to Cuba at the conclusion of the Cuban Missile Crisis); and Georgy Shakhnazarov, personal aide to General Secretary Gorbachev. The key participants on the American side were McGeorge Bundy, Robert McNamara and Theodore Sorensen, special counsel to President Kennedy, all of whom were members of ExComm. The conference provided new insights into the critical question of why Khrushchev decided to deploy the missiles in Cuba.

**27-29 January 1989; Moscow.** The conference brought together the U.S., Soviet, and Cuban sides of the Missile crisis where significant new facts about the crisis were disclosed. Burlatsky, Mikoyan, Shakhnazarov, Bundy, McNamara, and Sorensen, all of whom participated in the Cambridge Conference, also participated in the Moscow conference. Other participants included: on the Soviet side, former Foreign Minister Andrei Gromyko; former Ambassador to the United States Anatoly Dobrynin; former Ambassador to Cuba Aleksandr Alekseev; General Dimitry Volkogonov, head of the Soviet Ministry of Defense Institute of Military History; and Sergei Khrushchev, son of former Soviet Premier Nikita Khrushchev; on the Cuban side: Jorge Risquet, a member of the Cuban Politburo and a longtime comrade of Fidel Castro; Sergio del Valle, member of the Central Committee of the Cuban Communist Party and chief of staff of the Cuban Army in 1962; Emilio Aragones, secretary of the Cuban Central Committee in 1962 and a former aide to Che Guevara; and Jose Arbesu, chief of the Cuban Interest Section, Washington, D.C., and former deputy director of the Americas Department of the Cuban Central Committee. Significant revelations at the conference were that U.S. intelligence estimates of the number of Soviet troops in Cuba were far off; The Cubans expected the Unites States to invade and predicted up to eight hundred thousand casualties; At least twenty nuclear warheads were actually in Cuba but were never mounted on the rockets, the first confirmation that the Soviets had deployed warheads for the missiles. For a summary of the Moscow conference with references to the Cambridge Conference see Bruce J. Allyn, James G. Blight and David A. Welch, "Essence of Revision: Moscow, Havana, and the Cuban Missile Crisis," *International Security*, Vol. 14, No. 3 (Winter, 1989-1990), pp. 136-172, published by The MIT Press.

3-7 January 1991; Antigua. The conference was once again attended by American, Soviet and Cuban officials. The focus was the U.S.- Cuban and Soviet - Cuban dynamic and Cuba's role in the crisis.

9-12 January 1992; Havana, Cuba. In attendance at the conference held at the National Conference Center in Havana were Fidel Castro as well as former high-level officials from the United States, Cuba and the former Soviet Union.

Castro, who participated in all four days of the conference, provided unapparelled accounts of his personal role in the events, as well as that of Cuba as a nation. Among the more astounding revelations by the former Soviet Union was confirmation that the Soviets had installed short-range tactical nuclear weapons in Cuba, and that the local Soviet commander had the authority to fire those weapons without further direction from the Kremlin in the event of a U.S. invasion. The idea of a Havana conference was encouraged by two developments: the relative openness of Moscow under Gorbachev, and the desire of the Cubans to tell their side of the story in a setting that included senior American and Russian participants in the crisis. The Havana conference was distinguished by a degree of directness and civility, a journey back in time and space to Havana, Washington and Moscow in October 1962.

The first four conferences were organized by Professor James G. Blight, the last by James Blight, Janet Lang, and Brown University's Center for Foreign Policy Development.

———

Sources: Laurence Chang and Peter Kornbluh, editors. *The Cuban Missile Crisis, 1962*; Allyn, Blight, and Welch *Essence of Revision*; Blight and Lang *Dark Beyond Darkness*.

ATTACHMENT

Translated memorandum by the Soviet Ministry of Defense to Khrushchev, May 24, 1962. Troops, equipment and instructions for Operation Anadyr.

Top Secret
Special Importance
One Copy
To the Chairman of the Defense Council
Comrade N.S. Khrushchev

In accordance with your instructions the Ministry of Defense proposes:

1. To deploy on the island of Cuba a Group of Soviet Forces comprising all branches of the Armed Forces, under a single integrated staff of the Group of Forces headed by a Commander in Chief of Soviet forces in Cuba.

2. To send to Cuba the 43rd Missile Division [commander of the division Major General (Igor) Statsenko] comprising five missile regiments:
   — The 79th, 181st and 664th R-12 [SS-4] missile regiments with eight launchers each, in all 24 launchers.
   — The 665th and 668th R-14 [SS-5] missile regiments with eight launchers each, in all 16 launchers.
   — In all, 40 R-12 and R-14 launchers. With the missile units to send 1.5 missiles and 1.5 warheads per each launcher (in all 60 missiles and 60 warheads), with one field missile technical base (PRTB) per regiment for equipping the warheads and rocket fuel in mobile tanks with 1.75 loadings per R-12 missile and 1.5 per R-14

missile at each launcher. Deployment of the R-12 missiles is planned in the [illegible] variant with the use of SP-6. Prepared assembly-disassembly elements of the SP-6 for equipping the missile pads will be prepared at construction enterprises of the Ministry of Defense by 20 June and shipped together with the regiments. Upon arrival at the designated locations, personnel of the missile regiments will within ten days equip the launch positions by their own efforts, and will be ready to launch missiles. For deployment of the missile units armed with R-14 missiles, construction on site will last about four months. This work can be handled by the personnel of the units, but it will be necessary to augment them with a group of 25 engineer-construction personnel and 100 construction personnel of basic specialties and up to 100 construction fitters from State Committees of the Council of Ministers of the USSR for defense technology and radioelectronics. For accomplishing the work it is necessary to send:

— 16 complete sets of earth equipment for the R-14 produced by [the machine] industry in the current year;

— machinery and vehicles:

- Mobile cranes (5 ton) —10
- Bulldozers —20
- Mobile graders —10
- Excavators —10
- Dump trucks —120
- Cement mixers (GVSU) —6
- Special technical equipment for [illegible] and testing apparatuses

— Basic materials

- Cement —2,000 tons
- Reinforced concrete —15,000 sq. meters (not counting access roads)
- Metal —2,000 tons
- SP-6 sets —30
- GR-2 Barracks —20
- Prefabricated wooden houses —10

- Cable, equipment and other materials.

Further accumulation of missile fuel, missiles, and warheads for the units is possible depending on the creation of reserve space and storage in Cuba, inasmuch as it would be possible to include in each missile regiment a third battalion with four launchers. The staff of the Group and of the missile division can expediently be sent from the Soviet Union in the first days of July 1962 in two echelons: the 1st echelon (R-12 regiments) and the 2nd (R-14 regiments).

3. For air defense of the island of Cuba and protection of the Group of Forces to send 2 anti-aircraft divisions, including in their composition 6 anti-aircraft missile regiments (24 battalions), 6 technical battalions, one fighter air regiment with MiG-21 F-13 (three squadrons—40 aircraft), and two radar battalions. With the divisions to ship 4 missiles per launcher, in all 576 [SAM] missiles. To send the anti-aircraft divisions: one in July, and one in August, 1962.

4. For defense of coasts and bases in the sectors of probable enemy attack on the island of Cuba to send one regiment of Sopka ["little volcano"] comprising three battalions (6 launchers) with three missiles per launcher
   — on the coast in the vicinity of Havana, one regiment (4 launchers)
   — on the coast in the vicinity of Banes, one battalion (2 launchers)

On the southern coast in the vicinity of Cienfuegos to locate one battalion (2 launchers), [already] planned for delivery to Cuba in 1962. The Sopka complex is capable of destroying surface ships at a range of up to 80 km.

5. To send to Cuba as part of the Group of Forces:
   — a brigade of missile patrol boats of the class Project 183-R, comprising two units with 6 patrol boats in each (in all 12 patrol boats), each armed with two P-15 [trans: NATO SS-N-2 Styx] missiles with a range up to 40 km.;
   — a detachment of support ships comprising: 1 tanker, 2 dry-cargo transports, and 4 repair afloat ships;
   — fuel for missiles: fuel for the R-13 [trans: NATO SS-N-4 Sark]

and P-15—70 tons, oxidizer for the R-13— 180 tons, oxidizer for the P-15—20 tons, kerosene for the S-2 and KSShCh [trans: probably NATO SA-N-1 Goa]— 60 tons;
— two combat sets of the P-15 missile (24 missiles) and one for the R-13 (21 missiles).

Shipment of the missile patrol boats Project 183-R class, the battalions of Sopka, technical equipment for the missile patrol boats and technical batteries for the Sopka battalions, and also the missiles, missile fuel, and other equipment for communications to be carried on ships of the Ministry of the Maritime Fleet.

Shipment of the warheads, in readiness state 4, will be handled by ships of the Navy.

6. To send as part of the Group of Forces in Cuba in July-August:
— Two regiments of FKR (16 launchers) with PRTB, with their missiles and 5 special [trans: nuclear] warheads for each launcher. Range of the FKR is up to 180 km.;
— A mine-torpedo aviation regiment with IL-28 aircraft, comprising three squadrons (33 aircraft) with RAT-52 jet torpedoes (150 torpedoes), and air dropped mines (150 mines) for destruction of surface ships;
— An Mi-4 helicopter regiment, two squadrons, 33 helicopters;
— A separate communications [liaison] air squadron (two IL-14, five Li-2, four Yak-12, and two An-2 aircraft).

7. With the objective of combat security of our technical troops, to send to Cuba four separate motorized rifle regiments, with a tank battalion in each, at the expense of the 64th Guards Motorized Rifle Division in the Leningrad Military District, with an overall personnel strength of 7300. The regiments to be sent in June-July 1962.

8. Upon completion of the concentration of Soviet troops planned for Cuba, or in case of necessity, to send to Cuba on a friendly visit, tentatively in September:

A) A squadron of surface ships of the Navy under the command of Vice

Admiral G.S. Abashvili (deputy commander of the Red Banner Baltic Fleet) comprising:
— two cruisers, Mikhail Kutuzov (Black Sea Fleet) and Sverdlov (Red Banner Baltic Fleet);
— two missile destroyers of the Project 57-bis class, the Boikii and Gnevny (Black Sea Fleet);
— two destroyers of the Project 76 class, the Skromnyi and Svedush-chii (Northern Fleet);

Along with the squadron to send one refueling tanker. On the ships to send one full combat set of standard ammunition (including one combat set of KSShch missiles –24 missiles) and standard equipment. Sailing time of the ships 15 days.

B) A squadron of submarines, comprising:
— 18th Division of missile submarines of the Project 629 class [trans: NATO Golf or G-class] (7 submarines each with 3 R-13 [SS-N-4] missiles with range of 540 km.);
— a brigade of torpedo submarines of Project 641 class [NATO: Foxtrot or F-class] (4 submarines with torpedo armament);
— two submarine tenders.

Sailing time for the submarines, 20-22 days.
If necessary, the squadrons can be sent separately. Time for preparation to depart, after 1 July, is 10 days.
Upon arrival of the squadrons in Cuba, they would be incorporated into the Group of Soviet Forces.

9. For rear area security of the Group of Forces in Cuba to send:
— three hospitals (200 beds each);
— one anti-epidemic sanitary detachment;
— seven warehouses (2 for food, 1 for general storage, 4 for fuel, including two for automotive and aviation fuel and two for liquid fuel for the Navy);
— one company for servicing a trans-shipping base;

— one field bakery factory;

Create reserves:
— in the Group—fuel and provisions for routine maintenance of the troops for three months;
— in the troops—mobile (fuel, ammunition, provisions) by established norms;
— for follow-up secure provisions for 25 days.

10. The overall number of the Group of Soviet Forces in Cuba will be about 44,000 military personnel and 1,300 workers and civilians. For transport of the troops and combat equipment in summertime a simultaneous lift of about 70-80 ships of the Ministry of the Maritime Fleet of the USSR will be required.

11. To establish a staff of the Group of Soviet Forces in Cuba to command the Soviet troops. To form the staff of the Group convert the staff of the 49th Missile Army from Vinnitsa, which has a well qualified integrated apparatus with support and service elements. To incorporate into the staff of the Group a naval section, an air force section, and an air defense section. The Commander in Chief of the Group to have four deputies—one for general matters, one for the Navy (VMF), one for Air Defense (PVO), and one for the Air Force (VVS).

12. The form of dress envisioned for the troops sent to Cuba, except for the Navy, is one set of civilian clothes and one tropical uniform (as for troops in the Turkestan Military District).

13. Food for the personnel of the Group of Soviet Forces in Cuba will be arranged from the USSR.

14. Financial support will be paid on the same general basis as for other troops located abroad.

15. Measures for creation of the Group of Soviet Forces in Cuba will proceed under the codename Anadyr.

We request your review.

[signature]

R. Malinovsky
[signature]
24 May 1962 M. Zakharov
Prepared in one copy
on seven pages, no draft
Attested Colonel General S.P. Ivanov
[signature]

———-

BIBLIOGRAPHY

Books

Elie Abel. *The Cuban Missile Crisis*, J.B. Lippincott Company, 1966.

Kenneth Michael Absher. *Mindsets and Missiles: A Firsthand Account of the Cuban Missile Crisis*, Strategic Studies Institute, 2009.

Matthew M. Aid. *The Secret Sentry; the Untold History of the National Security Agency*, Bloomsbury Press, 2009.

Graham Allison and Philip Zelikow. *Essence of Decision: Explaining the Cuban Missile Crisis*, second edition. Addison-Wesley, 1999.

David M. Barrett, and Max Holland. *Blind Over Cuba: The Photo Gap and the Missile Crisis*, Texas A&M University Press, 2012.

James G. Blight, and Janet M. Lang. *Dark Beyond Darkness: The Cuban Missile Crisis as History, Warning, and Catalyst*, Rowman &Littlefield, 2018.

James G. Blight, and David A. Welch. *On the Brink: Americans and Soviets Reexamine the Cuban Missile Crisis*, Hill and Wang, 1989.

James G. Blight, and David A. Welch, (Editors). *Intelligence and the Cuban Missile Crisis*, Frank Cass, 1998.

Joseph F. Bouchard. *Command in Crisis*, Columbia University Press, 1991.

Dino A. Brugioni. *Eyeball to Eyeball: The Inside Story of the Cuban Missile Crisis*, Random House, 1991.

Laurence Chang and Peter Kornbluh (Editors). *The Cuban Missile Crisis, 1962, A National Security Archive Documents Reader*, The New York Press, 1992.

Ray S. Cline. *Secrets, Spies and Scholars: Blueprint of the Essential CIA*, Acropolis Books, 1976.

Robert A. Divine. *The Cuban Missile Crisis*, Quadrangle Books, 1971.

Michael Dobbs. *One Minute to Midnight: Kennedy, Khrushchev, and Castro on the Brink of Nuclear War*, Vintage Books, 2009.

William B. Ecker and Kenneth V. Jack. *Blue Moon Over Cuba: Aerial Reconnaissance During the Cuban Missile Crisis*, Osprey Publishing, 2012.

Daniel Ellsberg. *The Doomsday Machine: Confessions of a Nuclear War Planner*, Bloomsbury Publishing, 2017.

Alexander Feklisov and Sergei Kostin. *The Man Behind the Rosenbergs*, Enigma Books, 2001.

Carlos Franqui. *Family Portrait with Fidel, First Vintage Books, 1985.*

Aleksandr Fursenko and Timothy Naftali. *One Hell of a Gamble: Khrushchev, Castro, and Kennedy, 1958-1964*, W.W. Norton, 1997.

Douglas Garthoff. *Directors of Central Intelligence as Leaders of the U.S. Intelligence Community, 1946-2005*, Central Intelligence Agency Center for the Study of Intelligence, 2005.

Raymond L. Garthoff. *Reflections on the Cuban Missile Crisis, Revised Edition*, The Brookings Institution, 1989.

Alexander L George and Richard Smoke. *Deterrence in American Foreign Policy: Theory and Practice*, Columbia University Press, 1974.

Anatoli I. Gribkov and William Y. Smith, *Operation Anadyr: U.S. and Soviet Generals Recount the Cuban Missile Crisis*, Edition q inc.,1994.

Roger Hilsman. *The Cuban Missile Crisis: The Struggle Over Policy*, Praeger Publishers, 1996.

Peter A. Huchthausen. *October Fury*, John Wiley &Sons, 2002.

Robert F. Kennedy. *Thirteen Days*, W.W. Norton & Company, 1971.

Norman Klar. *Confessions of a Code Breaker: Tales From Decrypt*, BookSurge, LLC, 2004.

Mary S. McAuliffe (Editor). *CIA Documents on the Cuban Missile Crisis 1962*, CIA History Staff, 1992.

Gregory W Pedlow and Donald E. Welzenbach. *The Central Intelligence Agency and Overhead Reconnaissance; The U-2 and Oxcart Programs, 1954-1974*, CIA Archive.

Ronald R. Pope (Editor). *Soviet Views on the Cuban Missile Crisis: Myth and Reality in Foreign Policy Analysis*, University Press of America, 1982.

Thomas Powers. *The Man Who Kept the Secrets: Richard Helms and the CIA*, Knopf Doubleday, October 1979.

W. Craig Reed. *Red November: Inside the Secret U.S.-Soviet Submarine War*, Harper, 2011.

David Robarge. *John McCone as Director of Central Intelligence, 1961-1965*, CIA Center for the Study of Intelligence, 2005.

Pierre Salinger. *With Kennedy*, Doubleday & Co., 1966.

Jerrold L. Schecter and Peter S. Deriabin. *The Spy Who Saved the World: How a Soviet Colonel Changed the Course of the Cold War*, Scribner, 1992.

Sheldon M. Stern. *The Cuban Missile Crisis in American Memory: Myths versus Reality*, Stanford University Press, 2012.

Evan Thomas. *The Very Best Men: The Daring Early Years of the CIA*, Simon and Schuster, 1995.

H. Wayne Whitten. *Without A Warning: The Avoidable Shootdown of a U-2 Spyplane During the Cuban Missile Crisis*, Whitten and Associates, 2017.

Unclassified and Declassified Documents and Articles

Bruce J. Allyn, James G. Blight, and David A. Welch "Essence of Revision: Moscow, Havana, and the Cuban Missile Crisis," *International Security*, Vol. 14, No. 3.

David Alvarez. "American Signals Intelligence and the Cuban Missile Crisis." *Intelligence and National Security*, Vol. 15, No. 1.

Amazon.com review: "Project Boresight" by William Reed with W. Craig Reed.

Dwayne Anderson. "On the Trail of the Alexandrovsk," CIA *Studies in Intelligence*, Winter 1966.

Thomas Blanton, William Burr, and Svetlana Savranskaya. Soviet Northern Fleet Headquarters report, "About participation of submarines 'B-4,' 'B-36,' 'B-59,' 'B-130' of the 69th submarine brigade of the Northern Fleet in the Operation 'Anadyr' during the period of October-December, 1962," circa December 1962. *The National Security Archive Electronic Briefing Book No. 399*, October 24, 2012.

William Burr and Thomas S. Blanton, (Editors). "The Submarines of October: U.S. and Soviet Naval Encounters During the Cuban Missile Crisis," *The National Security Archive Electronic Briefing Book No. 75*, October 31, 2002.

William Burr and Thomas S. Blanton. "In The Depths of the Sargasso Sea" by Aleksei F. Dubivko, *The National Security Archive Electronic Briefing Book No. 75*, October 31, 2002.

Robert M. Clark. "Soviet Deception and the Cuban Missile Crisis: When Intelligence Made a Difference," *The Intelligencer, Journal of U.S. Intelligence Studies*, Winter/Spring 2021, Vol. 26, No. 2, Association of Former Intelligence Officers.

Denis A. Clift. "Ringside at the Missile Crisis," *US Naval Institute*, February 5, 2013.

J. Earman. "Inspector General's Survey of Handling of Intelligence Information During the Cuban Arms Build-up August to mid-October 1962," 20 November 1962, CIA archives.

Fritz W. Ermarth. Book review: "Essence of Decision: Explaining the Cuban Missile Crisis and Victims of Groupthink," CIA *Studies in Intelligence*. Vol. 18, Number 1, 1974.

Justin F. Gleichauf. "A Listening Post in Miami," CIA *Studies in Intelligence*. Winter-Spring 2001.

James H. Hansen. "Soviet Deception in the Cuban Missile Crisis: Learning from the Past," CIA *Studies in Intelligence*. 46, No. 1, 2002.

John T. Hughes and Dennis A. Clift, "The San Cristóbal Trapezoid," CIA *Studies in Intelligence*. 1992.

Thomas R. Johnson. "American Cryptology during the Cold War, 1945-1989, Book II: Centralization Wins, 1960-1972" *Center for Cryptologic History*, National Security Agency, 1995.

Thomas R. Johnson and David A. Hatch. "NSA and the Cuban Missile Crisis." *Center for Cryptologic History*, National Security Agency, May 1998.

Sherman Kent. "A Crucial Estimate Relived," CIA *Studies in Intelligence*. Vol. 8, No. 2, Spring 1964.

James R. Killian, Jr. "President's Foreign Intelligence Advisory Board Memorandum for the President and Report," 4 February 1963.

Helen Kleyla and Robert O'Hern. "History of the Office of Special Activities," CIA Directorate of Science and Technology Historical Paper, 1 April 1969.

Richard Lehman. "CIA Handling of the Soviet Build-up in Cuba, 1 July-16 October 1962," Memorandum to Director of Central Intelligence, 14 November 1962, CIA Archives.

Jean Lichty, Mike Peterson, Brad Burke and David A. Hatch. "Juanita Moody Oral History interview," NSA *Center for Cryptologic History* Oral History Program, 19 May 1998.

Harlow T. Munson and W.P. Southard. "Two Witnesses for the Defense." CIA *Studies in Intelligence.* Vol. 8, 1964.

Sean D. Naylor, "Operation Cobra: The untold story of how a CIA officer trained a network of agents who found the Soviet missiles in Cuba" *Yahoo News*, January 23, 2019.

No identified author. "Cuba 1962: Khrushchev's Miscalculated Risk," CIA DD/I Study, 13 Feb 1964. CIA archives.

No identified author. "The Air Force Response to the Cuban Crisis." USAF Historical Division Liaison Office Headquarters USAF. Undated.

No identified author. "The Naval Quarantine of Cuba, 1962." Office of Naval Intelligence history, undated.

No identified author. "The Soviet Missile Base Venture in Cuba," CIA DD/I Study, 17 February 1964. CIA archives.

No identified author. "The Military Buildup in Cuba," *Special National Intelligence Estimate. 85-3-62*, CIA Board of National Estimates, September 19, 1962, CIA archives.

No identified author. The President's Foreign Intelligence Advisory Board (PFIAB), "Chronology of Specific Events Relating to the Military Buildup in Cuba," Undated.

Alexander Orlov. "The U-2 Program: A Russian Officer Remembers," CIA, *Studies in Intelligence.* Winter 1998-1999.

Michael B. Petersen. "Legacy of Ashes, Trial by Fire: The Origins of the Defense Intelligence Agency and the Cuban Missile Crisis." Defense Intelligence Agency Historical Perspectives, Number 1, DIA Historical Research Support Branch, 2011.

Redacted name of author. "Into Politics with John F. Kennedy," CIA *Studies in Intelligence.* Date unknown.

Redacted name of author. "Reflections on Handling Penkovsky; Operating in Moscow in the 1960s." CIA *Studies in Intelligence.* Date unknown.

Redacted name of author. "Role of Intelligence During the Cuban Missile Crisis," 19 September 1966, CIA archive.

J.J. Rumpelmayer. "The Missiles in Cuba," CIA *Studies in Intelligence.* Vol. 8, Fall 1964.

Svetlana Savranskaya and Thomas Blanton. "Memoir of Lieutenant General Nikolai Beloborodov, Head of the Soviet Nuclear Arsenal in Cuba," circa early 1990s, *The National Security Archive Electronic Briefing Book, No. 449*, December 11, 2013.

Svetlana Savranskaya and Thomas Blanton. "Report of Major General Igor Demyanovich Statsenko, Commander of the 51st Missile Division, about the Actions of the Division from 07.12.62 through 12.01.1962." circa December 1962, *The National Security Archive Electronic Briefing Book No. 449*, December 11, 2013.

William F. Scott. "The Face of Moscow in the Missile Crisis: Observations of the attachés in the Soviet Union in the fall of '62," CIA *Studies in Intelligence.* Spring 1966.

David T. Spalding. "Early Direction Finding: From WWI Through the Cold War," Station Hypo, undated. https://stationhypo.com.

David T. Spalding "Thirteen Days? The Naval Security Group in the Cuban Missile Crisis," Station Hypo, Undated. https://station hypo.com.

David T. Spalding. "Find and Fix: Direction Finding in the Cuban Missile Crisis." Station Hypo, Undated. https://stationhypo.com.

David T. Spalding. "Naval Cryptology and the Cuban Missile Crisis," *Center for International Maritime Security*, January 14, 2016.

David T. Spalding. "USS Oxford: The Largest Producer of SIGINT in the Cuban Missile Crisis," Station Hypo, Undated. https://station-hypo.com.

H. Wayne Whitten. "Without A Warning: The Story of the Shoot Down of a U-2 Spy Plane During the Cuban Missile Crisis," Station HYPO, 5 August 2016. https://stationhypo.com.

Donald C. Wigglesworth. "The Cuban Missile Crisis: A SIGINT Perspective," *Cryptologic Quarterly*, undated, NSA archive.

David Wolman. "The Once-Classified Tale of Juanita Moody," *Smithsonian Magazine*, March 2021.

Amy Zegart. "The Cuban Missile Crisis as Intelligence Failure, " *Policy Review*, October & November 2012, Stanford: Hoover Institution (https://www.hoover.org/research/cuban-missile-crisis-intelligence-failure).

#1. Kennedy and Khrushchev first met at the Vienna Summit in June 1961. Less than one year later Khrushchev, possibly emboldened after his meeting with Kennedy, launched Operation Anadyr, a monumental miscalculation. (Image source: Wikipedia.)

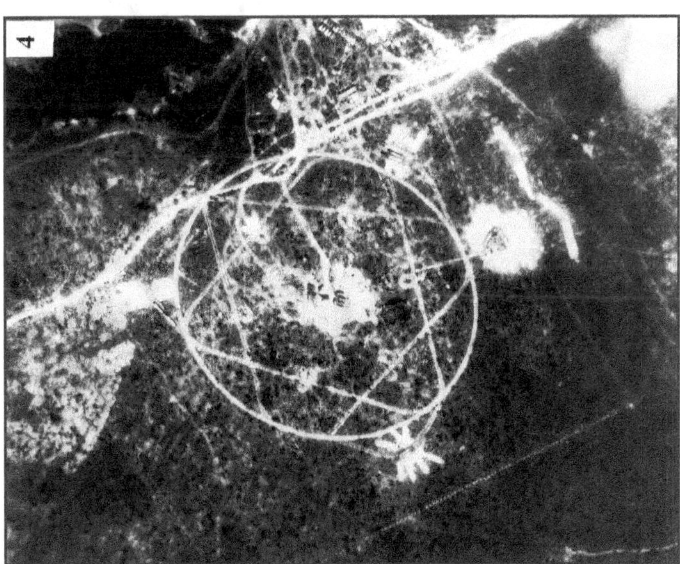

#2. First imagery of an SA-2 surface to air missile site shown under construction taken on 29 August 1962. DCI McCone believed the Soviet's installed the SA-2 missiles to keep the U-2 out of Cuban airspace preventing the U.S. from discovering the nuclear missiles. (Image source: The National Security Archive.)

#3. Soviet ship *Poltava* enroute to Cuba on 15 September 1962. The large-hatch and the ship riding high in the water were missed indicators that the ship may be carrying large, lightweight objects such as offensive missiles. (Image source: United States. Department of Defense. Department of Defense Cuban Missile Crisis Briefing Materials, JFK Library.)

#4. Sherman Kent. The CIA official responsible for the erroneous estimate of 19 September 1962 that predicted the Soviets likely would not send offensive missiles to Cuba. (Image source: McCone history, CIA archive.)

SECRET KIMBO

ELECTRICAL RELEASE
25 Sep 62
DIST:

FURTHER INFORMATION ON CARGO SHIPMENTS TO CUBA IN SOVIET SHIPS

1. An additional 13 Soviet merchant ships have been noted in COMINT en route or possibly en route Cuba. The following details concerning these ships are available. Read in six columns: Ship [C/S, Gross Tons]/Area of Departure/Port Declared/Cargo Declared/Known Cargo/Remarks.

BERDYANSK [UIWP, 5436]/Black Sea/xxxx/xxxx/xxxx/possibly en route Cuba; second trip

DVINOLES [UYSA, 4638]/Baltic/xxxx/xxxx/xxxx/second trip

KASIMOV [Unknown, 9254]/Baltic/xxxx/xxxx/xxxx/xxxx

GRUZIYA [UPOV, 11030]/Black Sea/xxxx/xxxx/xxxx/passenger ship; possibly en route Cuba; second trip

BELORETSK [USMZ, 10300]/Black Sea/xxxx/xxxx/2527 metric tons steel/second trip

DEPUTAT LUTSKIJ [UJYQ, 9935]/Black Sea/xxxx/xxxx/1462 metric tons pig iron and steel/xxxx

NIKOLAEVSK [URST, 4871]/Baltic/xxxx/xxxx/100 passengers sighted on deck/passenger ship; second trip

DUBOSSARY [UBFW, 7265]/Black Sea/Cuba/3400 tons general/xxxx/second trip

METALLURG BARDIN [UHDP, 12285]/Black Sea/Conakry/1707 tons general/xxxx/second trip; possibly Cuba

SEVASTOPOL' [UOJE, 7176]/Baltic/xxxx/xxxx/xxxx/second trip; possibly Cuba

INDIGIRKA [UWLP, 7661]/Arctic/xxxx/xxxx/xxxx/icebreaker/cargo ship

ORENBURG [UTXH, 11858]/Black Sea/Conakry/1988 tons general/xxxx/second trip; possibly Cuba

SIMFEROPOL' [UVTO, 6758]/Black Sea/Cuba/2288 tons general/2295 metric tons flour/xxxx

2. International commercial messages indicate that the BELORETSK, DEPUTAT LUTSKIJ, and SIMFEROPOL' loaded the above-mentioned tonnages of cargo for shipment to Cuba. This type of information has been largely absent from such communications

THIS DOCUMENT CONTAINS TWO PAGES

SECRET KIMBO

#5. NSA communications intelligence (COMINT) reporting on 25 September 1962 noting the exceptionally large number of Soviet merchant ships enroute to Cuba. (Image source: NSA archives.)

#6. Secretary of Defense Robert McNamara and Gen. Maxwell Taylor, chairman of the JCS. McNamara bridled at McCone's efforts to assume authority over intelligence agencies as President Kennedy had instructed him. (Image source: McCone history, CIA archive.)

#7. Soviet ship *Kasimov* with IL-28 bomber fuselages in crates on 28 September 1962. Photointerpreters recognized the crates as carrying IL-28 fuselages having seen them earlier in the USSR. (Image source: The National Security Archive.)

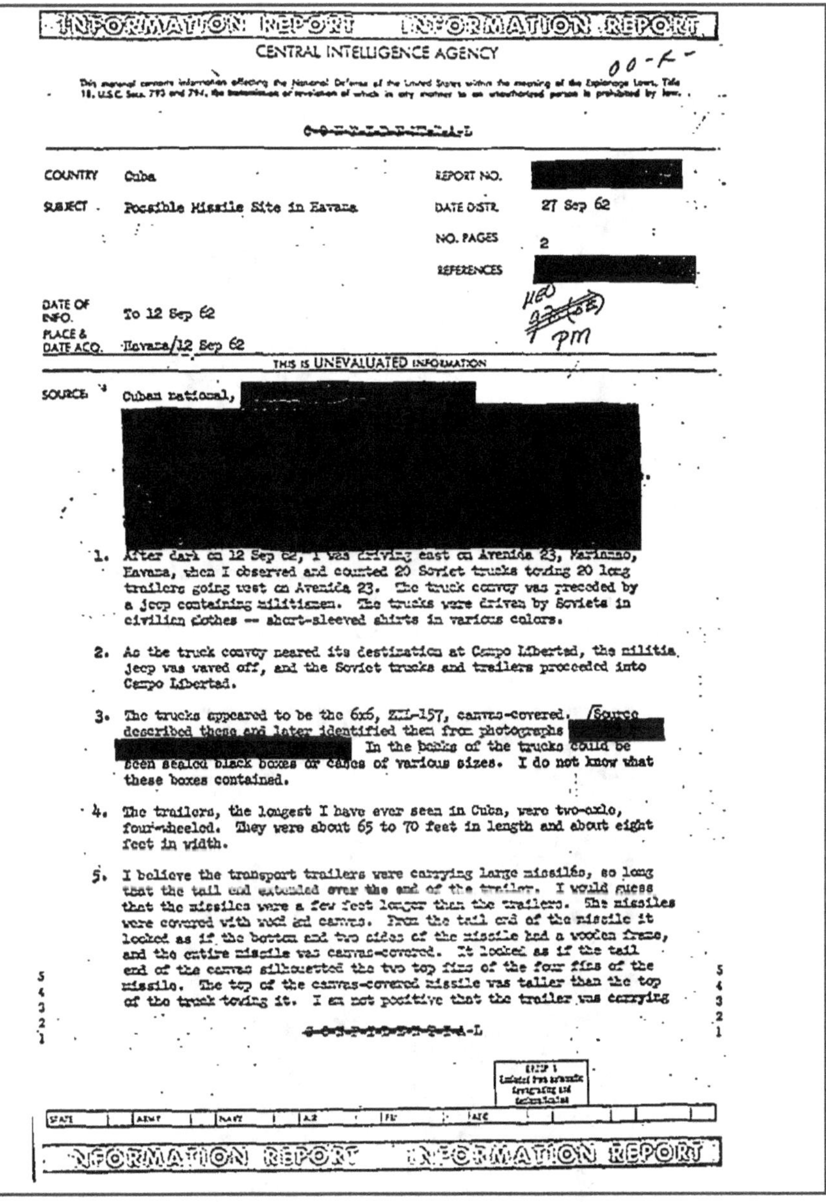

#8. Report of CIA agent in Cuba who on 12 September 1962 observed a convoy moving toward San Cristóbal and believed that the trailers he saw were carrying large missiles. Due to the time required to clandestinely transmit the report it was not received at CIA headquarters until 27 September. It was one of several that together led to the 14 October U-2 mission. (Image source: McCone history, CIA archive.)

#9. Soviet medium bomber Ilyushin IL-28 ("Beagle") (February 1963 photo). The U.S. considered the IL-28 to be an offensive weapon since it was capable of carrying a nuclear bomb. Protracted negotiations over the issue delayed final settlement of the crisis. (Image source: United States. Department of Defense. Department of Defense Cuban Missile Crisis Briefing Materials, JFK Library.)

#10. CIA Deputy Director Major General Marshall Carter served in McCone's absence during a critical period. (Image source: McCone history, CIA archive.)

#11. First hard evidence of offensive weapons in Cuba. Photo from the U-2 mission of 14 October 1962 showing indicators of Soviet Medium-Range ballistic missile (MRBM) launch site number 2 in San Cristóbal, Cuba. (Image source: United States. Department of Defense. Department of Defense Cuban Missile Crisis Briefing Materials, JFK Library.)

#12. SAC pilot Maj. Richard Heyser wearing a partial pressure suit beside a U-2. Heyser flew the 14 October mission in a "borrowed" CIA U-2C and brought back the film that showed evidence of MRBMs. (Image source: This Day in Aviation: Important Dates in Aviation History.)

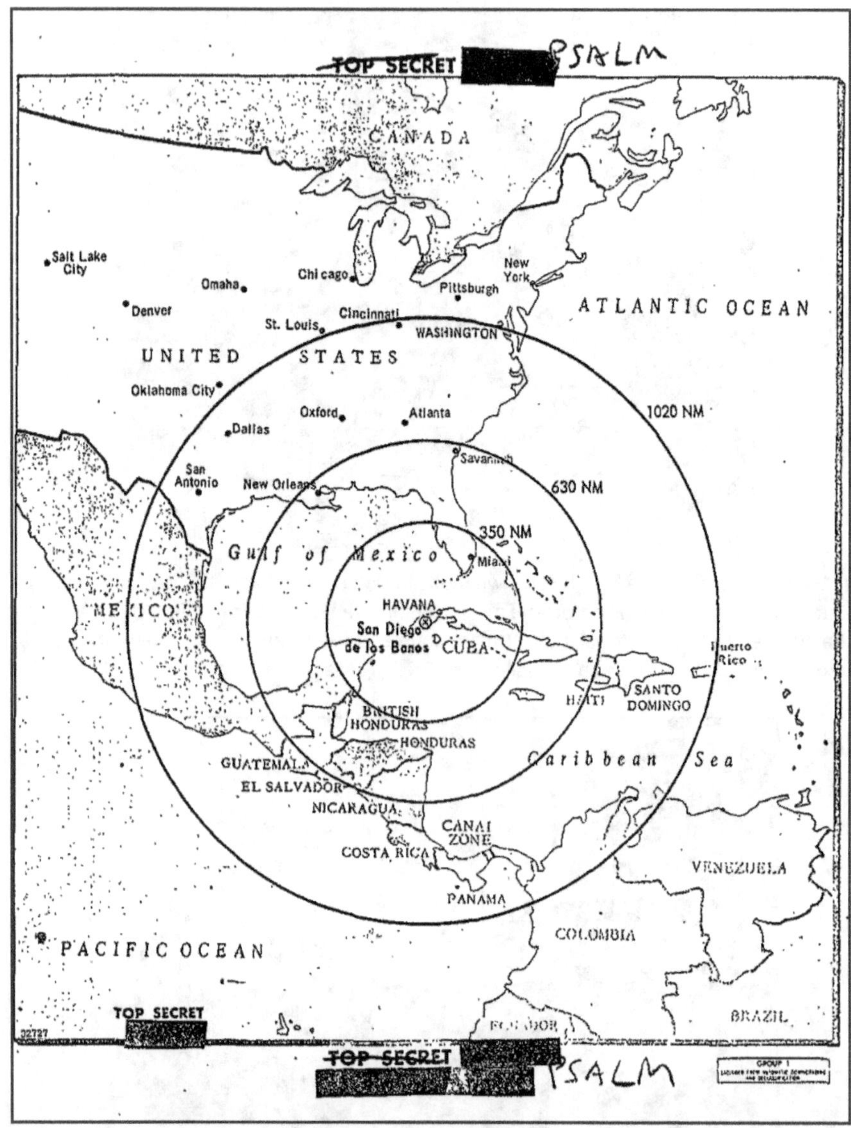

#13. Soviet MRBM's launched from Cuba could reach much of the Eastern U.S. including Washington. The range of Soviet IRBM's, not show on the map, could reach almost the entirety of the U.S. Note the "Psalm" caveat, the special codeword created at Kennedy's insistence for greater control of this sensitive information. (Image source: CIA documents.)

#14. Soviet medium-range ballistic missile (MRBM) on a transporter photographed in a Moscow parade (undated). Dimensions show the size of the missile. (Image source: United States. Department of Defense. Department of Defense Cuban Missile Crisis Briefing Materials, JFK Library.)

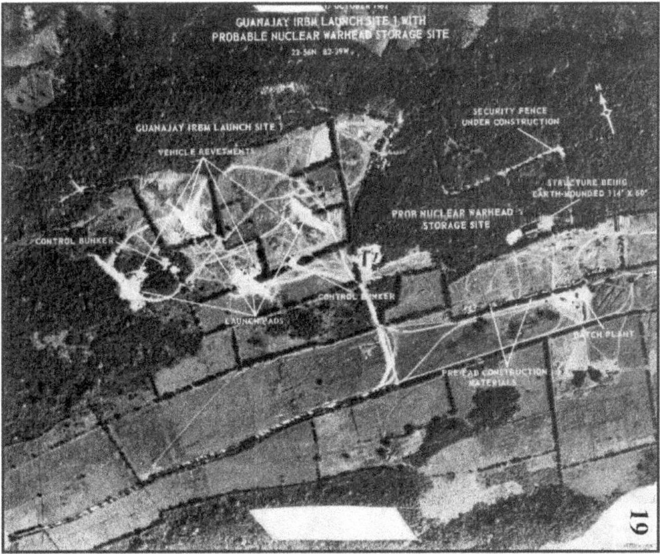

#15. First evidence of an Intermediate Range Ballistic Missile (IRBM) site shown under construction on 17 October 1962. IRBM missiles were delivered to Cuba but were never deployed to the field. (Image source: The National Security Archive.)

#16. President Kennedy meeting with Soviet Foreign Minister Andrei Gromyko on October 18, 1962 at the White House. (Clockwise from top: Kennedy, Gromyko; Vladimir Semenov, Deputy Minister of Foreign Affairs of the Soviet Union; Secretary of State Dean Rusk; Mikhail Menshikov, Soviet Ambassador to the U.S.) Kennedy was tempted to show the photo that he has in his desk of offensive missiles in Cuba, but decided not to reveal what he knew. Gromyko asserts that Soviet military assistance to Cuba is purely defensive. (Image source: Harvard Kennedy School's Belfer Center for Science and International Affairs.)

#17. Continuing IRBM launch site construction in Guanajay, Cuba. Shown as it appeared on 23 October 1962. (Image source: United States. Department of Defense. Department of Defense Cuban Missile Crisis Briefing Materials, JFK Library.)

#18. U.S. Navy begins low-level reconnaissance of missile sites on 23 October 1962. Shown is San Cristóbal site No.1. The reconnaissance photos were used in Ambassador Stevenson's presentation at the UN. (Image source: The National Security Archive.)

#19. Ambassador Adlai Stevenson (far right) described U.S. photos showing Soviet missiles in Cuba at the United Nations on 25 October 1962. An NPIC official stands next to the easels where the photos are displayed. Soviet Ambassador Valerian Zorin denies U.S. claims of offensive missiles in Cuba and is humiliated by the evidence presented by Stevenson. (Image source: Harvard Kennedy School's Belfer Center for Science and International Affairs.)

#20. Medium-range ballistic missile (MRBM) launch site number 3 in San Cristóbal, Cuba, as it appeared on 27 October 1962. Until immediately prior to Khrushchev's decision to withdraw missiles from Cuba, the Soviets continued at a feverish pace with the construction of their MRBM and IRBM bases. (Image source: United States. Department of Defense. Department of Defense Cuban Missile Crisis Briefing Materials, JFK Library.)

#21. R-14 (NATO SS-5) Intermediate Range Ballistic Missile (IRBM). Much larger and longer range than the R-12 MRBM. (Image source: Wikipedia.)

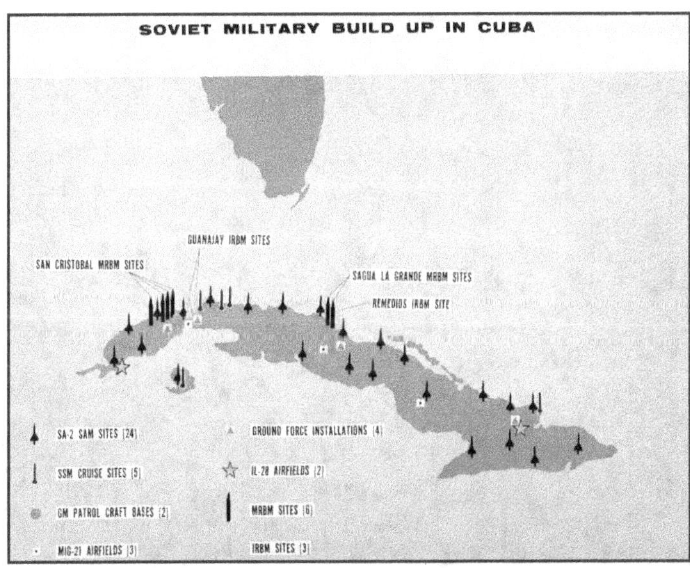

#22. Soviet MRBM and IRBM sites in Cuba. On 27 October 1962 construction of the MRBM sites was complete and at full combat readiness with all 24 MRBM launchers able to deliver a strike against the U.S. The construction of the IRBM sites was never completed; U.S. intelligence estimated that the IRBM sites would have become operational between late November and mid-December. (Image source: CIA documents.)

#23. ExComm meeting in the Cabinet Room at the White House. McCone is to the right near the fireplace. (Image source: McCone history, CIA archive.)

#24. McCone and the U.S. Intelligence Board (USIB) met every morning during the crisis to review the latest intelligence reports prior to McCone going to the White House for Ex-Comm meetings. (Photo is from January 1963. Image source: McCone history, CIA archive.)

#25. Director of Central Intelligence John McCone leaves the White House after an ExComm meeting. (Image source: McCone history, CIA archive.)

#26. A MONGOOSE operations team. MONGOOSE was a sustained covert action program of sabotage, propaganda, espionage, and work with resistance networks. (Image source: McCone history, CIA archive.)

#27. Brig. Gen. Edward G. Lansdale was in charge of MONGOOSE operations. MONGOOOSE was under Pentagon authority but was an interdepartmental effort in which CIA was very heavily involved. (Image source: McCone history, CIA archive.)

#28. On 22 October 1962 President Kennedy announced the U.S. discovery of medium-range nuclear missiles capable of striking major American cities and imposed a U.S. naval blockade, aka "quarantine," of Cuba. Thus opened the public phase of the Cuban Missile Crisis that for the next six days threatened to precipitate a nuclear war between the two superpowers. (Image source: Woodstockwisperer.info.)

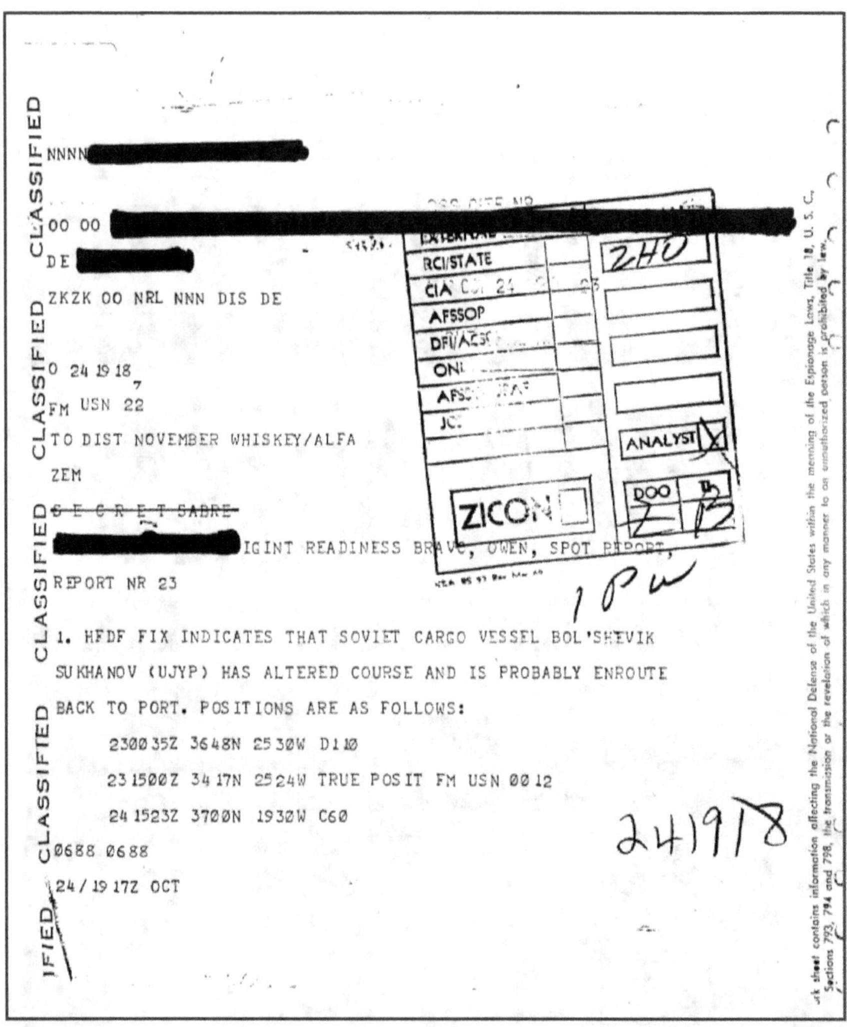

#29. This NSA cable is one of the earliest reports indicating Soviet cargo ships have stopped outside the quarantine line and were probably headed back to port. The report greatly relieved the anxiety of U.S. officials who feared that conflict over the blockade could lead to war since Khrushchev was defiant in opposition to it and said he would not instruct the captains of the Soviet ships to abide by the American demand. (Image source: NSA archives.)

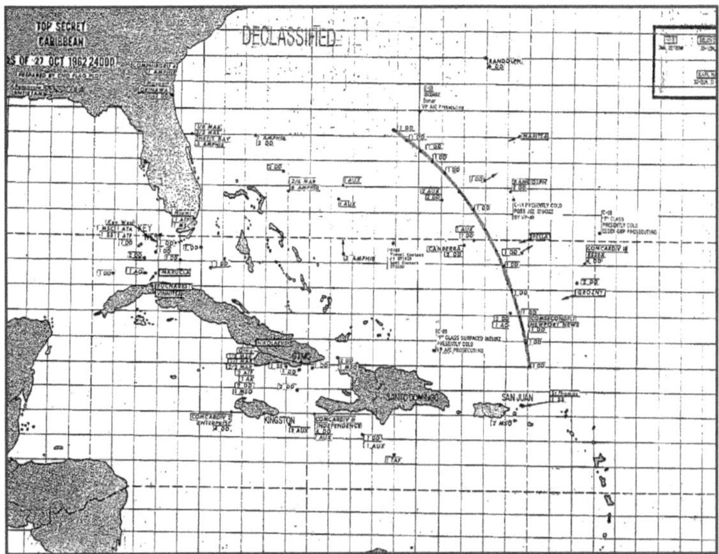

#30. Chart showing the positions of U.S. blockade and invasion forces together with Soviet ships and submarines on 27 October 1962. These were produced by "Flag Plot" and "ASW Plot," components of the office of the Chief of Naval Operations. (Image source: The National Security Archive.)

#31. The Soviet ship *Grozny* crosses the quarantine line on 27 October, but stops after U.S. Navy ships fire star shells across her bow. (Image source: The National Security Archive.)

#32. As an agent for CIA and the British MI-6, GRU Col. Oleg Penkovsky gave the West secret Soviet manuals related to the operation of their nuclear missiles. This intelligence enabled the U.S. to determine when the MRBM's in Cuba would be operational and able to be launched at the U.S. It happened that Penkovsky was arrested in the USSR on 22 October 1962, the day of President Kennedy's blockade announcement. (Image source: *Russia Beyond* citing the Central Intelligence Agency.)

#33. This military pass gave Col. Penkovsky privileged access to Soviet General Staff headquarters and the Defense Ministry where he stole classified information. (Image source: *Russia Beyond* citing the Central Intelligence Agency.)

RF-101 over Cuba. (Source: The Aviation Geek Club.)

US Navy RF-8 Crusader reconnaissance aircraft. (Source: Wikimedia Commons.)

#34. Navy RF-8 and Air Force RF-101 jet aircraft used in low-level reconnaissance of Cuba in 1962.

#35. Cuban anti-aircraft gun in front of the Hotel Riviera, Havana. U.S. low-level reconnaissance aircraft were repeatedly fired on and but for the inexperience of the gunners would have succeeded in shooting down U.S. planes. (Image source: The National Security Archive citing photo courtesy of Michael Dobbs.)

#36. Low-altitude reconnaissance photograph on 23 October 1962 showing a nuclear warhead bunker under construction, prefabrication materials, and construction personnel at site number 1 in San Cristóbal, Cuba. The U.S. was never able to determine with confidence whether nuclear warheads were present in Cuba, but nuclear warhead bunkers such as shown here were a strong indicator that they were. (Image source: United States. Department of Defense. Department of Defense Cuban Missile Crisis Briefing Materials, JFK Library.)

#37. Low-altitude reconnaissance photograph of medium-range ballistic missile (MRBM) launch site number 1 in San Cristóbal on 25 October 1962 showing missile shelter tents, launch pad, transporters, and other equipment. (Image source: United States. Department of Defense. Department of Defense Cuban Missile Crisis Briefing Materials, JFK Library.)

#38. San Julian Airfield in Cuba on 27 October 1962, showing Soviet IL-28 bombers still being assembled. (Image source: United States. Department of Defense. Department of Defense Cuban Missile Crisis Briefing Materials, JFK Library.)

#39. FROG (Free Rocket Over Ground; Soviet name Luna) missile mounted on a transporter-erector-launcher shown in the Moscow Parade of 7 November, 1965. This version is comparable to the nuclear-capable one deployed in Cuba. (Image source: The National Security Archive.)

#40. Soviet FROG missile with transporter and launcher first seen in Cuba on 25 October 1962. The U.S. knew that the FROG missile was capable of carrying a nuclear warhead, but did not know that those warheads were in Cuba and able to be fired at an invading U.S. force. (Image source: United States. Department of Defense. Department of Defense Cuban Missile Crisis Briefing Materials, JFK Library.)

#41. FROG missile transporters at a military camp near Remedios. (Photo is from 9 November 1962. Image source: The National Security Archive.)

#42. Nuclear-capable FKR *(frontovaya krylataya raketa/*front-line winged rocket) cruise missiles were deployed to a firing position 15 miles from Guantanamo. In an American invasion, FKR missiles would likely have destroyed the American naval base. (Image source: The National Security Archive citing photo courtesy of Michael Dobbs.)

#43. USS Oxford spy ship was the principal SIGINT collector during the crisis. It intercepted Cuban and Soviet communications and signals from the radars associated with the SA-2 missile. Signals from the Spoon Rest radar that the Oxford detected in the early morning hours of 27 October indicated to NSA that the radar was no longer undergoing testing but was operational. (Image is circa 1966-67.) Source: Terry Swann, CTR-1, USN (Ret.), Navy CT History.

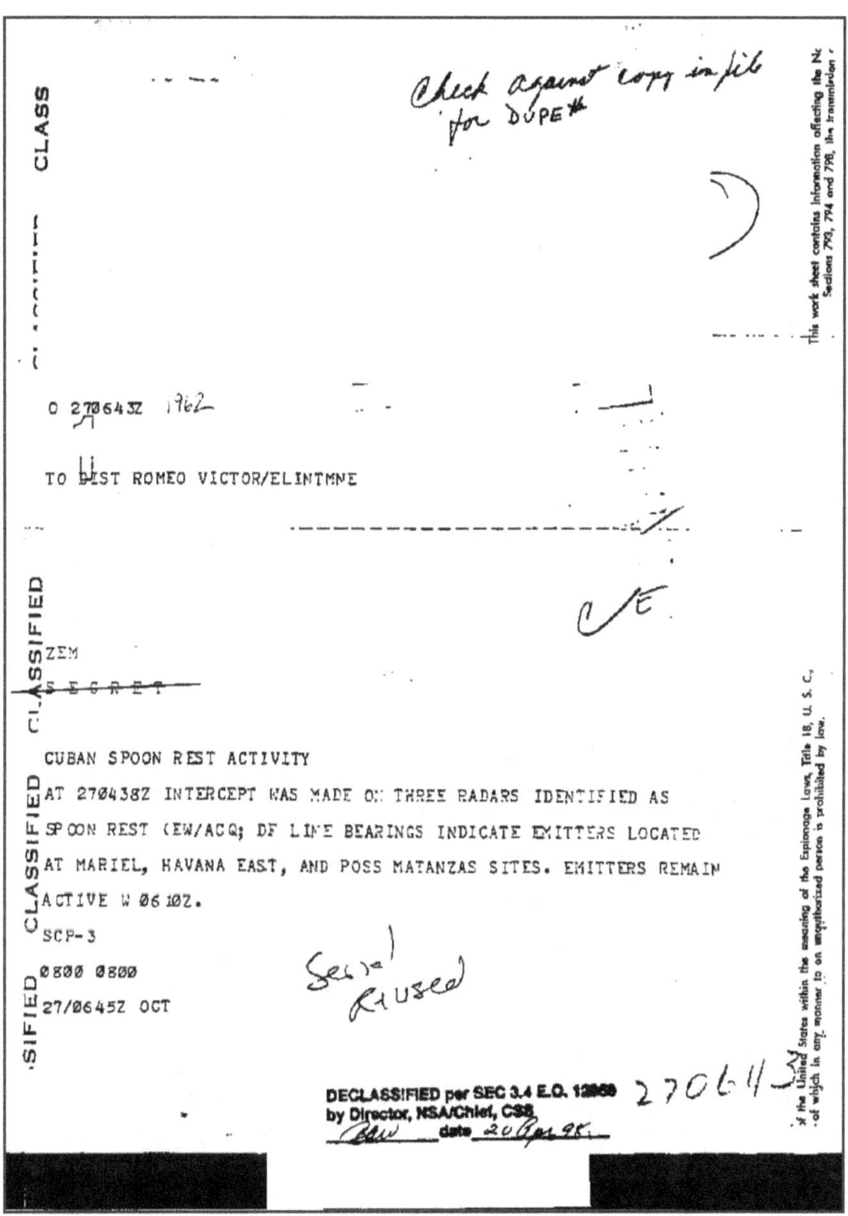

#44. NSA message reporting that the Spoon Rest radar (associated with the SA-2 missile) was detected early in the morning of 27 October and was now in an operational mode. Maj. Anderson's U-2 was detected by a Spoon Rest radar as it flew over Cuba and was shot down by an SA-2 that day. (Image source: NSA archives.)

#45. SAC RB-47H ELINT aircraft operated off of Cuba collecting electronic signals from radars that were part of the SA-2 system that shot down Maj. Anderson. Unfortunately, the RB-47 crew was unable to warn Maj. Anderson of the grave danger he was in. (Image source: National Museum of the USAF.)

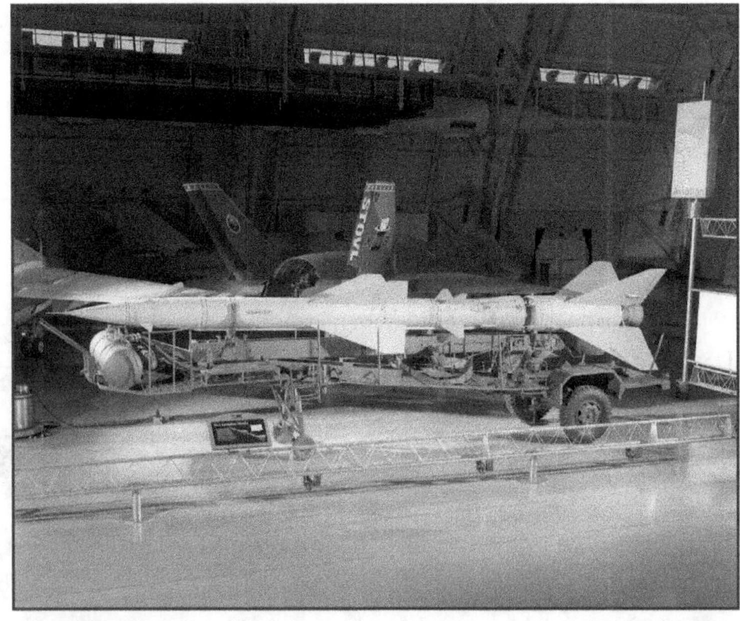

#46. SA-2 Guideline missile of the type used to shoot down Maj. Anderson. (Image source: Smithsonian Air and Space Museum.)

#47. Soviet Foxtrot submarine B-59 photo taken by U.S. Navy photographers circa 28-29 October. U.S. Navy ASW forces surfaced B-59 On "Black Saturday," one of the most dangerous days of the crisis as President Kennedy was intensifying threats to invade Cuba and Maj. Anderson's U-2 had just been shot down. No one on the U.S. side knew that the submarine carried a nuclear-armed torpedo. (Image source: The National Security Archive.)

#48. Typical antenna array (AN/FRD-10) of the "Classic Bullseye" program operated by the Naval Security Group for High Frequency Direction Finding (HFDF). (The operations building is shown in the center.) During the Cuban Missile Crisis Bullseye was used to track Foxtrot submarines unbeknownst to the Soviets. (Image source: Wikipedia citing Mark a Dorner - Own work, CC BY-SA 3.0, https://commons. wikimedia.org/w/index. php?curid=27948611.)

#49. Soviets are seen removing missile erectors and transporters at San Cristóbal on October 29, 1962 as they withdraw from Cuba. (Image source: The National Security Archive.)

#50. Photograph of 1 November 1962 showing destroyed launch pads at medium-range ballistic missile (MRBM) site number 2 in San Cristóbal, Cuba. (Image source: United States. Department of Defense. Department of Defense Cuban Missile Crisis Briefing Materials, JFK Library.)

#51. Soviet personnel and six missile transporters loading at Casilda port on 6 November 1962 for return to Russia. Shadow in the lower right is of a US Air Force RF-101 reconnaissance aircraft. (Image source: The National Security Archive.)

#52. Soviet ship *Volgoles* being inspected at sea on 9 November 1962 with the *USS Vesole* (DD 878) alongside. Crewmen of the *Volgoles* have pulled back the tarpaulin covering a missile so that it is easily seen by U.S. inspectors. (Image source: United States. Department of Defense. Department of Defense Cuban Missile Crisis Briefing Materials, JFK Library.)

#53. The *Poltava* turning back towards Russia carrying IRBM missiles (circled are the IRBM launch rings on trucks). The missiles were never offloaded from the *Poltava* because the IRBM sites were still under construction and not prepared to receive the missiles. (Image source: The National Security Archive.)

#54. Aerial photograph on 5 December 1962 showing the deck of the Soviet ship *Kasimov* at sea with dismantled crates exposed on the deck to show cargo inside. IL-28 bombers were among the last Soviet weapons to leave Cuba because of a dispute between Cuban and Soviet officials concerning their removal. (Image source: United States. Department of Defense. Department of Defense Cuban Missile Crisis Briefing Materials, JFK Library.)

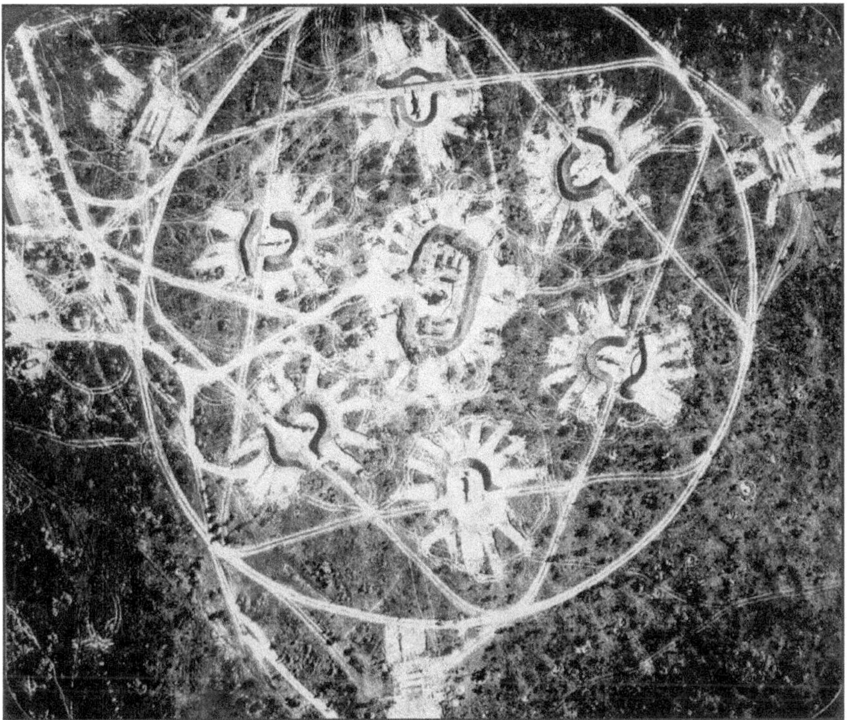

#55. Soviet surface to air missile site at La Coloma, Cuba on 10 November, 1962. Following the withdrawal of offensive weapons, Soviet SA-2 missile systems remained on the island. This worried U.S. officials who continued to fly U-2 missions looking for any signs that the Soviet withdrawal was not complete and that offensive weapons were not being reintroduced. (Image source: United States. Department of Defense. Department of Defense Cuban Missile Crisis Briefing Materials, JFK Library.)

www.ingramcontent.com/pod-product-compliance
Lightning Source LLC
Chambersburg PA
CBHW050906260726
48660CB00001B/54